Information Sciences Series

Editors

ROBERT M. HAYES
University of California
Los Angeles, California

JOSEPH BECKER
President
Becker and Hayes, Inc.

Consultant

CHARLES P. BOURNE
University of California
Berkeley, California

Joseph Becker and Robert M. Hayes:
INFORMATION STORAGE AND RETRIEVAL

Charles P. Bourne:
METHODS OF INFORMATION HANDLING

Harold Borko:
AUTOMATED LANGUAGE PROCESSING

Russell D. Archibald and Richard L. Villoria:
NETWORK-BASED MANAGEMENT SYSTEMS (PERT/CPM)

Launor F. Carter:
NATIONAL DOCUMENT-HANDLING SYSTEMS FOR SCIENCE AND
TECHNOLOGY

Perry E. Rosove:
DEVELOPING COMPUTER-BASED INFORMATION SYSTEMS

F. W. Lancaster:
INFORMATION RETRIEVAL SYSTEMS

Ralph L. Bisco:
DATA BASES, COMPUTERS, AND THE SOCIAL SCIENCES

Charles T. Meadow:
MAN-MACHINE COMMUNICATION

LITERATURE AND BIBLIOGRAPHY OF THE SOCIAL SCIENCES

Thelma Freides

School of Library Service
Atlanta University

A WILEY-BECKER & HAYES SERIES BOOK

MELVILLE PUBLISHING COMPANY
Los Angeles, California

Copyright © 1973, by John Wiley & Sons, Inc.
Published by Melville Publishing Company,
a division of John Wiley & Sons, Inc.

Library of Congress Cataloging in Publication Data

Freides, Thelma.
    Literature and bibliography of the social sciences.

    (Information sciences series)
    "A Wiley-Becker & Hayes series book."
    1. Social sciences—Theory, methods, etc.
2. Social sciences—Bibliography. I. Title.
H61.F635   300'.1'8   73-10111
ISBN 0-471-27790-8

Printed in the United States of America

10 9 8 7 6 5 4 3 2 1

To the memory of
PATRICIA KNAPP
who showed the way

Information Sciences Series

Information is the essential ingredient in decision making. The need for improved information systems in recent years has been made critical by the steady growth in size and complexity of organizations and data.

This series is designed to include books that are concerned with various aspects of communicating, utilizing, and storing digital and graphic information. It will embrace a broad spectrum of topics, such as information system theory and design, man-machine relationships, language data processing, artificial intelligence, mechanization of library processes, nonnumerical applications of digital computers, storage and retrieval, automatic publishing, command and control, information display, and so on.

Information science may someday be a profession in its own right. The aim of this series is to bring together the interdisciplinary core of knowledge that is apt to form its foundation. Through this consolidation, it is expected that the series will grow to become the focal point for professional education in this field.

Preface

The aim of this book is to describe the literature and bibliography of the social sciences, and the strategy of literature searching, against a background of some basic ideas about communication in science. It is an attempt to anchor the study of bibliographic organization in a view of science as a social activity centered on communication, and of scientific literature as an artifact of a communication system. Ideas such as these occur often in the discourse of information science and are commonplace assumptions in studies of the uses and users of scientific literature, but they have had little impact on day-to-day operations at library reference desks, or on the content of subject literature courses in library schools. This is the gap to which the present work addresses itself.

To experienced scholars, habituated to the styles and customs of the academic world, the idea of scholarly literature as a system of communication logically related to the processes of investigation, criticism, and consensus formation in science is likely to seem elementary and rather obvious. Through close and continuing acquaintance with the creative processes in his field, the scholar comes naturally to a view of publications as contributions to an ongoing discussion. He takes it for granted that a piece of writing is not just "about" a subject, but conveys a much more specific message, and that the most important and interesting characteristic of any single work is apt to be its place in a larger mosaic. In consequence, the experienced literature searcher tends to conceptualize his goal not as locating "some information," but as reaching an identifiable phase of the scientific forum. Even in a relatively unfamiliar field he will generally be fairly clear about what he is seeking and know when he has found it, because he knows what there is to be found.

In contrast, the concept of a "knowledge enterprise" producing and shaping the array of printed matter on library shelves in accordance with distinctive purposes of its own is often quite foreign to the experience of students and not at all self-evident. In the absence of an integrating framework, the publications and bibliographic tools of scholarship are perceived as an unstructured collection of "sources of information," and it is difficult to conceptualize the investigation of a topic as anything more than the gathering up of whatever seemingly relevant writings come to hand and summarizing them somehow. Accordingly, the book attempts to articulate for the novice the conceptual underpinnings that the sophisticated literature user takes for granted, and in this way to offer an account of literature and bibliography grounded in a comprehensible underlying reality.

If scientific literature is seen as the vehicle of an ongoing discussion, then "looking up" a subject, or "searching the literature" means "tuning in" on the phase of the discussion corresponding to the searcher's problem, using bibliographic tools as location devices. It follows that effective use of the bibliographic record requires awareness of the character of the writings reached by it, which rests in turn on comprehension of the nature of scientific activity and the character of the discussion carried on through the literature. On this rationale, the book treats three major topics, each viewed as laying the groundwork for the one that follows it: the nature of the scientific enterprise (Part I); the communication roles of the various forms of scientific publication (Part II); the functioning of bibliographic records as identifying devices (Part III).

Part I sets forth some basic points concerning the nature of scientific work and the meaning of knowledge in science, and the patterns of organization and communication characteristic of the scientific world. It considers the ways in which the attributes of science manifest themselves in the social sciences and describes, briefly and generally, the evolution of scientific perspectives in social science. Readers already acquainted with these matters will find little that is new here. On the contrary, it will probably be observed that the picture is a simplified one, and tends to stress the rationality and functional efficiency of scientific interaction while underplaying some of the less orderly realities of the scientific world. Yet the perspective does not seem inappropriate in the light of two additional considerations. The first is that scientific literature, as a system of formal communication, reflects the rational, structured side of the scientific enterprise for the most part. In addition, so little is known about the bibliographic structure of social science, beyond a few rudimentary generalizations, that a highly complex picture of science would not only be superfluous, but might well have the effect of obscuring the basic relationships that a simple, even oversimplified, representation is able to suggest.

Part II describes the forms of publication which comprise scientific literature, and considers their functioning as communication instruments. The sequence follows the basic pattern of discourse in science, beginning with the reporting of research and introduction of new information and ideas via technical reports and journals, followed by several stages of assessment and synthesis as conveyed by review publications, handbooks and the like, and culminating in the inclusive, highly generalized accounts of "accepted" knowledge as presented in textbooks, encyclopedias, and dictionaries. Many specific works are described, particularly in the bibliographic appendices which supplement the text, but the principal intention, here as in the account of bibliographic tools in Part III, was not to identify all useful publications, but only to use examples to clarify and add substance to the description of the system. It was hoped in this way to offer the reader a framework capable of accommodating new materials as they are encountered, in preference to an exhaustive catalogue of the existing literature. In general, the aim was to mention all the major continuing publications, such as review journals and comprehensive serial bibliographies, which may be said to have a unique function in relation to a given field of study, but to include only representative examples of one-time works, such as histories of disciplines or retrospective bibliographies of limited subjects, whose function is shared by a large number of publications. It should be added that the perspective is very much that of American libraries, with consequent stress on American and English-language publications. To aid (and encourage) readers to examine at first hand the materials which are described, Library of Congress classification numbers are given for most of the works cited in the appendices and bibliographic footnotes.

Part III presents bibliographic publications as compressed, abbreviated representations of the literature, in a sequence which parallels that of the discussion of the literature in Part II. The inclusive serial bibliography or abstracting journal is considered first, as the bibliographic representation of a field's literature in its entirety. This is followed by discussion of more selective forms of bibliographic publication, which identify limited segments of the literature from specialized perspectives just as cumulating components of the literature, such as handbooks and textbooks, focus selectively on substantive knowledge. A summarizing chapter at the conclusion of this section looks at the bibliographic arrangements of the several disciplines in relation to the over-all picture, and suggests some factors which may underlie some of the more striking differences.

The meaning of all this for use of the literature as an information resource is considered in the conclusion, which notes the parallels between literature and bibliography as communication instruments, as well as the differences between them, and attempts to show how the concept of the literature as a communication system can be used to give direction and coherence to literature searching.

Throughout, the discussion encompasses seven basic social science disciplines—anthropology, economics, geography, history, political science, psychology and sociology—plus education, as an applied area of social science whose large literature shares many of the qualities characteristic of the other fields. Other applied and interdisciplinary areas are mentioned from time to time, usually to illustrate particular points. However, the emphasis is very much on the common communication pattern, rather than on its specific manifestations in the various fields. This may seem a disadvantage to the prospective literature user interested mainly in familiarizing himself with the bibliographic capabilities of his own field. On the other hand, the distinctive idiosyncracies of each discipline's bibliographic structure stem more from specific historical circumstances than from any fundamental differences, and if the basic model of scientific communication is viewed as the key to a rational, coherent view of bibliographic tools and searching procedures, this argues for emphasis on the common, cross-disciplinary patterns. I hope also that the book's broad focus can direct attention to each discipline's literature against the larger common background, and in this way illuminate not only what exists now, but also unfilled needs and promising directions for further development.

One additional feature of the book may warrant explanation. Attention throughout centers on scholarly literature, understood to mean the writings of scholars addressed to their peers. General social commentary and debate on public issues are excluded as are, more significantly, the multitude of publications, such as government documents and news reports, which are sources of social data—the facts of social life—rather than analysis and explanation. The second exclusion is a major departure from custom. Traditionally, consideration of information resources and information seeking practices in social science has encompassed both "literature," strictly defined, and data, and the difference between them, while recognized, has not been made much of. However, it seems to me that a view of scientific literature as a system of communication among a community of scholars requires a conceptual separation between literature and data, even though the publications relevant to the study of social science belong to both categories, and the search for either one may take the form of consulting printed volumes in libraries.

The distinction poses no fundamental difficulty, since it is quite consistent with the way the social scientist seeks and uses information. That is, the scholar will know, in a given instance, whether he needs raw facts or scientific analysis, and one does not substitute for the other. (Beginning students may be less aware of the distinction and its importance but that, again, probably bears on the lack of focus and direction which are so often sources of difficulty for inexperienced literature users.) But most important, a view of literature and data as separate information systems which need not be considered simultaneously can greatly facilitate comprehension of both in rational terms.

If scholarly literature is viewed as separate and distinct from social data, then concepts relating to the goals and communication patterns of science can usefully be employed to account for the content and organization of scientific literature. This does not hold if data sources are brought into the picture since, unlike the literature, the data sources are not the creation of the scientific community and are not shaped in response to scholarly needs. Rather, these materials are generated by a myriad of activities in the larger society, normally without reference to the uses social scientists are able to make of them. A systematic account of data sources would begin not with the character of science and scientific communication, but with the characteristics of the societal activities that generate records and the collection of information. Very little study along these lines has been undertaken, and it would be extremely valuable, but it is outside the scope of the present work. This book deals only with the social science literature, on the dual premise that the distinction between literature and data is too significant to be disregarded, and that a necessary first step toward adequate comprehension of either realm of information is a clear grasp of the difference between them.

The book has its roots in efforts to explain the organization and use of social science bibliography at a very practical level, originally to graduate students in social science, and more recently to prospective librarians. A summary of this history may shed some further light on the work's basic orientation, as well as provide the occasion to thank a number of people who have helped along the way.

My first formal attempts to articulate a relationship between bibliographic structure and the structure of scientific communication were made in the context of a graduate course in concepts and methods of political science in which the students needed to locate writings pertinent to the linkages between specifically political concepts and broader constructions in social science. The problem brought into sharp focus both the limitations of conventional, subject-centered approaches to literature searching and the logic of the communication system model. In an effort to spell out the latter idea in relation to bibliographic searching more fully than could be done in a single "library lecture" to the class, I wrote a brief descriptive guide to political science research resources, which was reproduced and distributed by the Wayne State University Library in 1965. This led to involvement with the bibliographic requirements and difficulties of several courses, in political science and other social science fields. At the time my intention was to follow the bibliographic guide with a companion piece discussing sources of political and social data, but events led in another direction, as will be recounted shortly.

In truth the guide went only a little way toward solving the problems of its intended beneficiaries, but the experience was certainly instructive for me, and I am most grateful to Professor Theodore Fleming, whose classes provided the initial impetus, for the opportunity to learn from his students, and for his sympathetic and constructive advice.

The approach to bibliographic instruction represented by these efforts owed much to the work of other librarians with whom it was my good fortune to be associated at the time. The late Patricia Knapp, who devoted a professional lifetime to the search for ways to make the library educationally meaningful, and who had then recently completed the Monteith Library Project, was a boundless and truly inspiring source of insight, challenge, and encouragement, in approximately equal proportions. I learned a great deal also from Vern Pings, who was then lecturing to Wayne State University medical students on the history and organization of scientific communication and their ramifications for the literature user. My appropriations from both these colleagues are considerably greater than can be recompensed by acknowledgement here, however gratefully given, as is apparent throughout the book. Less evident, perhaps, but no less real, is my vast indebtedness to Howard Sullivan, whose lunch-hour tutorials, then and since, have been the heart of my professional education. And a special word of thanks is due Robert Grazier who, as Associate Director of Wayne State Universities Libraries, worked hard to create the ambience in which a relatively junior member of the staff was free to pursue an idea where it led, unhampered by hierarchical constraints.

My attentions to bibliographic structure broadened from political science to the social sciences at large when I began to teach the literature of the social sciences at the Atlanta University School of Library Service in 1967. In an effort to help the students to cope simultaneously with the underlying principles which I saw as the foundation of bibliographic expertise and the huge array of materials with which prospective librarians are expected to familiarize themselves, I began to distribute the basic lectures in written form so as to free as much class time as possible for consideration of specific, practical issues. This brought into being a hefty course syllabus which formed the basis of the present work. I am greatly indebted to my students, who were really my teachers, and also to Dean Virginia Lacy Jones of the School of Library Service for her steadfast support of a difficult and not always entirely promising venture.

Several friends and colleagues have commented helpfully on the manuscript at various stages of its completion. Once again, Patricia Knapp was more than generous, painstakingly analyzing an early draft and suggesting some very substantial improvements. Charles Bunge, Karl Orgren and Howard Sullivan read diverse versions and offered useful suggestions. My husband, David Freides, reacted to draft after draft from the point of view of a literature user, and deserves thanks for much more than the forbearance customarily credited to authors' spouses. That these able folk could not eliminate all my errors and follies in no way diminishes my gratitude, and I unhesitatingly claim all the book's faults as my own.

Atlanta, Georgia   Thelma Freides

Contents

Part II.　Structure and Components of the Social Science Literature

Chapter Three

Research Reports: Scholarly Journals, Technical Reports,
　　and Books

Appendix B

Selected List of Social Science Journals

Chapter Four

Cumulating Publications (1): Research Reviews and
　　Handbooks

Part III. Literature Retrieval and the System of Bibliographic Records

LITERATURE AND
BIBLIOGRAPHY OF
THE SOCIAL SCIENCES

PART I

Science, Scientific Literature and Social Science

THE SCOPE OF THE BOOK, AND SOME BASIC DISTINCTIONS

The phrase "literature of the social sciences" refers to the published writings of social scientists. Like scholars in all other fields, social scientists write and publish in order to report their investigations, compare their findings with those reported by others, argue about the meaning and interpretation of what has been found. In short, they sort out and set down "what is known" in an area of study. The literature thus functions as a system of communication among the scholars in a field, providing a means for them to carry on the discussions necessary to their work.

These observations form the basic premise of the present work, which seeks to explain the social science literature and its use as an information resource by considering first the nature of the scholarly discussion in the social sciences and, on that foundation, the organization of the literature to convey the discussion and the use of bibliographic records to identify and facilitate access to the literature.

1

As the foregoing suggests, the phrase "literature of the social sciences" is used here in a somewhat restricted sense, to refer to works written by social scientists, addressed to other social scientists, and dealing with matters of mutual scientific interest. While this conception accords generally with what scholars are apt to think of as "their" literature, it excludes substantial amounts of material which readers might expect to find treated in a work such as the present one. As the exclusions are not arbitrary, but rest on some fundamental differences between the scholarly literature of social science and other publication covering a similar range of subject matter, some further consideration of what is involved can help bring the picture of the literature, as viewed here, into sharper focus.

Literature and Data

The first distinction to be made is between literature and data. As used here, "literature" refers to writings intended to analyze and comment on social life; "data" refers to the written records of the society. A large body of material ordinarily found in the social science collections of libraries—such items as laws, statistics, newspapers, the published correspondence and memoirs of statesmen, annual reports of corporations, governmental records of all kinds—belong to the category of social data. These are the records generated by the myriad public and private activities carried on in the society. They are brought into existence to disseminate the laws, report the news of the day, support the activities of government and the various sectors of the economy, and so forth. Social scientists are able to make use of these materials for purposes of their own, and in some fields of study depend on them almost entirely to supply the basic information needed in research. However, in terms of the present discussion, the critical point is that the data sources do not originate in the social scientists' communication system and are not fashioned in accordance with the needs of science. While understanding of the operations of science and scientific communication can be the basis for comprehending the scientific literature, these ideas are not relevant to comprehension of the characteristics of the social record, and on that basis the latter does not enter into consideration here.

Scholarly and Popular Literature

Within the realm of discussion and analysis there is a further distinction to be made between scientific writing addressed to specialists in a field, and discussions of public affairs and social issues addressed to the community at large. The distinction here is not an individious one. Because the work of social scientists often concerns subjects of widespread public interest, such as crime, racial conflict, or war and peace, the concerns of social science may not be readily distinguishable from the issues that engage the attention of political leaders and journalists. In consequence it might be assumed that the chief difference is that the scholar approaches these matters with greater intellectual detachment and the analytic skills of the trained researcher, so that his work puts more emphasis on thorough scrutiny of the facts, documentation of sources, and strictly logical, systematically reasoned argument, while the popular writer might allow himself more unsubstantiated expression of opinion. An alternative assumption might be that the scholar is an "ivory tower" theorist and logic-chopper, while the "hard-headed" politician or journalist is apt to have more useful ideas about the subject because he is more in touch with reality. Either way, the conception is erroneous. Both scholarly and popular writing can be soundly or poorly reasoned, well informed or ignorant, and can appeal to facts which are reliable and adequate or faulty and insufficient. The difference between them relates not to their quality, but to their audience and intent and, in consequence, to their content.

The social commentator addressing himself to the public at large deals with his subject as a matter of concrete social importance and tangible current interest. His aim, whether directly or indirectly, immediately or more remotely, is to persuade his readers to his point of view and influence their attitudes regarding the issue in question and what should be done about it. The social scientist is also a member of the general public, of course, and, as such, he has opinions and social and political preferences like anyone else. In addition, he may at times take on the role of social commentator, writing articles for popular magazines about current issues relating to his area of expertise. But when he writes as a scientist and addresses himself to other scientists he approaches his subject from a significantly different persepctive.

In his professional role, the social scientists directs his attention to matters such as poverty, or racial or international conflict, not as tangible issues about which important public decisions must be made, but as opportunities for learning more about how some aspect of society operates. His interest in such topics may be stimulated by his personal social and ethical values, but his approach to them in the scientific framework is a specialized one, outside the arena of general public discussion and subject to the special standards and values of the scientific system. Though his subject may impinge on matters of great public interest, the social scientist's efforts will have more in common with the historian's account of an event of the tenth century or the psychologist's observation of rats in mazes than with public debate as carried on in the public press. That is, the scientist aims to influence the other scholars working in his speciality, rather than the public at large, and what he seeks to persuade them of is not the fairness or righteousness of his views or the wisdom of the course he advocates, but the usefulness of his observations and explanations as a way to account for what goes on. If he writes with an eye to the judgment of history, it is not the history of his place and time he has in mind, but the history of his discipline.

All of this means that the specialized professional literature of social science, and the general public discussion of social issues, represent two separate arenas of conversation, carried on among different groups of participants in pursuit of different ends. The first category, scientific literature, is shaped in response to the goals and methods of operation of the scientific enterprise; the other belongs to another realm of discourse and requires another sort of framework for its comprehension. Only the former—scientific literature—figures in the examination of the social science literature to be undertaken here.

Chapter One

Some Characteristics of Science
and Scientific Communication

Several of my statements describing the activities of social scientists point to attributes of science which strongly influence the character of scientific literature, and it will be helpful to look at these more closely before proceeding to direct consideration of the literature. What follows is a necessarily brief and superficial survey of several large and rather formidably complex matters, intended to do no more than suggest some basic qualities of the scientific enterprise in general and of the social sciences as fields of scientific work. A number of distinctions that are in themselves notable and important are under-played or ignored, in an attempt to concentrate on the qualities broadly characteristics of science as a whole which most directly shape scientific literature. A list of books that treat more fully the philosophy and organization of science and social science, and the scope and current status of the social science disciplines, appears as Appendix A.

SCIENCE AS EXPLANATION

I have suggested that the aim of science is to account for what goes on—to explain. This idea is central to scientific work, but it is not always very clearly understood. Science does not consist, as is sometimes assumed, of a collection of facts. Rather, science uses facts to suggest and support explanations. A statement of fact—for example, most mid-western farmers vote Republican—is not, whether accurate or not, scientific, and it would not be more scientific if stated more precisely or in numerical terms—for example, twice as many mid-western farmers vote Republican as vote Democratic. Factual observations such as these take on scientific interest when they are attached to explanatory ideas, such as, in this instance, the role of traditional party attachments in voter choices, or the relation of regional or economic partisan patterns to the operations of the American political system.

The focus on explanation is evident in the language of scientific discourse. Terms such as concept, theory, and law all have to do with the relation between facts and their meaning. Roughly speaking, a concept is an abstract term that seems to summarize some aspect of reality in a meaningful way. Examples are role, self-image, social class. Concepts are thus categories which serve to guide the selection and ordering of facts. They provide the scientist with a frame through which he can look at the vast range and diversity of observable facts, and think about what they might mean. A theory, again speaking very roughly, is an explanatory statement expressing some relationship among concepts—for example, an idea that child-rearing practices in a culture are related in systematic ways to the adult personality patterns prevalent in the culture. A law is similar, though the term is usually applied to relatively positive and definite relationships such as the "law" of supply and demand which states that under specified conditions the price of a good will be that which clears the market. The meaning of terms such as these may vary with the circumstances of their use, and the distinctions made here may shade into one another. The general point is that these terms (and others, such as "ideal type," "model," "hypothetical construct") refer to ways of explaining what may be observed, and are thus focal points on which the scientific discussion centers.

The scientist offering an explanation of what he has observed must manage to persuade other scientists that the facts really are as he has reported them, and that all the facts pertinent to the situation have been considered. This raises several questions. Can the observations be repeated? Would what was seen also be apparent to others who observed the same phenomenon? Does the investigator's report include all there was to be observed, or might there have been additional factors whose presence was unknown and whose influence, therefore, could not be taken into account? Considerations such as these have given rise to a number of procedural requirements and customs associated with scientific work. These are sometimes referred to as "scientific method," but the term really relates to the fundamental rationale of inquiry and explanation, and not to any specific operations.

A chemist sterilizing laboratory containers, a historian studying the water-mark on a document and a sociologist pretesting a questionnaire are all doing about the same thing as far as science is concerned, dissimilar though these activities may be in other respects. That is, all are taking steps to assure that the observations they will report are as accurate and complete as other scientists will expect them to be, in order to support the explanations based on them. The chemist uses a sterile flask in order to be sure of what the flask contains. For the historian, the watermark is an indicator of the authenticity of his document; he wants to be sure that the document is what he takes it for. Likewise, the sociologist pretests his questionnaire as a way of ascertaining that the questions communicate what he intends and that the answers, accordingly, can be taken as responses to what he thinks he has asked.

A similar concern with the ability of facts to support an explanation underlies the use of experiment as a technique of investigation. An experiment is a way of manipulating data so as to be able to observe the effects of actions which are specified and controlled by the experimenter, and in this way to make the explanation of what occurs more convincing. When direct experiment is not feasible, as is often the case in the social sciences, but also in physical science fields such as astronomy and geology, analogous attempts are made to isolate selected factors for observation. Often this entails "controlled observation," which means finding situations as alike as possible except for the factors to be considered in the explanation, and comparing them. If the expected differences are found it is assumed that they are due to the known differences in the situations, since all the other elements believed to be relevant are alike and presumed to operate in the same way. This is exactly the assumption the experimenter makes in attributing the changes he observes in his data to his manipulations.

The general point is that there is no single "scientific method." The term really means whatever methods and procedures scientists accept as adequate to assure that the same results would always be obtained under like conditions, and that the explanation rests on appropriate observations.

The concern of science with explanation affects scientific literature in several ways. In the reporting of research, considerable space and attention is apt to be given to description and justification of the procedure employed by the researcher. This may permit other scholars to repeat the procedure and verify the observations, should they wish to do so. It serves to strengthen the argument for the validity of the explanation by assuring potential critics that the observations on which it is based are accurate and sound.

Since it is desirable that explanation rest on specific observation, the scope of scientific studies is usually rather narrow, limited to the range of data which can be systematically observed and whose role in the resulting explanation can be spelled out in detail. Non-scientists may be surprised and disappointed when research studies touching matters of widespread interest, such as race riots or school achievement, turn out to be addressed to very limited questions and to produce results which have no apparent connection with what the layman sees as important about the topic. The underlying reason is the necessity imposed by the scientific system to limit the explanation to what the data will support, and the difficulty of dealing with more than a limited number of variables in any single investigation.

CUMULATIVENESS IN SCIENCE

The explanation a scientist offers as the result of his observations does not consist of whatever might occur to him and seem plausible. His view of the possibilities is very much influenced by what has been learned about the subject in the past, as, indeed, is his initial choice of the problem—the idea that it presents a question worth investigating—and his method of approaching it. The scientist, who seeks to contribute to the "advancement of knowledge" in his field, is aware that knowledge in science is cumulative. This means that new knowledge is seen not as the unique product of its creator's personal insight, but as a part of a larger whole, arising out of what has gone before and contributing in its turn to the foundation and impetus for further movement.

Cumulativeness is a highly significant attribute of science and the quality which, probably more than any other, distinguishes science from other forms of intellectual activity. Because scientific knowledge is cumulative, new discoveries have, on occasion, been predicted before they were actually made, and similar or identical work has sometimes been done at the same time by investigators who were not even aware of each other's existence. Moreover, an idea in science is never regarded as complete in itself, the way a work of creative art or literature normally is. Instead, scientific ideas depend for their value and validity on their meaning in relation to the larger body of knowledge. Also, works of art, or even systems of philosophical or religious thought may be vastly different from each other yet each may be valid and acceptable in its own terms so that there can be no objective way of choosing one over the other, while the existence in science of incompatible ideas is always temporary. Though competing theories may exist for a long time, it is always assumed that the inconsistency will be resolved eventually when additional knowledge is gained and the matter in question comes to be better understood.

The difference between science and the creative arts from this point of view is quite clear cut and easy to see. The contrast with humanistic areas of scholarship is more ambiguous. Certainly it is true that all scholarship is done in a social environment, so that all scholars work in the context of a wider body of knowledge, are influenced by their predecessors, and expect in their turn to influence those who come after them. Yet it is generally accepted that these matters are considerably more consciously and deliberately articulated in science than in such fields as philosophy or literary criticism. Knowledge in science moves in more definitely demarcated channels; the place of a given idea among others, and the over-all result of a body of related efforts are of greater concern and are more clearly spelled out in science than in the humanities. The position of the social sciences can probably be described as intermediate. That is, cumulativeness is almost universally highly valued among social scientists, but it is less universally characteristic of scholarship in the social science disciplines. Nonetheless, this quality is reflected in some significant aspects of the organization of the social science literature, and on that ground it is useful here to regard the social sciences as essentially cumulative in nature, even though this is not uniformly the case in practice.

The idea of knowledge as cumulative also means that whatever is learned from research not only answers a specific question but also drives the investigative process forward. When the results of many studies all seem to point in the same direction, this forms the basis for more generalized ideas and explanations. At the same time, acquisition of new knowledge may reveal problems which were unrecognized earlier, and thus generate new questions to be investigated. In the final analysis, scientific progress means the uncovering of new opportunities for exploration. The value of an idea in science is judged in terms of its ability to lead to additional ideas, rather than on the basis of any absolute or permanent standard of validity.

There are not only additions to knowledge, but also replacements and deletions; science is not static, but dynamic. Again in contract to the artist, the scientist does not create for the ages or hope that his work will endure forever. The idea that new knowledge is mainly a springboard for further study means that even the greatest scientific achievements can be expected to do no more than serve for a time and then cease to be useful. Since it is usefulness in the creative process, and not "correctness" as such, which determines the standing of an idea in science, discovery of contradictions does not in itself invalidate a scientific explanation, and it is not unusual for an idea to continue to be used as though it were correct, even though its defects and inconsistencies are widely recognized. In general, a scientific idea is discarded only when a more fruitful replacement is put forward. Permanence can never be assumed, however, and principles which have existed for centuries (an example is Archimedes' theory of displacement)[1] must nonetheless be regarded as tentative and liable to be altered at some time in the future.

The quality of cumulativeness in science has several notable effects on scientific literature. First, it exerts an important influence on the subjects treated in scientific publications. Since science builds on existing knowledge, scholars tend to choose their problems for study in the light of issues brought to the fore by previous investigations. Such questions may or may not coincide with the larger society's views of what is important about the subject and may or may not produce the kind of information society needs to deal with its problems. But unless the cumulative processes in the field have advanced to the level where they can provide concepts and techniques for dealing with the problem, the scientist sees himself as having no special contribution to make or expertise to offer. Accordingly, he tends to concentrate on problems he can solve and areas where his research can be successful by the standards of science, even though these may seem far less interesting and important to laymen than other matters.

The idea of cumulativeness also relates to the differing approaches that several disciplines might take to the same subject, and thus to the aspects of a topic treated in each discipline's literature. The meaning of the disciplinary divisions, and their impact on the scientific enterprise, will be further considered below. Here it may be noted in passing that while a given subject may fall within the range of several disciplines, in each one the questions raised about the topic and the prevailing ideas regarding possible explanations will reflect the distinctive history and environment of the field, its background of previous investigation, and its own body of general principles representing its cumulation of "what is known."

As was suggested earlier, the cumulative principle means that scientific explanations are put forward and considered at several levels, from the specific and limited inferences drawn from a single research study to successively broader and more generalized ideas. Reflecting this, scientific publications take several forms, each designed to serve as the vehicle for a particular level of discussion, a particular phase of the development and formulation of cumulated knowledge. It is thus possible to view the publications as differentiated in terms of their functions, and to see scientific literature as a coherent system of communication. This is the key element in the explanation of the literature to be presented here.

Finally, because science is cumulative, scientific literature is especially strongly affected by the passage of time. The meaning and importance of a work must always be seen in relation to the current state of knowledge, and not to the scientific environment to which the work originally addressed itself. This applies irrespective of subject matter, to historical accounts of the events of centuries past as well as to studies of more contemporary affairs. It applies to humanistic fields as well as to science, of course, but the more fully the cumulative principle operates in a discipline, the more significant a consideration this is likely to be. In science, particularly, a work described as solid and useful or highly authoritative at the time of its publication, cannot be assumed years later to have retained these attributes.

SCIENCE AS A COLLECTIVE ENTERPRISE

The idea that science is a collective undertaking has been suggested at several points. I have described scientific literature as the communications a scientist addresses to his fellows and have noted that the scientist aims to persuade other scientists, and derives his rewards from the recognition of the scientific community. The collective character of the scientific enterprise is extremely significant, not only in the sense that the work of each participant is guided by and responds to the work of others, but also because the content of scientific knowledge—what scientists know—rests on the consensus judgment of the community of scientists.

As stated earlier, a scientist bases his investigations on the cumulative results of previous studies and offers his findings, in turn, as a stepping stone for others. An experiment done by one scientist may be repeated by another to verify the findings, or may be repeated with certain modifications to see what the differences in the outcome would be. The results obtained in one study will be matched up against those stemming from comparable efforts. As research relating to the question accumulates, judgments are formed about the meaning of the evidence and the explanations the evidence can support. Certain ideas and interpretations become widely known among scholars who concern themselves with the subject, and succeed in gaining their acceptance. Those ideas are taught in courses, set down in textbooks, and generally presented as part of "what is known" among the authorities on the subject, that is, as part of the scientific consensus.

The processes by which the scientific community arrives at consensus judgments are entirely tacit and informal. It really cannot be sufficiently stressed that there is nothing orderly, organized, or systematic about what occurs. Many people think of science as a collection of information that is "true," or "proven." This is probably because they have studied from textbooks in which the subject is presented in a systematic, well-ordered fashion, and few students recognize that the orderliness is not intrinsic to the information but has been imposed, for purposes of clarity and comprehensibility, by the author of the text. In fact, the concept of "truth," of a definitive bar of judgment at which it can be decided what truth is and is not, is quite foreign to the operations of science. A given idea may be accepted by some scientists and rejected by others, equally qualified and equally authoritative. A question may remain in dispute for many years, with fierce argument raging all the while and new evidence ceaselessly gathered and put forward by the adherents of the various positions. By the same token, as mentioned above, ideas long established and universally accepted may be discarded and replaced when scientists come to believe, for a number of possible reasons, that the new theory is more useful than the one it replaces. Scientists have evolved a number of standards governing what is acceptable by way of evidence and reasoning, and there is, in general, wide agreement on these. Application of the standards to particular cases is not automatic, however, and, as noted, there is no final authority who decides.

In all of this, moreover, factors in addition to objective rationality and even-handed weighing of the evidence may play a role. No scientist can be totally familiar with all the evidence and possible alternatives relating to all the propositions he finds useful, and much of what he "knows" consists of ideas he has accepted without question in the course of his training, or as the outcome of work with which he is not directly involved. The reputation of an eminent scientist may at times persuade other scientists of the correctness of his arguments quite as much as the concrete evidence he offers. The "somewhat cranky Harvard professor of the 1870s (who) used to tell his class that 'the reason everyone now believes in the wave theory of light is that all those who once believed in the corpulcular theory are dead' "[2] made a point that few would dispute. Nonetheless, at bottom there exists a process by which the scientific community exercises its collective judgment to determine "what is known" in science, and this is the only basis on which scientific knowledge can be defined.

SCIENTIFIC LITERATURE

One way to summarize everything that has been set down thus far would be to characterize science as a kind of continuous open forum for the reporting of research findings and the consideration of explanations. The central importance of communication is thus apparent. For this reason, scientific communication arose virtually simultaneously with modern scientific investigation, in the seventeenth century. At first the system was mainly informal. Those engaged in scientific work—mostly amateurs for whom science was an avocation—wrote each other letters describing their experiments and the conclusions to be drawn from them. They formed societies, and reported their discoveries in letters to the society's officers and directly to other scientists at society meetings. In time, regularly published journals containing research reports replaced the letters, forming a pattern which, in essence, persists to this day.

As scientific activity has grown, it has become increasingly institutionalized and professionalized. Scientists are no longer amateurs, but almost invariably are people who earn their living by research—chiefly as members of university faculties, but also on staffs of special research institutes and in research enterprises maintained by government and industry. The communication activities begun in the seventeenth century by such groups as the Royal Society in England and the French Académie royale des Sciences are now conducted by a great many scientific organizations in a multitude of specialized fields. They hold meetings for direct reports and discussions, and sponsor numerous publications. The scientific journal continues as the major means for communicating the results of research, and other forms of publication—reviews, texts, histories, encyclopedias—have been devised to carry other communications, such as discussions of the implications of research findings, assessments of progress in a field, and formulation of the basic principles of a subject. This system of publications is what is known as the "literature" of a field of study.

The scientific literature serves the scientific community in a dual capacity. It is both working instrument and repository. As working tool, it is the medium by which scientists communicate with each other. The private thoughts of an individual are not science, and can only become part of science by being communicated to other scientists for examination and judgment. Likewise, an individual who performed experiments to satisfy his own curiosity but kept the results to himself would not be engaged in science in any meaningful sense of the term, no matter how meticulous his work. Communication is required for the creative processes of science to go forward, and for the scientific consensus to form. Publication is not the only medium of scientific communication (scientists also meet face-to-face at meetings, and groups of scientists may correspond with each other directly) but it is the principal one, and the one which creates a permanent, public record. The scientific literature, then, serves as repository for the collective intellectual property of the scientific community—the content of science, "what is known." For this reason it is often said that "science is the scientific literature."

SCIENTIFIC DISCIPLINES

The discussion to this point has repeatedly made reference to scientific "fields," and these figure very importantly in the literature, which is mainly organized along disciplinary lines. It is therefore worthwhile not simply to recognize the existence of these divisions, but to examine their meaning with some care. In an ultimate and very generalized sense, the continuing discussion of research findings and their meaning which constitutes the scientific enterprise embraces all scientists, past and present, and all subjects to which scientists have turned their attention. In the long run, and in broadest perspective, all knowledge is interrelated and there is "a scientific community" which has collective jurisdiction over scientific knowledge in its entirety. In practice, however, the concerns of science are too extensive and complex for an individual to be able to comprehend and participate in the scientific enterprise across its entire spectrum. For most purposes, the world of science consists of a number of specialized groups, each functioning as the scientific community in relation to a limited area of knowledge and a limited range of scientific concerns.

These groups or "fields," are often assumed to be distinguishable in terms of their subject matter. One thinks of a biologist as a student of the nature and functioning of living organisms, a sociologist as concerned with the characteristics and behavior of human groups and institutions, an economist as engaged in studying the creation and distribution of material goods, and so forth. While this is the case to some extent, there are few, if any, subjects which are squarely and exclusively the province of a particular branch of science. The brain is an element in the functioning of living organisms, and thus a subject for study by physiologists. It is also a critical factor in behavior, and thus part of the subject matter of psychology. The outbreak of a war is an event in a country's history and historians are concerned with it in that context, but the same war is an instance of a type of political relationship among nations, and hence of interest to political scientists. The propensity of consumers to buy or not buy a particular item under given conditions is an aspect of the functioning of an economic system and a subject of concern to economists. It is also an aspect of individual choice and decision making, and thus a problem in psychology, as well as a manifestation of the values of the social groups and culture of which the individual is part, and thus interesting to sociologists and anthropologists. Similar examples could be cited endlessly. In each instance a given subject—brain functioning, war, consumer choice—can be viewed as part of the subject matter of several branches of science. What distinguishes one field from another is not subject matter as such, but a distinctive approach that relates particular concepts and ideas to the subject and gives the subject its interest as a focus of inquiry. Each discipline views its subject matter through the unique lens provided by its history as a field of study and the explanatory propositions it has created. In consequence, each raises its own questions about a subject, seeks answers in distinctive ways, and relates what is found to its own body of cumulated knowledge.

As a rough illustration, consider the possibility that a political scientist and a sociologist become interested in the subject of voter participation, or why some people vote more regularly than others. This subject may interest a political scientist because of possibilities it suggests for increased understanding of such matters as differences in the types of government operating in various communities, the fate at the polls of certain types of issues or candidates, and the like. Because his interest is in the functioning of the political system, the political scientist will see the problem as one of learning about the composition of the electorate and the factors determining its composition. Does the tendency to vote or not vote vary from one place to another? What are the differences between men and women, among various ethnic groups, among people of different ages? How do all of these factors interrelate with such matters as election propaganda, or the issues raised in a campaign?

In raising such questions, the political scientist is aware that the answers will account for only a portion of the behavior he is studying; whatever general patterns he finds, there will be people whose actions as voters are not described by them. However, the deviant cases do not claim his attention. From his perspective, the significant point is that large numbers of people behave in similar ways, and that this pattern of behavior can account for certain other occurrences which interest him. Since the deviations do not appear to affect the over-all pattern in any systematic or consistent way, they are viewed as random events; that is, they are assumed to result from circumstances unrelated to the question under study. Accordingly, the political scientist would ignore the exceptions and concentrate his efforts on exploring the nature and implications of the general pattern.

This does not mean that deviations from general patterns of voting participation are really believed to be random. On the contrary, they are just as subject to investigation and systematic explanation as any other phenomenon and might lead another scholar, say a sociologist, to interest himself in the question "who votes" from another point of view. He might see the act of voting as a manifestation of the way an individual relates to the society around him and might undertake to explore the connection between the two as a way of learning more about the individual's perception of society and his role in it, and the factors governing this perception. Here the causes and circumstances of individual deviation from a general group pattern—the aspect of the subject disregarded by the scholar interested in its political implications—are of central concern, while the precise characteristics of the group pattern might not be considered. The sociologist is aware that the nature of the pattern may vary from one time or place to another or among various segments of the population, but from his perspective the important thing is that some general pattern exists and some people conform while others deviate. In the absence of reasons to think otherwise, he will view variations in the pattern as random events unrelated to conformity or nonconformity to a group norm. Accordingly, he ignores the details of the pattern's characteristics and focuses on the factors associated with individual conformity and deviation.

The two scholars in this hypothetical example may be regarded as studying the same subject—political participation—or different subjects—the political system, on the one hand, and the development of social perceptions and identifications on the other. It is clear that whatever differences there are between them relate fundamentally to the web of ideas and perspectives out of which their questions arise, and also therefore to the portions of the scholarly audience to whom their work is addressed. A field of study, then, may be described as a group of scholars who tend to converse primarily with each other about a limited range of knowledge. In so doing they tend to develop certain ways of formulating questions, making observations, and assessing and interpreting data. They come to regard these as most suitable to their range of interests, and their concepts and methods are continually added to and sharpened by the discussion and criticism that are focused on them. At the same time, the scholars in a given field are relatively much less informed about and influenced by the similar discussions taking place in other circles.

The division of the scientific enterprise into separate, limited discussions serves a practical end. It is only in this way that scientific work is possible at all. The basic scientific activity is observation. In any situation, the number of things taking place is infinite, and observation and explanation of all of them simultaneously is beyond human capability. To observe any part of the situation with accuracy and precision, it is necessary to focus on that part alone and to eliminate all other elements from consideration. Generally speaking, the narrower the range of observation, the greater the degree of precision that can be achieved. This is the purpose of the laboratory and the experiment: to create a situation that brings into sharp focus the variables under consideration and to remove all others from the range of attention. Something very similar is accomplished when a group of scholars—the members of a "field"—focus their attention on explanation of the nature and operation of a limited range of variables.

Yet it is readily understood that knowledge is nowhere neatly divisible; it is quite apparent that the work of each of the scholars may have relevance and implications for the other. Awareness of the factors governing conformity and deviation may suggest to the political scientist additional possibilities for explaining the pattern of political participation. More knowledge of the nature and range of variation in a general social pattern may suggest to the sociologist aspects which might affect conformity to group norms. For this reason a scholar's recognition of the usefulness to his field of results obtained in another can be a very significant achievement in science, since it may raise new questions and open new channels of investigation in several directions at once. Moreover, larger questions, such as "why do people vote" are likely to require a fitting together of explanations generated by numerous lines of investigation.

In this sense the division of science and scientific knowledge into "fields" is wholly arbitrary and artificial, and there is constant crossing of the boundaries as scientists attempt to apply to their work insights derived from other areas of study. Yet it is only by virtue of the division that science is possible at all, and each accretion to knowledge brings to light further questions susceptible to ever closer and more specialized exploration. Thus the scientific system generates a constant tension between tendencies toward broader generalization and increased range and depth of knowledge, and toward narrower specialization and increased precision. A consensus defining "scientific knowledge" on any point may emerge from the deliberations of any group, and the likelihood of its acceptance depends largely on whether or not other groups coalesce in support of competing ideas. This points out once again the inherent instability and looseness surrounding "what is known" about questions in science.

The participants in a group that may collectively carry on the processes of investigation and consensus formation in science cannot be specified in advance. With regard to a given point or question the group may consist of those engaged in the study of particular problems (such as poverty, or crime), or whose interests focus on the operation of a range of variables in particular circumstances (such as group dynamics, or Rennaissance history), the adherents of a particular approach or point of view (such as Skinnerian psychologists, or Marxist economists), or those making use of similar methodologies (such as opinion sampling or content analysis).[3] The most stable and enduring divisions, and the most significant in many respects including that of the organization of scientific literature, are the major fields of study, or "academic disciplines," such as psychology, history, and so forth. It is usually in terms of their disciplines that scholars identify themselves. A man will seldom describe himself as a scientist or social scientist, but is likely to say instead that he is a psychologist or a historian. In so doing, he also indicates the range of concerns with which he feels obliged to be at least somewhat familiar, the arena of deliberation and judgment he regards himself as qualified to enter, and, in turn, the group to which his own work is addressed.

A number of factors, social and institutional as well as intellectual, account for the importance and pervasiveness of the academic disciplines as the main structural units of the scientific system. Since universities tend to be organized on the basis of disciplinary departments, the discipline is the framework in which scholars are trained. The graduate student is ordinarily exposed extensively to the range of knowledge in his discipline and much less so, if at all, to work being done in other fields. In consequence he tends to acquire, from the beginning of his career, the outlook and assumptions prevailing in his discipline.

Similarly, the discipline is the main basis on which professional societies devoted to the discussion and advancement of scientific work are organized. Every discipline has its own national organization (e.g., the American Psychological Association) and these are frequently part of world-wide associations (e.g., the International Political Science Association). Although there are also scientific organizations that represent a range of interests narrower than that of an entire discipline or comprised of strands from several disciplines (for example, the Society for Research in Child Development; the American Association for Public Opinion Research) members of such groups are almost invariably also members of the general associations of their respective disciplines. Thus, again, through participation in scientific meetings and personal association with colleagues, a major part of the scholar's contact with the world of science occurs within a disciplinary framework.

Finally, perhaps because the factors mentioned above, and possibly also because a large portion of scholarly employment is in university departments organized along disciplinary lines, the discipline is the major source from which the scholar receives acceptance and recognition of his work. The scientific community at large tends to look to each discipline for evaluation of the work of its members. Accordingly, the widest audience which a scholar addresses, and the group he seeks ultimately to convince of the validity and significance of his efforts, is his discipline.

Thus science, the collective enterprise, consists of a number of collectives that function separately and relatively independently. These groups have no fixed extent or boundaries and may vary in scope from one purpose or occasion to another, but the generally stable and enduring components of the scientific system tend to be the academic disciplines.

FOOTNOTES

1. Although this may be common knowledge to some, the present writer is specifically indebted for the example to Gordon Tullock, in The Organization of Inquiry (Durham, N.C.: Duke University Press, 1966) p. 163.

2. James B. Conant, Science and Common Sense (New Haven: Yale University Press, 1951) p. 29.

3. For an interesting view of the growth of a new research area from roots in several disciplines, see the account of the development of the field of organization studies in James G. March's introduction to the Handbook of Organizations (James G. March ed., Chicago, Rand McNally, 1965). That discussion is especially germane to the matters being considered here because it is based on an analysis of publications and citation patterns.

Chapter Two

The Social Sciences as Branches
of the Scientific Enterprise

THE SOCIAL SCIENCE DISCIPLINES

The disciplines customarily designated "social sciences" are psychology, anthropology, political science, economics, geography, and history. The boundaries delineated in this way are only approximate and roughly indicative of the range of social science. Psychology, anthropology, and geography overlap at various points with areas of natural science, and history is sometimes placed with the humanities. Demography might be seen as another social science discipline, or as a subfield of sociology; business could be considered a separate field or a part of economics, and so forth. There is no single way to define or enumerate the social sciences. Very generally, they are the fields whose interest centers on observation and explanation of the actions of people in society: what people do and why, and under what circumstances they do one thing rather than another. The most general custom is to designate as social sciences the seven disciplines enumerated above.

Each of the disciplines approaches the study of social life from its own perspectives, and in so doing carves out its own segment of the broad field of social inquiry. Allowing for the inevitable crudeness and inaccuracy of distinctions of this kind, psychology can be described as primarily concerned with the behavior of individuals, while sociology focuses on the function of groups and institutions, and anthropology centers on the characteristics of thought and behavior which distinguish societies or cultures from one another. Political science deals with the formulation of concepts relating to the distribution and use of power, and economics is much the same applied to material goods. Geography examines the interactions between man and his physical environment.

Explanation of almost any of these matters in chronological, developmental terms is the concern of history.

Several other fields of study, closely related to the major divisions of social science mentioned above, devote their attention to patterns of behavior operating in particular types of institutions and social relationships. These are the "applied" fields, so called because they concentrate on the practical issues arising in some portion of the social arena, and attempt to apply scientific knowledge to the solution of concrete problems. Fields such as business and public administration, labor and industrial relations, social work, education, and, in some degree, law, can be numbered in this group.[1]

Another range of concerns is described by the term "policy sciences," designating areas of scholarship that direct particular attention to problems relating to public policy. Broadly speaking, the work of policy scientists draws on concepts and ideas developed in numerous disciplines, mainly but not exclusively within the social sciences, and brings these to bear on efforts to comprehend and elucidate the goals, determinants, decision processes, and effects of public policy. Policy scientists may work in operational settings, such as government departments, in which case their activities would probably also fall within the "applied" category described above, or they may devote themselves entirely to basic research and the search for underlying theory. In either case, the areas of study designated policy sciences are those centering on policy issues and processes.

The term "behavioral science" (or "the behavioral sciences") has a specific historical origin which will be explained further on, but is often used to refer to areas of social inquiry that draw their data mainly from direct observation of behavior, rather than from written records. By this criterion, much of the work in such fields as psychology and anthropology would come under the rubric "behavioral science," while the activities of economists and historians characteristically would not. The distinction can be useful at times, but it is not fundamental.

Social science utilizes data drawn from direct observation, and collected expressly for the purposes of the investigation, when people are asked to perform certain tasks in a laboratory or respond to an interviewer's questions, or when a researcher watches and records certain activities in a classroom, club meeting, hospital ward, tribal ceremony, or other accessible locale. In other studies, the data are derived from written records compiled originally for purposes other than research: demographic or economic statistics, the minutes and resolutions of a political body, the diaries and correspondence of a statesman. The activities of a scholar examining a group of historical documents may look quite different from those of another researcher who is reading instrument dials in a laboratory, but the work of the two men is actually much the same. Both are attempting to observe some aspect of behavior and explain what they have observed. Both are attempting to answer questions raised by previous attempts of scholars to answer other questions, and in this way to add to an existing body of knowledge and also to generate new problems for further investigation.

Most generally, then, social science may be described as the cumulative formulation of propositions to explain social life. It is the application to a particular range of data—those relating to human behavior and interaction—of scientific styles of inquiry. This characterization of the social sciences as essentially identical in outlook and practice to other fields of science is one which would probably find agreement among most present-day social scientists as well as many scientists in other fields, but it is not beyond question or dispute. The meaning of science in relation to social inquiry, and whether the social sciences are, can be, or ought to aspire to be scientific are matters which have been long and extensively debated, both within and outside the social science disciplines. The account of the social science literature to be presented here is grounded in an assumption that the social sciences are indeed sciences, or, at the least, that their communication patterns are essentially those characteristic of scientific fields, designed in response to the requirements of scientific work. This is done for two reasons: first, because this view of social sciences as true sciences is, I believe, more nearly accurate than any other, and, second, because the scientific model can supply a logical and highly useful framework in which to comprehend the literature. At the same time it must be recognized that the literature as the reader actually encounters it owes its character not only to the needs and attributes of science, as postulated by a hypothetical, generalized model of scientific communication, but also to the traditional and customary patterns of investigation and discussion, as these have evolved in a particular field. Accordingly, it will be useful to give some attention here to the background out of which current perspectives have developed.

What follows is a necessarily truncated and superficial review of the history of social science and of the idea of science in relation to the study of society. The unique attributes of the several fields have mainly been glossed over, in the interests of delineating a broad, common pattern which may be related to significant qualities of the literature. The backgrounds and current concerns of the various disciplines are more extensively explored in the works listed in Appendixes A and D.

THE DEVELOPMENT OF SCIENTIFIC PERSPECTIVES IN THE SOCIAL SCIENCES

Because many areas of social science have undergone noticeable change in relatively recent times, the idea of the social sciences as scientific fields may seem very modern, associated with a contemporary world of computers, survey teams, and personality tests, and contrasting sharply with an older image of "professors . . . (who) sit in chairs writing books about each other's books."[2] Actually, attempts to develop a science of society are as old as science itself, and it is really not at all inaccurate to say that the history of social science during the three centuries of the existence of modern science has been the history of efforts to be scientific. The specific goals and practices of social scientists have changed with changes in the prevailing conceptions of the character of science and the scientist's work, but an orientation toward the natural sciences as models for social science to emulate is quite long standing and consistent.

The Philosophical System-Building Tradition

To the social philosophers of seventeenth- and eighteenth-century Europe, science was the discovery of the basic laws governing the universe. A "science" of society was understood to mean an overarching cosmological system built with watertight logic and consistency from a set of fundamental postulates. These basic principles, or laws, were assumed to govern behavior and social relations in much the same inescapable and immutable fashion as physical laws, such as those of gravity or motion, were thought to shape and control the physical world. In this regard it is of interest to note that Auguste Comte, the French philosopher of the early nineteenth century, who is generally credited with the founding of sociology, called his proposed new science "social physics."

Despite their interest in science, the approach of the social philosophers differed from that of the physical scientists in at least one highly significant respect. In the developing physical sciences, ways were increasingly found to use detailed observation as the source of explanatory principles and to verify hypotheses by experiment. By contrast, in the realm of social analysis "laws" were arrived at by deductive reasoning from fundamental principles whose validity was assumed but not demonstrated—for example, the idea that man behaves rationally. Writers supported and illustrated their arguments with such evidence as they were able to muster, but the "facts" cited in support of conclusions derived from casual observation and personal experience, rather than systematic investigation. In consequence, social thought remained oriented to construction of comprehensive cosmological systems, while natural science moved increasingly to incremental investigation and solution of narrow, precisely stated problems.

Nonetheless, social theories often reflected prevailing ideas in natural science, or were analogies to physical principles. For example, the concepts of economic equilibrium, and of checks and balances as a political principle, both important eighteenth-century ideas, are essentially mechanical conceptualizations, reflecting the mechanical orientation of the physical science of the time. In the late nineteenth and early twentieth centuries, interest in evolutionary theory in biology was reflected in social theories based on analogies between society and biological organisms. The work of the English philosopher Herbert Spencer affords the most notable example. Spencer saw society as an organism which evolved from simpler to more complex forms by a process of natural selection, in the same way as biological organisms. Accordingly he proposed that the controlling principle of social, as of physical, life, was adaptation of the individual to change in the environment. These ideas, and others influenced by them, came to be known as "social Darwinism," and the familiar phrase "survival of the fittest" is actually Spencer's, not Darwin's. Another notable social theory based on a biological analogy was formulated by the German historian Oswald Spengler, whose Decline of the West, published in 1918, described civilizations as passing through an inevitable life cycle from birth through maturity and decay. Marxist theory, grounded in the concepts of economic class conflict and dialectical materialism, is another nineteenth century example of the construction of an all-embracing explanation of society on the basis of immutable universal principles, though not, in this instance, biologically inspired.

Global theories of society constructed on the basis of fundamental laws had a distinctly normative, evaluative character. That is, they were directed as much toward prescribing what ought to be as toward explaining what was actually observable. Having set forth certain relationships as universal and inevitable laws, it was natural to argue for particular social arrangements on the basis of their alleged compatability with those laws, and to reject alternatives as contrary to the natural and inevitable order of the universe. Thus the approach to social analysis represented by abstract speculation, though it often employed the rhetoric of science, was in large measure a form of moral philosophy aimed principally at distinguishing between the proper and improper ordering of society. Modern social science has largely turned away from this orientation, but it is a major current in the background of today's perspectives.

The Fact-Gathering Approach

Another major tradition in social science was one that stressed the collection of facts, rather than the formulation of theories. This approach, too, was based on a conception of science; one that defined the essence of science as exact knowledge derived from precise and unbiased examination of definite facts, uncontaminated by abstract, "armchair" theories or the prior opinions of the investigator. In this view, scientific work consisted of the collection and orderly classification of all the facts obtainable, which could then speak for themselves to reveal their meaning. This outlook exercised a strong influence in the social sciences during the nineteenth and early twentieth centuries.

In the aftermath of the political and social upheavals associated with the French Revolution, historians, early in the nineteenth century, began to reject the use of history as a source of moral lessons and patriotic indoctrination, and to seek a firmer foundation for their knowledge in factual comprehensiveness and precision.

> ... (In) every age history is taken to be a story of actual events from which a significant meaning may be derived; and in every age the illusion is that the present version is valid because the related facts are true, whereas former versions are invalid because based on inaccurate or inadequate facts. . . . Finding the course of history littered with the *debris* of exploded philosophies, the historians of the (nineteenth) century, unwilling to be forever duped, turned away (as they fondly hoped) from 'interpretation' to the rigorous examination of the factual event, just as it occurred. Perfecting the technique of investigation, they laboriously collected and edited the sources of information, and with incredible persistence and ingenuity ran illusive error to earth . . .[3]

The new approach stressed the inclusion of all facets of social life in the historical record and, of highest importance, the full and impartial recording of facts, without expression of opinion by the historian or attempts to judge and interpret past epochs from the perspectives of a later time. The German historian Leopold von Ranke, writing in the 1820s, used the words "wie as eigentlich gewesen" (as it really was) to characterize the proper standard of historical research, and this phrase became a kind of slogan for historians of the new persuasion, who called their work "scientific" or "objective" history.

The rise of the fact-centered approach to historical study coincided with the establishment of a number of major governmental archives, organized and opened to historical researchers during the nineteenth century. The close scrutiny and editing of documents and other historical source materials became a major area of historical work. As the statement above, by the twentieth-century historian Carl Becker suggests, the assumption was that the "true" historical picture would emerge "when all the facts were in."

The nineteenth century also saw a great upsurge in interest in the facts of contemporary social life. Growing industrialization and urbanization brought many changes in living conditions and numerous social problems. One consequence was an expansion in the range of governmental activity and concern, with concomitantly larger needs for information about conditions in the society. Government programs for the collection of social statistics, by population censuses and other means, were substantially enlarged and improved during the nineteenth century in both Europe and America. This work provided employment for social scientists as well as opportunities to develop techniques for collecting and presenting data, and in this way tended to reinforce the idea of fact-collecting as the focus of social inquiry.

The collecting and reporting of the facts of social life was of great interest also to people concerned about social betterment and amelioration of the many social defects of the new industrial society. Advocates of social reform believed that their efforts would gain support if the true extent of poverty, disease, and general social disintegration were made know, and, in consequence undertook social investigations aimed at discovering such facts. A monumental example of work in this vein is Charles Booth's Life and Labour of the People in London, a comprehensive report on the economic and social conditions of the London population, published in seventeen volumes between 1889 and 1903. Booth was a businessman and philanthropist with strong avocational interests in social research, who conducted many studies of social problems during the latter half of the nineteenth century and also served as president of the Royal Statistical Society. His study of London life was intended to show how occupational and employment patterns were causing misery and social decay. To collect his information, Booth took up residence in the London slums and conducted extensive interviews with the inhabitants, as well as with school attendance officers, welfare workers, and others acquainted with local conditions. His survey encompassed over one million families, and was the most extensive systematic social investigation undertaken up to its time.

Though ordinarily not conducted on the massive scale of Booth's study, the collection of facts as a catalyst for social change was an important and pervasive element in nineteenth-century social inquiry. The National Association for the Promotion of Social Science, founded in England in 1857, and the American Social Science Association, founded in 1865, played major roles. Though spurred by a basic concern with social improvement and reform, the activities of these groups centered around the "social survey," or collection of information concerning social conditions, and they rejected any connection to a philosophical or ideological position. The assumption was that proper social policies would be evident to men of good will once the "true facts" concerning social conditions were brought out.

By the start of the twentieth century professional scholars in the social sciences had formed their own organizations and had largely separated themselves from lay groups such as the two named above, whose orientation was chiefly philanthropic. However, basic assumptions similar to those that characterized the social survey movement remained significant in academic social science at least into the 1920s and 1930s. That is, many scholars saw research as a process of collecting and classifying facts, on the assumption that correct answers to questions could be arrived at by impartial consideration of all the facts pertaining to a problem. One example of a scholarly enterprise of this nature was the "Harvard Barometer," a periodic report on economic conditions issued during the 1920s. As described by the economic theorist Joseph Schumpeter, "The constructors of the Harvard Barometer emphasized for the benefit of their readers and also believed themselves that they were not using any of that discredited and discrediting monster, economic theory." He adds, "As a matter of fact . . . they did use a theory that was all the more dangerous because it was subconscious,"[4] but this expresses a view of the relation of theory to fact which became apparent only to a later generation of scholars. As recently as thirty or forty years ago a belief that facts "speak for themselves" was still fairly widespread among social scientists.

System Building and Fact Collecting Compared

To major traditions in social science had been formed by the beginning of the twentieth century: sweeping, abstract theory building grounded in moral philosophy, and extensive and painstaking amassing of facts, allegedly uninfluenced by theory. Both these tendencies were manifested, in one form or another, in virtually all the social disciplines. In some fields the two approaches were the focus of overt conflict. This was notably the case, for example in economics in which a famous and much discussed methodenstreit (methodological conflict) divided the field into two opposing camps during much of the late nineteenth and early twentieth centuries. On one side were ranged the "neoclassical" economists, principally English, whose work stressed abstract, deductive theory in the classical tradition of Adam Smith and Ricardo. Opposing them were the "Austrian" or "institutional" school, whose approach centered on economic history and the reporting and classifying of concrete facts of economic behavior. In other instances the two approaches simply coexisted, with little mutual contact or interest between the philosophers, on the one hand, and the fact-finders on the other.

While very different in some respects, these two approaches to the study of society had more in common than may appear at first glance. Both had a decidedly evaluative and moralistic stance, in which prescription was at least as important as description or explanation. For the "philosophical" school, as has been seen, it was but a short step from the delineation of universal social laws to the passing of moral judgments, since the social order clearly had to follow alleged universal principles. Advocates of the factual approach stressed their freedom from preconceived opinions, but much of their work was grounded in, and strongly influenced by, interests in social reform, and they were quite confident in their belief that the proper course of social action would be evident once the facts were known. As the remark by Professor Schumpeter suggests, the fact-finders' claim to be uninfluenced by theory largely meant that their own values and presuppositions tended to be accepted, unconsciously and unquestioningly, as universals. The significant common ground between the two approaches is their shared belief that correct social policies could be arrived at through scientific methods; in other words, that science provides a way to answer what later came to be seen as essentially moral and evaluative questions. The view more characteristic of present-day social science is that many issues in society rest on value judgments and ethical preferences whose validity cannot be either demonstrated or refuted by scientific means.

Another way in which the philosophical and factual approaches resembled each other and differed from modern social science is that neither of the older traditions placed much emphasis on, or directed attention to, a cumulative or collective concept of scientific work. Rather, each investigation or theory stood separately. In the philosophical tradition, the grand, all-embracing social systems were each constructed from the ground up on the basis of a unique set of starting principles. Each system was thus self-contained and the rival and competitor of the others, with its own group of adherents, or "school of thought," convinced of the rectitude of its own position and of the fundamental wrongness of the rest. The merits of rival theories could be, and were, interminably argued but it was not seen as either possible or particularly necessary to relate new ideas to an existing body of knowledge, or to seek the source of theoretical differences and the ways to reconcile them. In the framework of the factual approach each investigation likewise tended to stand on its own, unconnected to previous work. Since facts as such, rather than interpretive conceptualizations, were stressed, each new body of facts was a new and separate contribution to knowledge.

It is also noteworthy that both the older approaches reflected a more static conception of knowledge than is characteristic of modern science. In the earlier traditions the facts and laws presented as scientific knowledge were regarded as true in a relatively universal and permanent sense. There was little of the idea, since become prevalent, that a scientifically true statement is simply a working tool, useful for a time to generate new ideas which will eventually bring about the replacement of the original theory. This conception is largely a twentieth century development, in natural as well as social science.

The substantial similarities notwithstanding, the philosophic and factual traditions in social science present some marked and significant contracts. They differ most notably with regard to the givens and the unknowns of social investigation, so that what appears in one approach as the main problem and object of study is seen by the other as relatively obvious and incidental, and vice versa. For the abstract philosophers and system builders, the facts of social life were readily accessible to any reasonably intelligent and observant person, and the real work of science consisted of discovering the underlying causal principles. The factual orientation turned this perspective on its head, and regarded science as the collection of precise, accurate facts, the meaning of which would be apparent to any intelligent and unbiased observer.

On this score, both older approaches differ significantly from modern social science, which regards both facts and their interpretation as problems for investigation, thus, in a sense, bridging the gap between the earlier traditions. In the perspectives of the present day, facts alone are seen as rather uninformative. Some sort of explanatory idea is required in order to determine which facts are to be looked at and how they are to be analyzed, and it is regarded as necessary that the assumptions governing the selection and interpretation of facts be deliberately chosen and articulated, rather than unconscious and unquestioned. From this point of view Booth's Life and Labor . . . , although, for its time, a great achievement of data gathering, foretold what would come to be seen as the great weakness of the fact-collecting approach. In the words of a modern critic:

> Booth did not accomplish what he set out to do, namely to show the link between conditions of living and type of employment; much data was collected which is relevant, but the connection is not made, except in the most general way. And this criticism may be related to an even more general one, namely that he had no sociological framework in mind in the first place. The fact is that seventeen volumes of data is far too many, and it would have been much less cumbersome and much more useful if data had been collected with a greater sense of theoretical relevance.[5]

At the same time, it is not now considered sufficient to derive generalizations about how people behave by logical deduction from assumed fundamental principles. From a modern perspective, for example, the great defect in Spencer's evolutionary theory is the assumption that, given some evident analogies between biological and social life, what is demonstrable for the one must necessarily hold for the other. By current standards, the proposed evolutionary principle would need to be argued on the basis of systematic scrutiny of evidence; logic and anecdotal example would not be sufficient. Similarly, explanations involving broadly inclusive abstractions such as, for example, "national interest" as a basis for foreign policy, tend to be regarded as positing moot issues of little value unless a concept such as national interest can be spelled out in terms which are measurable against concrete, observable actions of states in their foreign relations. Theoretical abstractions are considered useful chiefly to the extent that they can be connected to actual observations and thus supply a tool for explaining what is observed.

The general point is that modern social science questions all of the elements entering into an explanation: the facts considered, the adequacy of the observations and analytic methods, the logic of the inferences drawn from the facts. In contract to earlier approaches, none of these are assumed or taken for granted; all are problematic elements requiring overt consideration and empirical demonstration.

An early example of this more modern approach to social inquiry was the study Suicide by the French sociologist Emile Durkheim published in 1897. Durkheim viewed suicide as representing a breakdown of the individual's connection to the social order. On this assumption he examined the police records of suicides and was able to show that rates of suicide varied consistently with factors, such as religious ties, which would seem relevant to such a connection. This approach was a major new departure in social research. Unlike the factually oriented investigators, Durkheim did not simply assemble statistics in the expectation that they would "speak for themselves" and reveal the cause and meaning of suicide. He used the figures to substantiate a set of ideas about an aspect of society's functioning. Moreover, in contrast to earlier styles of theory building, the concept put forward in Suicide was not a component of an all-embracing social system, derived deductively from assumed principles and resting on evident plausibility and anecdotal examples. Rather, Suicide presented a limited explanation, verifiable by systematic examination of a specific body of evidence. All this is much in the pattern of today's social science. However, Durkheim's work was prophetic as well as pioneering, since about another half-century was to elapse before the orientation represented by Suicide was to become generally prevalent in social science.

Professionalization and Disciplinary Specialization

The years around the turn of the last century were a time of substantial, university-centered, development of the social sciences as academic professions. Many university departments in the various social science disciplines were established during the late nineteenth and early twentieth centuries. Growing professionalization was reflected also in the founding of learned societies in the disciplines: the American Historical Association, founded in 1884, the American Economic Association, 1885, the American Psychological Association, 1892, the American Sociological Society, 1895, the American Anthropological Association, 1902, the American Political Science Association, 1903. A related development was that academic study of social topics became increasingly separated from general social commentary and the writings of journalists, political figures, or independent gentlemen-scholars. Professionalization and disciplinary specialization brought into existence in each field relatively cohesive groups of scholars possessing similar training and intellectual background, for whom the advancement of their particular branch of social knowledge was a continuing, full-time preoccupation. A specialized professional literature consisting of technical communications presuming extensive prior knowledge of the subject could exist because there was an identifiable audience for esoteric work of that kind. Professionalization and disciplinary specialization were thus important preconditions for the evolution of a collective, cumulative outlook in social science, and for the development of the institutions and cognitive styles of modern science.

Ideas of Science in the Twentieth Century

The number of social scientists, and the academic recognition accorded them increased markedly during the first quarter of the twentieth century, but, despite this, many social scientists were discontented with the nature of their work and the size of their achievements. The two generally prevalent styles of work—speculative theory building and detailed collection and classification of facts—seemed to produce endless debates among warring ideological schools on the one hand, and a plethora of specific information on the other, but there was little in social science that could be compared with the achievements of the natural sciences in adding new ideas to old and creating a steadily growing stock of reliable and useful explanations.

For many social scientists, thoughts along these lines were confirmed very concretely by the experience of the First World War. The social scientists able to make the most visible contributions to the war effort were psychologists, with their skills in mental testing, and economists, who were able to manipulate statistical data to deal with problems of wartime regulation and planning. Those disciplines appeared to equip their members with tangible, useful skills, in contrast to the other social sciences, which appeared to produce mainly intuitive ideas on which the "experts" often did not agree. Economics and psychology were also the areas of social science that made the most use of quantitative methods. It seemed evident that the most substantial progress was being shown by the fields of social inquiry that most resembled the natural sciences in their style of operation, and that all areas of social science could profit from attempts to move in a similar direction. Consequently, the 1920s and succeeding decades were marked by intensified interest in the principles of scientific inquiry, and the possibilities of applying scientific methods to the subject matter of social science.

Two organizations founded during the 1920s, the National Bureau of Economic Research and the Social Science Research Council, played important roles in efforts to develop social inquiry along more scientific lines. The National Bureau of Economic Research was established in 1920 through the efforts of a group of businessmen and academic economists, for the purpose of conducting "exact and impartial" investigations into economic conditions. Its creation was a direct outgrowth of the wartime experience, when the economists and statisticians called into government service found that the available economic data were often too scanty and unreliable to provide the needed basis for planning. Some solid statistical advances had been made during the war, but it was feared that these would dissipate with demobilization and the "return to normalcy." The major announced aim of the National Bureau was to collect reliable and comprehensive statistics, but its efforts to develop ways to use economic data to increase understanding of the workings of the economy were highly significant. Wesley Clair Mitchell, an outstanding economic theorist, was a founder of the bureau and its research director during its first quarter-century of existence. Under his leadership, and subsequently, the organization produced a large number of important and influential studies exemplifying the relation of quantitative data to theory, and the uses of both to generate and give support one to the other.

In 1923, the Social Science Research Council was formed, with funds provided by several philanthropic foundations, by representatives of seven learned societies in the social sciences: the American Anthropological Association, American Historical Association, American Political Science Association, American Psychological Association, American Sociological Society, and American Statistical Association. The principal organizer was Charles Merriam, a political scientist who was profoundly dissatisfied with the philosophical and legalistic leanings which characterized his discipline. Merriam believed that the methodological and theoretical weakness prevalent throughout the social sciences could be shored up by concerted effort and interdisciplinary contact. The interdisciplinary emphasis stemmed from the idea that since traditional approaches dominated within each discipline, innovative breakthroughs could occur most readily at the interdisciplinary borders, and also from a belief that a multi-disciplinary framework would enable each field to benefit from advances in the others. Through its awards of research grants and fellowships, and its direct sponsorship and organization of several major research projects, the council has been a major influence in development of systematic methodology and empirical research.

Interest in strengthening the social sciences through cross-disciplinary contacts gave rise to another major undertaking of the inter-war years, the Encyclopedia of the Social Sciences, published in fifteen volumes between 1928 and 1933. This was intended to be a comprehensive, systematic summary of the full range of existing social science knowledge. A very significant element in its underlying rationale was the idea that by bringing together the work done in the various disciplines, each could be stimulated and strengthened by the others. While much of the encyclopedia's content is hardly scientific by today's standards, the aim of developing a science of society and the search for scientific directions are in evidence at many points.

Along with the search for scientific approaches to social inquiry, understanding of the goals and distinctive qualities of science was undergoing significant change. Earlier conceptions of science as a set of immutable universal laws, or a body of precise factual information, were repeatedly criticized by philosophers and theoreticians of science as erroneous and misleading as to the actual nature of scientific practice. Natural science fields such as biology and chemistry began to move away from an emphasis on empirical description and classification as ends in themselves, and to concentrate on the search for broader, underlying concepts. A virtual revolution in physics culminated in the view that there are no such things as universal laws, and earlier conceptions of mechanistic determinism were replaced by concepts of relativity. It also came to be recognized that even the process of knowing is not absolute; that the relation between the investigator and the object of his study is an interaction, so that the act of measuring itself affects what is being measured.

These developments greatly affected the social sciences. Growing awareness that science is not synonymous with the collecting and ordering of facts was one major source of change. It came to be seen increasingly that facts can become knowledge only in relation to an explanatory framework which must be supplied by the investigator and does not arise spontaneously from the data. A landmark of the recognition by social scientists of this altered viewpoint, one which may serve here to illustrate a more general trend, was the 1931 Presidential Address delivered by Carl Becker before the American Historical Association. Becker characterized the "scientific" history of the nineteenth century, with its focus on "rigorous examination of the factual event, just as it occurred," as "hoping to find something without looking for it, expecting to obtain final answers to life's riddle by resolutely refusing to ask questions . . . surely the most romantic species of realism yet invented." He strongly urged historians to acknowledge that "it is . . . not the undiscriminated fact, but the perceiving mind of the historian that speaks."[6] Carl Becker's address was a forceful and memorable statement of a point of view that was gaining widespread currency in all areas of social science. From this new perspective, theory began to appear not as something inimical to objective, empirical inquiry, but rather as its indispensable partner.

A development of equal importance was the loosening of the idea that science must mean the discovery of unvarying, universal laws. In its place there came recognition that many bona fide and useful scientific generalizations describe probabilities rather than certainties, or postulate specific limiting conditions, which might or might not obtain in a given instance. From this perspective it was possible to generalize about human actions without the necessity of assuming that human behavior must have a uniformity and determinism comparable to that of gases or celestial bodies. The view, once quite taken for granted, that

> a true science . . . would enable us to predict the essential movements of human affairs for the immediate and indefinite future, to give pictures of society in the year 2,000 or the year 2,500 just as astronomers can map the appearance of the heavens at fixed points of time in the future . . . and we should be powerless to change it by any effort of will[7]

came to be thought of as a misconception of the nature of most scientific work, "so that astronomy is taken as the paradigm of any science worthy of the name" even though "the circumstances which permit long-range predictions in astronomy do not prevail in other branches of natural science."[8] The more modern view could accommodate the idea that a generalization can be quite accurate as regards large numbers of people, notwithstanding individual variations and the clear impossibility of predicting the behavior of specific individuals. From the new perspective, theory came to be seen less as a matter of constructing airtight, logical, all-embracing, universal conceptualizations, and more as a means of accounting for a specified range of facts. The historian H. Stuart Hughes described the effects on his discipline of "the vast upheaval in scientific thinking . . . after the turn of the century" in terms that could apply equally to all the social sciences:

> When the natural scientists themselves had redefined nature's laws as mere hypotheses, when they had begun to substitute relativity, plural explanations, and eventually even indeterminacy for the earlier certitudes of a consistent universe, the science-minded historians had no recourse but to follow.[9]

In this way the dichotomy between facts and abstract theory, formerly the poles of social inquiry, declined in importance, and what had been opposing conceptions of science began to merge and acquire a combined role in the newer approaches.

The shift from a deterministic to a probabilistic orientation coincided with, and was undoubtedly stimulated and aided by, substantial and rapid advances in statistical theory during the first half of this century. Expansion of statistical knowledge made possible the development of much more refined and precise methods of sampling and of identifying and measuring correlations than had existed previously. With the new techniques came many new possibilities for analysis of large and complex bodies of data and for detailed, precise testing of theoretical ideas against actual experience.

In its over-all thrust the new perspective was essentially a recognition that the fundamental qualities of science relate to ways of ordering experience and asking questions, rather than to concrete and specific operations. This meant that the study of human behavior, in all its diversity and complexity, presented many difficult methodological problems but no intrinsic barriers to a scientific approach. On this basis, new answers began to be given to a number of traditional objections to the possibility of scientific status for the social sciences. Such conditions of social inquiry as limitations on the ability to experiment, the interest and involvement of the investigator in the outcome of his research, and the possibility that behavior could be affected by the very fact of studying it, came to be regarded as specific manifestations of methodological problems encountered in science generally.[10] They were seen as problems which could be subjected to scientific investigation, rather than conditions which could make such investigation impossible. This point of view led to greater awareness of and concern with procedural and epistemological questions. The idea that the subject matter of social science in itself precluded objective inquiry became increasingly unimportant.

In summary, the social science of the mid-twentieth century had a number of qualities which rather sharply differentiated it from earlier patterns of social analysis, and which brought social inquiry closer to the styles of investigation and discourse characteristic of natural science. A stress on explanation, grounded in concrete, verifiable experience, tended to replace the earlier concentration on noninterpretive description, on the one hand, and abstract philosophy, with its strong moralizing overtones, on the other, while incorporating elements of both traditions. A corollary development was greatly increased attention to methodological problems and the underlying logic connecting fact and theory. Yet another major consequences was a more restricted view of the range and scope of scientific inquiry. Many fundamental and long-standing problems concerning the nature of social life and human relationships came to be regarded as outside the realm of science, on the ground that scientific processes can reveal relationships between means and ends, but cannot choose among ends or make moral judgments. Also, scientific investigation was of necessity limited to questions capable of being investigated by means of specifiable procedures and evidence. As was suggested in the preceding chapter, all these factors strongly influence the character of scientific literature. Accordingly, as the twentieth century advanced, the literature of social science came increasingly to manifest the special, distinctive qualities of scientific communication, a point to be commented on more specifically a bit further on.

Science or Scientism

This cursory and much compressed account of the background of current perspectives in social science may convey the mistaken impression that the new scientific orientation was adopted almost automatically, as an inevitable consequence of fuller understanding of the nature of science. In actuality the development was a tortuous and contentious one. The views prevailing today of the basic qualities of science and their relation to social science were built only gradually, and as much from trial and error experience as from a priori intellectual insight.

In practice it proved extremely difficult to subject the infinitely complex and diverse facts of social life to systematic analysis governed by articulated and rigorous logic. Scientific procedures worked best when only a strictly limited number of variables needed to be taken into account, and when observation could likewise be limited to only those facts that could be encompassed by the analysis. This meant that the questions selected for study were often so narrow that they could be related only to artificial, hypothetical situations, and not to anything in the real world. Critics pointed out that the methodological elegance of "scientific" research often outran the interest or significance of the question dealt with, so that exhaustive, painstaking effort was expended on trivial questions, and elaborate constructions of charts and mathematical symbols might do no more than confirm what was already apparent on the basis of ordinary experience and common sense. Efforts to develop a precise terminology corresponding to the precision of scientific concepts produced considerable graceless jargon which often seemed to express no other meaning that what was conveyed by ordinary language. The disparaging term "scientism" came into use to describe what was seen as posturing with the trappings and vocabulary of science, at the expense of substance.

Writing in 1938, in a world of vast social disintegration and with world war about to begin, the sociologist Robert Lynd produced a widely noted book called Knowledge for What?, which contained passages such as the following:

> If social science has tended to acquire humility as it has shifted from a priori theorizing to empirical observation and analysis, it is by way of reassuming its lost assurance through its erudite devotion to statistical manipulation. The beautiful precision of this procedure, as more and more variables are drawn within its intricate net, may, and does in some cases, operate to distract attention from the need for candid, and if need be radical, revision of implicit assumptions.[11]
>
> No informed person questions nowadays the indispensability of objective data-gathering and of the exhaustive statistical analysis of those data for all they are worth. The only question that is being raised here concerns the need to ask, "What are they worth for what?" Objective empiricism can become as much of a blind alley as can logical speculation. And if the social sciences are to be judged by their adequacy in helping man to resolve his difficulties, they will be only weakened by a policy of rationalizing one's way out of blind alleys by asserting that "more knowledge about anything is a self-justifying pursuit and there is no sure basis for saying that any one datum is more important than another."[12]

Some twenty years later the issues raised by Lynd were still alive in some areas of social science, as illustrated by the following passage from the preface to a book on international politics published in 1959:

> This is an old-fashioned kind of book. . . . The author has not used a single IBM facility in the book's preparation, nor has he conducted any interviews for it, whether in depth or otherwise. There has not been any polling, nor have questionnaires been distributed. As a matter of fact, the book does not contain a single chart, graph, map, diagram, table or statistical figure. It is simply the product of the application to problems and subject matter at hand of whatever intelligence was available.[13]

Nonetheless, partisan positions on both sides were tending to modify with time and experience. Growing familiarity with the techniques of investigation and analysis led to development of methods and conceptual models better suited to the characteristics of the social world and less dependent on literal imitation of natural science. Summarizing in 1959 the trends manifested in a comprehensive survey of psychological theory, the psychologist Sigmund Koch took note of the changes that had occurred:

> From the earliest days of the experimental pioneers, man's stipulation that psychology be adequate to <u>science</u> outweighed his commitment that it be adequate to man . . .
> The history of psychology, then, is very much a history of changing views, doctrines, images about <u>what to emulate in the natural sciences—</u>especially physics.[14]

Yet Koch also pointed to a newer outlook, which, in effect, responded to Lynd's critique of two decades earlier:

> No one is prepared to retreat one jot from the objectives and disciplines of scientific inquiry, but most are inclined to reexamine reigning stereotypes about the character of such objectives and disciplines. . . .
> <u>For the first time in its history, psychology seems ready—or almost ready—to assess its goals and instrumentalities with primary reference to its own indigenous problems.</u> It seems ready to think contextually, freely, and creatively about its own refractory subject matter, and to work its way free from a dependence on simplistic theories of correct scientific conduct.[15]

It need hardly be said that these changes did not occur at one stroke, but were the slowly evolving result of the operation of many factors. Refusal "to retreat one jot from the objectives and disciplines of scientific inquiry" more or less required recognition that knowledge could advance only incrementally and on its own terms, and that many of society's pressing problems were, due to their complexity, both unreachable by the scientific tools thus far developed and unlikely to reward investigation by contributing new knowledge to the existing stock. On these assumptions, the answer to Lynd's question "knowledge for what" had to be, in effect, that while social science might at times be able to contribute to the search for human betterment, much of the time those responsible for decisions in the practical world would have to proceed on the basis of intuition and general experience, with little specific help from science, and that much scientific research had to be regarded as useful only in the ultimate, but not the immediate sense. One development which probably served to some extent to mitigate conflict over the relation of values and ideology to science was formation, outside the mainstream of academic social science, of several organizations expressly devoted to consideration of the public issues of the day in the light of developing scientific knowledge: the Society for the Psychological Study of Social Issues, founded in 1935, the Society for Applied Anthropology, founded in 1941, and the Society for the Study of Social Problems, founded in 1951.

A most important stimulus for the new scientific orientation was its own success in producing meaningful results. A growing body of research gave evidence of solid, potentially cumulative results, more nearly comparable to the precision of natural science than anything achieved by the older styles of social science. The natural science model, as it came to be understood by social scientists toward the middle of the twentieth century seemed to hold out the promise of something truly new. There now seemed to be a real possibility of developing for the social sciences a body of specialized expertise, demonstrably and unquestionably different from the general knowledge possessed by intelligent and educated laymen. This prospect attracted increasing numbers of social scientists, espeically young scholars at the start of their careers, to the research areas offering the best opportunities for empirical and methodologically rigorous study. As the products of these efforts grew in number and stature it became increasingly difficult to dismiss them as trivial or "demonstrating the obvious." For example, Paul Lazarsfeld, one of the major pioneers of empirical social research, was able to point out, in 1949, that a large-scale and elaborate statistical study of the army in World War II had produced a number of noteworthy findings which would not have been anticipated on the basis of "common sense" and ordinary observation, or at least that "common sense" might as readily have pointed in a diametrically opposite direction. His comment was, "Obviously something is wrong with the entire argument of 'obviousness'."[16]

As experience with the new methods accumulated, many social scientists became convinced that quantification and methodological rigor were not alternatives to, or substitutes for, imaginative and knowledgeable approaches to meaningful problems, but were, on the contrary, invaluable aids and supports for creative thought. The British geographer David Harvey wrote recently:

> Some people may flinch at the term "scientific method" so let me make it clear that I interpret this in a very broad sense to mean the setting up and observing of decent intellectual standards for rational argument. Now it is obvious that we can observe these standards without indulging in quantification. Good geographers have always observed them. But the curious thing was that it took quantification to demonstrate to me how extraordinarily lax my own standards were . . . I believe that the most important effect of quantification has been to force us to think logically and consistently where we had not done so before.[17]

Developments in the larger society also encouraged a scientific stance for social science. The Second World War, like the first, offered new opportunities to social scientists, and these were mainly in empirically oriented areas such as intelligence and personality testing, aptitude studies, propaganda analysis, and economic controls. The wartime experience added to the competence, confidence, and visibility of workers in those fields.

Following the war the greatly increased research funds that became available gave further impetus to development of a scientific posture, since large-scale research projects making heavy use of quantification seemed more up-to-date and promising to funding agencies than the narrative techniques and unarticulated methodologies of the older social science tradition. When, in the late 1940s, the Ford Foundation instituted a very large-scale program in support of social research, a new term, "behavioral sciences," was coined to describe the undertaking, in order to stress its empirical orientation and its separation from the historical-philosophical connotations of "social science." In similar fashion, areas of social science that most nearly resembled natural science in their aims and methods of operation were best equipped to acquire government funds for research, under the relatively large-scale programs instituted during the 1950s and 1960s. It is of interest in this connection that in 1946 the Senate amended the bill establishing the National Science Foundation to delete any reference to social science. A well-known sociologist commented at the time that the action reflected "the common feeling that the social and physical sciences have nothing in common and that at best the social sciences are a propagandist, reformist, evangelical sort of cult."[18] Yet in 1960, mirroring the shift in emphasis that has taken place virtually across the board in social science, a Division of Social Science was established within the National Science Foundation.

At present there is little doubt that the dominant orientation in social science is one which consciously emulates a natural science model as developed during this century, albeit with some softening and modification of earlier rigidities. Indeed, the precepts of science are now so firmly implanted as established orthodoxy in social science that in recent years a counter-movement of younger scholars has begun to advocate a more humanistic and socially relevant posture, which would abandon scientific detachment in favor of involvement in the clashes and debates of the larger society. In a charge reminiscent of that which the mentors of today's "establishment" once put forward against an earlier conception of science, the new radicals assert that a commitment to "scientific objectivity" serves mainly to mask an unspoken adherence to the values of the existing social order. For example:

> . . . the conventional economist, because he sees harmonies of interest almost everywhere can visualize himself as a neutral technician, applying his techniques as objectively as possible. If class or group conflicts do not exist, one can, of course, work for the "general interest."[19]

It is further argued that the "scientific" stance is, in effect, the ideology of successful and prosperous social scientists, who use the "neutral" values of science to rationalize their aversion to fundamental social criticism and change.[20] Conceivably, views such as these could bring about major change in the styles of research and writing in the social sciences in the years to come, but such an outcome cannot now be predicted. Many social scientists continue to maintain, as those who look to science as a model have consistently done, that concern with the critical social issues of the day requires more, not less, attention to the precepts of science. The essence of the argument is that the system of inquiry and analysis represented by science offers the most powerful tool available for arriving at meaningful answers to hard questions, and thus for moving social science beyond the clash of opinions and interests to a realm of solid, and hence usable, knowledge.[21] The view expressed by the sociologist Robert Friedrichs is probably not unrepresentative. Friedrichs notes that the radical challenge may well serve as a useful corrective to complacency, and stimulate increased senstivity to unexamined preconceptions in sociology, but adds:

> The . . . discipline . . . will almost certainly continue over the imme-diate years ahead to continue to perceive of itself as a science intimately linked to the natural sciences through its dedication to the delineation of order in the social word . . . The major shift will be the increasingly open admission that neither sociology nor any other science has operated nor can operate simply from within its own functional integrity for its normative standards, if one would sustain the values that the West derives from its Hellenic and Hebraic roots and other cultural traditions.[22]

It is of great interest to note that these issues are arising at a time when natural scientists have begun to show increased concern with the social and ethical values implicit in their work, and the impact of scientific activity on the larger society. Again, one may observe the influence of the example of natural science on social science.

SCIENTIFIC COMMUNICATION AND THE SOCIAL SCIENCE LITERATURE

Some effects of the changes in basic scientific orientation on the com-munication patterns and literature of social science have been implied at various points in the preceding account, and these may now be recapitulated more explicitly. As research becomes synonymous with detailed observation of specific data, and theory comes increasingly to mean step-by-step elaboration of explanatory propositions in a cumulative framework, the range of subject matter which can be encompassed in a single investigation or discussion is inevitably narrowed. Reflecting this, scholarly writing in social science has tended increasingly to focus on specific and closely defined problems, and the individual book or article tends to be not an account of a topic which is complete in itself, but a contribution to an ongoing stream of investigation and analysis. A study of the contents of leading sociological journals between 1895 and 1964 reported:

> (The) most evident trend is a precipitous decline in purely speculative articles about society in general . . . Contemporary sociologists definitely are not atheoretical, but they are more likely to confine their theorizing to identifiable sustantive specialties.[23]

A related point concerns enlargement and sharpening of the distinction between knowledge and action in social science, and increasing recognition of the limitations of science as a source of solutions to social problems or answers for the decision maker. The economist Max Millikan, describing the not infrequent mutual misunderstandings between officials responsible for policy and the experts called upon to provide a scientific basis for action, distinguishes between "useful" and "interesting" questions. He suggests that the former, the significant public issues and decisions of the day, are often lacking in scientific interest "since in the present state of our knowledge they must inevitably rest . . . largely on intuition, partially articulated insights, and informal common sense . . ." Scientifically "interesting" questions, on the other hand, are those lending themselves to "rigorous scientific conclusions, unambiguously communicable in a language developed for precise communication and capable of demonstration by repeatable experiment or by reference to incontrovertible evidence." In "the present state of social science" these "necessarily relate to exceedingly simple and hence operationally unimportant phenomena controlled to exclude all but a few variables capable of treatment by the tools of a single discipline."[24]

One response to this dichotomy has been the development of theoretical and applied fields of research as somewhat separate realms of discourse, with the former geared mainly to cumulative developments in science and influenced only indirectly by the needs and interests of the larger society, and the latter focused on the concrete problems of the time, blending scientific knowledge with "intuition, partially articulated insights and informal common sense" as required. Translated into terms of the literature, this means that "pure" or "academic" social science has tended to move away from direct concern with major social issues as a consequence of growing awareness of, and interest in, the requirements and practices of science. Significant differences in aims and perspective are recognized between theoretical and applied science, as well as between both of these and the general public discussion of social policy, and in each of these arenas the literature manifests its own distinctive qualities.

Another noteworthy phenomenon is the increasingly technical and esoteric tone of the scientific literature, and hence its increasing incomprehensibility to nonspecialists. The economist George Stigler analyzed articles in economics journals during the years 1892-1963, and reported as follows:

Only one article in twenty used even graphs or simple algebra at the beginning of our period; today only one article in three still finds the language of words sufficient. The shift to more mathematical techniques began in the decade of the 1920s and shows no sign of retardation.[25]

This development may be viewed as both a consequence of the professionalization of social science and as a necessary condition for the cumulative advance of knowledge, since cumulativeness requires that the writer assume the reader's familiarity with the prior development of the subject, and professionalization, as mentioned earlier, creates an audience for highly specialized and technical writing.

In a similar vein, the economic historian Joseph Schumpeter has observed with regard to both the content and the subject matter of modern scholarship:

The economic theory of our own time and of all future times can never again be so fascinating to the wider public as it had been in the time when it was understandable to every educated person and when it seemed to establish directly "eternal laws" and practical rules. Everyone can understand A. Smith. Only specialists can understand the matrix calculus and functional equations. Everyone is interested in free trade or protection. Only specialists are interested in questions of determinateness and stability.[26]

To summarize, then, as the social sciences have moved closer to the model of contemporary science in their styles of investigation and discussion, the social science literature has increasingly taken on the attributes characteristic of scientific communication. The literature today tends to be marked by a focus on narrow, often technical topics, by substantial attention to problems of methodology and analytic logic, by the attempt to place single contributions into the context of a developing, cumulative stream of knowledge. It tends to constitute a separate realm of discourse, independent of and readily distinguishable from the reporting and discussion of social issues in the general public media. Yet, though these are dominant qualities, there are also deviations and variations, suggestive of other modes and values that have figured in the development of social science: abstract, normative speculation on broad issues, factual, minimally interpretive descriptive accounts; polemical arguments relating to public policy and the issues of the day. This variability will be evident from time to time in the examination of the literature that follows.

FOOTNOTES

1. Library science, viewed as the study of the organization and transmission of the products of the intellect, and the application of the knowledge so derived to the operation of a particular social institution, might also be regarded as a member of this group, and a number of writers have advanced this view with considerable logic. (See, for example, Pierce Butler, An Introduction to Library Science, Chicago, 1933; Jesse Shera, Libraries and The Organization of Knowledge, Hamden, Conn., 1965). Conventionally, however, library science tends not to be numbered among the social sciences, either theoretical or applied.

2. Stuart Chase, The Proper Study of Mankind (New York: Harper, 1948) p. 43.

3. Carl Becker, "Everyman His Own Historian," American Historical Review 37 (1932): 232.

4. Joseph A. Schumpeter, History of Economic Analysis (New York: Oxford University Press, 1954) p. 1165.

5. G. Duncan Mitchell, A Hundred Years of Sociology (London: Gerald Duckworth, 1968) p. 132.

6. Carl Becker, "Everyman His Own Historian," American Historical Review 37 (1932): 233-234.

7. Charles A. Beard, The Nature of the Social Sciences, 1934, quoted in Ernst Nagel, The Structure of Science (New York: Harcourt, 1961), p. 460.

8. Nagel, Op. cit., pp. 460-461.

9. H. Stuart Hughes, History as Art and as Science (New York: Harper and Row, 1964), p. 15.

10. Extensive consideration of these points would be beyond the scope of the present discussion. Consult Ernst Nagel, The Structure of Science (New York: Harcourt, Brace and World, 1961) especially chapters 13-15, and Abraham Kaplan, The Conduct of Inquiry (San Francisco: Chandler, 1964).

11. Robert S. Lynd, Knowledge for What? The Place of Social Science in American Culture (Princeton: Princeton University Press, 1939) p. 126. (Copyright 1939 (c) 1967 by Princeton University Press; Princeton Paperback 1970. Reprinted by permission of Princeton University Press.)

12. Ibid., pp. 128-9.

13. John Herz, International Politics in the Atomic Age (New York: Columbia University Press, 1959), p. v.

14. "Epilogue" in Sigmund Koch, ed., Psychology: a Study of a Science (New York: McGraw-Hill, 1959) vol. 3, p. 784.

15. Ibid., p. 783.

16. Paul Lazarsfeld, "The American Soldier—an Expository Review," Public Opinion Quarterly 13 (1949): 380.

17. David Harvey, Explanation in Geography (London: Edward Arnold, 1969) p. vii.

18. George Lundberg, quoted in Robert W. Friedrichs, A Sociology of Sociology, (New York: Free Press, 1970), p. 86.

19. John G. Gurley, "The State of Political Economics," American Economic Association Papers and Proceedings 1970, American Economic Review 61, (1971): 55.

20. For elaboration of the "radical" position see Marvin Surkin and Alan Wolfe, eds., An End to Political Science (New York: Basic Books, 1970); J. David Colfax, ed., Radical Sociology (New York: Basic Books, 1971); Howard Zinn, The Politics of History (Boston: Beacon Press, 1970); and the journals Politics and Society and Review of Radical Political Economics.

21. For example, Charles L. Schultze, "The Reviewers Reviewed," American Economic Association Papers and Proceedings 1970, American Economic Review 61, (1972): 50: "Paradoxically, it is precisely as economics turns its attention to such social problems as health, education, and poverty in the midst of affluence, that it must begin to approach more closely the experimental methodology of the hard sciences."

22. Robert W. Friedrichs, A Sociology of Sociology (New York, Free Press, Copyright (c) 1970) p. 312.

23. James L. McCartney, "On Being Scientific: Changing Styles of Presentation of Sociological Research," American Sociologist 5, (1970): 30.

24. Max F. Millikan, "Inquiry and Policy: the Relation of Knowledge to Action," in Daniel Lerner, ed., The Human Meaning of the Social Sciences (New York: World Publishing Co., 1959), p. 178

25. George Stigler, "Statistical Studies in the History of Economic Thought," in his Essays in the History of Economics (Chicago: University of Chicago Press, 1965), pp. 47–48.

26. Joseph A. Schumpeter, History of Economic Analysis (New York: Oxford University Press, 1954), p. 1144.

Appendix A

Selected Books on the Organization and Operations of Science

THE SCIENTIFIC ENTERPRISE

Conant, James B. Science and Common Sense. New Haven: Yale University Press, 1951. Q175.C64

An explanation for nonscientists of the "strategy and tactics of science." Describes the nature of science as an organized activity, and traces the evolution of modern conceptualizations of "scientific method" through leading historical examples.

Hagstrom, Warren O. The Scientific Community. New York: Basic Books, 1965. Q180.A1H3

The goals, values, and operating characteristics of science as a social system; "the influence of scientific colleagues on the conduct of one another's research" (p. 1).

Kuhn, Thomas S. The Structure of Scientific Revolutions. 2d ed., enlarged. Chicago: University of Chicago Press, 1970. Q175.K95 1970

Patterns of scientific work, and the processes by which knowledge is developed in science.

Nagel, Ernest. The Structure of Science; Problems in the Logic of Scientific Explanation. New York: Harcourt, Brace and World, 1961. Q175.N22

The nature and logical structure of scientific explanations, and their application in a wide range of scientific fields. Three chapters are devoted to methodological and epistomological problems in the social sciences and history.

Storer, Norman. The Social System of Science. New York: Holt, Rinehart, Winston, 1966. Q147.S74

"Generalized description of the patterns of interaction that characterize science and of the forces that maintain them" (p. 7).

Tullock, Gordon. The Organization of Inquiry. Durham, N.C.: Duke University Press, 1966. Q180.A1T78

The social organization of science; characteristics and patterns of operation of the scientific community.

Ziman, John. Public Knowledge; an Essay Concerning the Social Dimension of Science. Cambridge, Eng.: At the University Press, 1968. Q175.Z54

Key characteristics of the scientific enterprise, from the point of view of the practicing scientist.

THE SOCIAL SCIENCES

Behavioral and Social Sciences Survey Committee. The Behavioral and Social Sciences; Outlook and Needs. Englewood Cliffs, N.J.: Prentice-Hall, 1969. H62.5.U5B4 1969b

Report of a comprehensive review and appraisal conducted by the Committee on Science and Public Policy of the National Academy of Sciences and the Problems and Policy Committee of the Social Science Research Council. "The survey is directed to two tasks: first, to assess the nature of the behavioral and social science enterprise in terms of its past growth, present size, and anticipated development; and second, to suggest ways in which these sciences might contribute both to basic understanding of human behavior and to effective social planning and policy-making" (p. 2. © 1969 National Academy of Sciences. Quoted by permission of Prentice-Hall, Inc.) The survey consists of this summary report, and specialized reports for anthropology, economics, geography, history, political science, psychology, psychiatry, sociology, and the social science aspects of mathematics and statistics. Description of the mathematics report follows; the others are listed below under the various disciplines.

Behavioral and Social Sciences Survey Committee, Mathematical Sciences Panel. Mathematical Sciences and Social Sciences. Edited by William Kruskal. Englewood Cliffs, N.J.: Prentice-Hall, 1970. H61.B44

Relevance of mathematics to social science; work of social statisticians; problems and advances in statistics and computational techniques.

Brown, Robert. Explanation in Social Science. Chicago: Aldine, 1963. H61.B68

The relation of explanation to observation and description, and the characteristic forms of explanation.

Duverger. Maurice. An Introduction to the Social Sciences, With Special Reference to Their Methods. New York: Praeger, 1964. H61.D913

Theoretical background and fundamental assumptions of the social sciences, and techniques of observation and analysis.

Kaplan, Abraham. The Conduct of Inquiry; Methodology for Behavioral Science. San Francisco: Chandler, 1964. H61.K24

Discusses the underlying logic of methodological concepts, and their functions in inquiry and analysis.

Lerner, Daniel, ed. The Human Meaning of the Social Sciences. Cleveland: World Publishing Co., 1959. H35.L54

Essays by ten scholars dealing with various aspects of the history and application of social science.

Lyons, Gene M. The Uneasy Partnership; Social Science and the Federal Government in the Twentieth Century. New York: Russell Sage Foundation, 1969. H53.U5L9

History of federal support for social science research, and the role of social science in government policy formation.

Madge, John. The Tools of Social Science. London: Longmans, Green, 1953. H16.M42

Principal research techniques used in social science, introduced by an analytical discussion of their supporting logic.

Main Trends of Research in the Social and Human Sciences: Part 1, Social Sciences. The Hague, Mouton, 1970. H62.M243

A UNESCO project, the book consists of essays describing the background and current situation of the social sciences viewed over-all, and of several social science disciplines. An introductory chapter by Jean Piaget discusses "The Place of the Sciences of Man in the System of Sciences." Other contributors address themselves to the subject matter and theoretical and methodological development of sociology, political science, psychology, economics, demography, and linguistics, to interdisciplinary and "problem-focused" research, and to issues relating to the organization and financing of research. A projected second volume will treat legal and historical sciences, and the humanistic disciplines.

THE SOCIAL SCIENCE DISCIPLINES

(See also the articles on each of the disciplines in International Encyclopedia of the Social Sciences, New York: Macmillan, 1968. H40.A2I5)

Anthropology

Behavioral and Social Sciences Survey Committee, Anthropology Panel. Anthropology. Edited by Allan H. Smith and John L. Fischer. Englewood Cliffs, N.J.: Prentice-Hall, 1970. GN24.B43

Current status, trends, and problems, as reported by the committee.

Pelto, Pertti J. Anthropological Research: the Structure of Inquiry. New York: Harper, 1970. GN33.P36

A text in methodology emphasizing the logical principles involved in forming generalizations, and the relation between general scientific postulates and the subject matter of anthropology, rather than details of techniques.

Pelto, Pertti J. The Study of Anthropology. Columbus, Ohio: Charles E. Merrill, 1965. GN33.P37

Basic account of history, methods, and results of scholarship in anthropology, designed to acquaint elementary and secondary social studies teachers with current scholarly perspectives.

Economics

Behavioral and Social Sciences Survey Committee, Economics Panel. Economics. Edited by Nancy D. Ruggles. Englewood Cliffs, N.J.: Prentice-Hall, 1970. HB171.B364

Current status, trends, and problems, as reported by the committee.

Boulding, Kenneth. Economics as a Science. New York: McGraw-Hill, 1970. HB71.B658

Seven essays intended "to introduce those who already have some acquaintance with economics to what might be called the larger scientific background of the subject . . . (or) the significance and the background of the discipline" (p. v). Essays treat economics as a social science, ecological science, behavioral science, political science, mathematical science, and moral science; and economics and the future of man, presenting the kinds of questions considered by economists, and the basic organizing ideas in the discipline.

Martin, Richard S. and Reuben G. Miller. Economics and Its Significance. Columbus, Ohio: Charles E. Merrill, 1965. HB171.5.M36

A basic account of the character and history of economics, designed to acquaint elementary and secondary social studies teachers with current scholarly perspectives.

Geography

Behavioral and Social Sciences Survey Committee, Geography Panel. Geography. Edited by Edward J. Taaffe. Englewood Cliffs, N.J.: Prentice-Hall, 1970. G74.B38

Current status, trends, and problems, as reported by the committee.

Broek, Jan O.M. Geography, Its Scope and Spirit. Columbus, Ohio: Charles E. Merrill, 1965. G73.B83

A basic account of the field, designed to acquaint elementary and secondary social studies teachers with current scholarly perspectives.

Harvey, David. Explanation in Geography. London: Edward Arnold, 1969. G70.H34

Philosophy of scientific explanation as related to the subject matter and problems of geographical research.

History

Behavioral and Social Sciences Survey Committee, History Panel. History as Social Science. Edited by David S. Landes and Charles Tilly. Englewood Cliffs, N.J.: Prentice-Hall, 1971. D16.B43

Current status, trends, and problems, as reported by the committee.

Berkhofer, Robert F., Jr. A Behavioral Approach to Historical Analysis. New York: Free Press, 1969. D16.B46

Considers the applicability of behavioral constructs and techniques to historical study.

Gottschalk. Louis, ed. Generalization in the Writing of History; Report of the Committee on Historical Analysis of the Social Science Research Council. Chicago: University of Chicago Press, 1963. D13.S595

Essays by a number of historians on problems of generalization in all historical writing and in specialized fields of history, with an extensive bibliography.

Hexter, J.H. The History Primer. New York: Basic Books, 1971. D16.H48

Analysis of problems of historical explanation.

Hughes, H. Stuart. History as Art and as Science; Twin Vistas on the Past. New York: Harper & Row, 1964. D16.H775

Essays on various aspects of the nature of historical writing.

Nugent, Walter T.K. Creative History: an Introduction to Historical Study. Philadelphia: Lippincott, 1967. D16.2.N8

Basic discussion for beginning students of philosophical and methodological issues in historical study.

White, Morton. Foundations of Historical Knowledge. New York: Harper, 1965. D16.W59

Discussion of the logic and language of historical investigation and writing.

Political Science

Behavioral and Social Sciences Survey Committee, Political Science Panel. Political Science. Edited by Heinz Eulau and James G. March. Englewood Cliffs, N.J.: Prentice-Hall, 1969. JA88.U6B45

Current status, trends, and problems, as reported by the committee.

Dahl, Robert A. Modern Political Analysis. Englewood Cliffs, N.J.: Prentice-Hall, 1963. HM271.D34

The basic concepts, ideas, and analytical tools that form the focus for research and theory in this discipline.

Platig. E. Raymond. International Relations Research; Problems of Evaluation and Advancement. Santa Barbara, Calif.: Clio Press for the Carnegie Endowment for International Peace, 1966. JX1291.P55

Characteristics of international relations as a field of study, and its problems of methodology and communication.

Ranney, Austin, ed. Political Science and Public Policy. Chicago: Markham Publishing Co., 1968. JA84.U5P6

Papers presented at two conferences sponsored by the Committee on Governmental and Legal Processes of the Social Science Research Council, on questions relating to the "professional expertise and obligations, if any, of political scientists to study, evaluate, and make recommendations about the contents of public policies" (p. vii).

Sorauf, Francis J. Political Science: an Informal Overview. Columbus, Ohio: Charles E. Merrill, 1965. JA88.U6S6

   Basic discussion of the subject matter of political science and history and methods of research, designed to acquaint elementary and secondary social studies teachers with current scholarly perspectives.

Psychology

Behavioral and Social Sciences Survey Committee, Psychiatry Panel. Psychiatry as a Behavioral Science. Edited by David A. Hamburg. Englewood Cliffs, N.J.: Prentice-Hall, 1970. RC327.B4

   Current status, trends, and problems, as reported by the committee.

Behavioral and Social Sciences Survey Committee, Psychology Panel. Psychology, edited by Kenneth E. Clark and George A. Miller. Englewood Cliffs, N.J.: Prentice-Hall, 1970. BF38.B43

   Current status, trends, and problems, as reported by the committee.

Hyman, Ray. The Nature of Psychological Inquiry. Englewood Cliffs, N.J.: Prentice-Hall, 1964. BF38.H95

   Discussion of the underlying rationale of psychological inquiry, with some general consideration of methodological issues and procedures, and examples from the history of psychology.

Sociology

Behavioral and Social Sciences Survey Committee, Sociology Panel, Sociology. Edited by Neil J. Smelser and James A. Davis. Englewood Cliffs, N. J.: Prentice-Hall, 1969. HM24.B385

   Current status, trends, and problems, as reported by the committee.

Friedrichs, Robert W. A Sociology of Sociology. New York: Free Press, 1970. HM24.F74

   Consideration of the character and history of present-day sociology in relation to basic ideas about the structure and operation of the scientific enterprise, particularly as advanced by Thomas Kuhn in The Structure of Scientific Revolutions (above).

Gouldner, Alvin. The Coming Crisis of Western Sociology. New York: Basic Books, 1970. HM24.G65

   "An historically informed critique of sociology as a theory and as a social institution" (p. 12).

Inkeles, Alex. What is Sociology? An Introduction to the Discipline and Profession. Englewood Cliffs, N.J.: Prentice-Hall, 1964. HM66.15

   Brief account of subject matter, basic theoretical assumptions, and methods.

Reynolds, Larry T. and Janice M. Reynolds, eds. The Sociology of Sociology; Analysis and Criticism of the Thought, Research, and Ethical Folkways of Sociology and its Practitioners. New York: David McKay Co., 1970. HM24.R48

Essays by a number of authors presenting a variety of points of view regarding the relationship between social factors and the theory and practice of sociology.

Rose, Caroline B. Sociology: the Study of Man in Society. Columbis, Ohio: Charles E. Merrill, 1965. HM51.R82

Basic account of subject matter and history of sociology, designed to acquaint elementary and secondary social studies teachers with current scholarly perspectives.

PART II

Structure and Components of the Social Science Literature

The literature of a field of study is the communications system of the scholars working in the discipline. In consequence, the literature derives its form from the character of scientific communication. This means that the various types of publications comprising the literature correspond to several types of messages carried by the communications system. Just as scientific knowledge begins with the observation of specific instances and cumulates from this base into broad statements of established principles, so the record of this knowledge, the scientific literature, builds from reports of single studies to comprehensive accounts of everything that is known about the subject. In this progression there is discernible a patterned structure of publications, each having a more or less distinctive role in the communications network. Thus comprehension of the literature of social science has been described as

> . . . the simple act of seeing, within all these tiered rows of books, a highly organized system of communicating information. Some elements of the system are sources which exist to report research; others exist to take such reports and piece them together into competent summaries of present knowledge; still others, to list or review new publications, explain the nomenclature, or perform some other helpful function. Each type of source, in short, has its job to do.[1]

In the chapters following, the forms of publication most commonly encountered in the literatures of the social science disciplines will be considered from the point of view of the "job" done by each in relation to the others, and the role of each publication form in the over-all process of scientific communication. This concept of the literature as a system is extremely useful for comprehending the kinds of information which can be found in scholarly writing and for distinguishing among superficially similar publications in ways that aid in using them effectively in literature searching. However, it is important to remember that the "system" is only a conceptual abstraction, and not a concrete entity. In reality, publications are instituted independently of each other, by individuals or groups who recognize a need and are able to command the necessary resources. There is no authority or master intelligence to parcel out the various phases of communication and prevent duplication or omission. The system, such as it is, results not from rational and deliberate design, but from certain basic characteristics of science as an enterprise.

The collective, cumulative quality of scientific work gives rise to several fairly distinctive forms of communication, and over the course of time a number of forms of publication have evolved as the traditional and customary means of conveying the various types of messages. Over all, these publications may be seen as comprising a coherent and functionally differentiated system, and there are advantages to be derived from this view. But because the systematic conceptualization does not create the publications, but is imposed on them, defects in the system and deviations from its alleged structure are not infrequently encountered.

The communication system to be described here as the organizing framework for the scientific literature derives from the view of science set forth in the preceding chapters; that is, briefly, the conception of science as a collective enterprise in which knowledge is developed cumulatively and by consensus. Accordingly, it is to be expected that the literature will fit the systematic framework approximately to the extent that the actual activities of scientists conform to the model described. Yet, as the account above indicated, the goals and methods of science are not fixed and immutable, or imposed uniformly by designated authority, but instead evolve in largely unpremeditated fashion as the general effect of many independent individual actions. Here, then, is one major source of discrepancies between the literature as it actually is and a hypothetical system or structure.

In addition, while the patterns of science may be applicable to the social sciences viewed over all, there are substantial differences at more specific levels. Each discipline has its own distinctive qualities of structure and operation—the result of myriad factors such as the field's subject matter, its size, the time and place of its origins, and early development, its degree of connection to, or insulation from, the concerns of a larger public. All this shapes the field's communication practices and its literature, and opens innumerable possibilities for variation in an assumed standard pattern.

Finally, a given publication may be adaptable to roles and uses other than that for which it was specifically designed, and may therefore be capable of carrying out a given communication function, particularly in the absence of better alternatives, even though it may differ in substantial ways from more "typical" examples of the category in question.

For all these reasons, it is important in examining publications and considering their characteristics as sources of information, to bear in mind that the aim is to use the idea of a logical, functionally differentiated communication system as an aid to understanding of the literature, but not to define categories or affix labels as ends in themselves. It may be taken for granted that, just as few, if any, generalizations about groups apply with equal force to each individual member of the group, few, if any, publications described as performing a given role in communication will be "perfect" examples of that type or function. However, generalizing about publications makes it possible to fit them into a rational scheme which can lend itself to logical analysis of information problems and systematic searching procedures, and this, rather than creation of a rigid, logically airtight typology, is the purpose of the present undertaking.

Chapter Three

Research Reports: Scholarly Journals, Technical Reports, and Books

In the same way as a detailed study of a specific situation is the basis of scientific knowledge, reports of such studies are the basic elements of scientific literature. Because science is a collective enterprise, the reporting of results is an intrinsic part of the research process. A scholar who conducts a study does not consider the work completed until he has communicated his findings to other members of the scientific community, and thus made his efforts available for their consideration and response.

There are several ways in which a researcher may choose to report his work. He may send his report directly to other scholars whom he knows have an interest in the subject, or he may read the paper before a meeting of his discipline's learned society. He may attempt to interest a publisher in issuing his study as a book. Most commonly, however, he will submit his report for publication as an article in a scholarly journal.

SCHOLARLY JOURNALS

Journals are the major vehicles for the reporting of research, and as such may be said to constitute the foundation and mainstay of the scholarly communication system. The history of these publications extends back to the seventeenth century, or approximately the time of the beginning of organized scientific activity. Originally, journals were mainly a device for announcing the current books, but their scope has expanded and diversified over the years to encompass current scientific activity in general, with emphasis on the detailed reporting of research.

To understand the role of journals in scientific communication, it is helpful to distinguish between specialized, scholarly periodicals and general magazines. The differences, while not always entirely clear-cut, are substantial and important. Typically, the scholarly journal is not a profit-making venture, and it is most often issued by a learned society or academic institution, rather than a commercial publishing firm. Editors of journals are not full-time journalists, but distinguished scholars in the discipline of the journal, who perform the editorial work in addition to their other research and teaching activities and are not paid for this work, except in honor and prestige. Normally the editor does not plan the contents of the journal, or assign writers to prepare specific articles.[2] Instead, the articles appearing in the journal are the reports that come in, unsolicited, from scholars in the field, dealing with whatever topics their authors have elected to study and discuss. In most cases, authors are neither paid for their contributions (except, again, in professional advancement and prestige) nor required to pay to have their work published. Articles may be rejected by the editor, usually in consultation with associates who assist him in reviewing manuscripts, on the ground that their quality is inadequate or their subject matter outside the scope of the journal, but the essential idea is to open the pages of the journal to the scholars in the field, as the reporting vehicle for their research.

In line with their basic function of disseminating current news of scholarly activity, journals frequently include a variety of materials in addition to research reports. Book reviews are a source of information about current work, and that is why many scholarly journals publish them. Some journals also contain notices of articles on relevant subjects appearing in other publications, and a few publish comprehensive current bibliographies. Because journals are widely read by specialists in their respective fields, they are also frequently the means for communicating general professional news, such as appointments, deaths, announcements of meetings, establishment of new organizations, and the like. However, their primary function is the reporting of current research, and their major content is the research article.[3]

The typical research report published as a journal article is an attempt to answer a question by examination of some relevant evidence, which is presented in the article. There is usually a brief introductory account of the current state of research on the problem and the specific gap or contradiction in existing knowledge toward which the study being reported is directed, followed by a description of the method of analysis to be used and the reasons the method can be expected to yield a valid answer. Most of the paper consists of exposition of the data, the observed facts, and a discussion of their meaning in relation to the problem being investigated. Finally there is a statement of the extent to which the data and analysis have answered the question. These components of a research report may not always be set forth as explicitly as they are outlined here, but they comprise the general content of most such articles in scholarly journals.

A variant form is the theoretical paper, which focuses on interpretation of already-known facts rather than on presentation of new evidence. In such an article, the author examines data which is already in the literature, i.e., reported in previous studies, to show that the data can support a conclusion or explanation which was not presented in earlier reports.

Virtually all journal articles, whether research reports or theoretical studies, are attempts to find new knowledge, to take up where the existing content of a subject leaves off and investigate what is unknown, or partially known, or questionable. As this requires systematic, detailed observation, the subject of articles are generally problems which lend themselves to such treatment—that is, very specific, narrowly defined questions which can be encompassed in a single investigation. Because articles are used to introduce new information and new ideas, they are likely to include a full presentation of the data underlying the author's conclusion. But for the same reasons, the conclusion itself is likely to appear not as a broad principle or firm concept, but rather as a limited, tentative statement subject to further investigation and verification. Thus the role of articles in the communication system governs the kind of information likely to be found in them.

Because they are regularly distributed by subscription, journals reach a wide audience among specialists in a given field, and therefore scholars tend to prefer publication of research in this form over others. However, other considerations may lead to alternative choices.

The principal "other consideration" is that the size of the scientific community has, on the whole, grown more rapidly than the number of journals, with the result that competition for space in journals may be quite severe, with long waits for publication and substantial numbers of rejected manuscripts. In order to announce his findings without waiting the six months or year or even longer that may elapse between submission of an article to a journal and its publication, an author may mimeograph his report and send copies to scholars known to him to have an interest in the topic. Papers of this kind are called "preprints," and they may or may not appear subsequently as articles.

Scholars sometimes present their latest work by reading a report to a scientific meeting. In some cases the society holding the meeting publishes the proceedings. When this is not done, the author of the report may later submit it to a journal for publication, or he may content himself with distribution of a small number of copies to those attending the meeting and others who may happen to hear of the paper and request copies.

TECHNICAL REPORTS

Not infrequently, institutions which employ researchers—government agencies, university research bureaus, business firms—publish the research done within the institution, sometimes as separate papers, and sometimes in a continuing series. Materials in this form are called "technical reports," and usually have relatively limited distribution. Work issued originally in the report format may reappear subsequently as a journal article or book, but this happens rather infrequently.

In the opinion of many scholars, an essential and very significant difference between technical reports and other informally circulated materials on the one hand, and journal articles on the other, is that the former enter the literature solely at the discretion of their authors and subject only to their control, while the latter are judged by someone other than the author to be suitable contributions to the literature. It is argued that the privately generated literature is comparable to the private correspondence that was the main means of scientific communication prior to the development of an institutionalized, public literature centered in journals, and thus is a retrogressive phenomenon, which undermines the open, collective quality essential to scientific progress. An opposing view holds that the clogged and overcrowded channels of conventional publication are themselves formidable barriers to openness and collectiveness in science, and that devices such as preprints and technical reports are essential for maintaining the free flow of communication. In most fields of social science the volume of technical report literature, while growing, is quite small in comparison to journal publication, so that for all practical purposes condieration of "the literature" begins with journals. However, it is well to remember that alternative, less formal means of research communication do exist and are employed to some extent.

BOOKS

Research reports and theoretical studies essentially very similar to those published as articles may also appear as books.[4] Another form, more or less intermediate, is the "monograph," a form of publication that tends to be longer than most articles and shorter than most books, and that usually appears as a physically separate entity within a series of related works.[5]

In the literature of the social sciences, books and journal articles (and their several variants, as described above) are used almost interchangeably as vehicles for original reports of research findings. This differs somewhat from the pattern of the natural sciences, in which books and articles tend to have rather more clearly differentiated roles in communication. In those fields, research—the search for new information—is nearly always reported in articles or technical reports, and books are nearly always a format for summary and interpretation of previously reported data. But in the literature of the social sciences, although there are probably many more books devoted to summary and synthesis than to the reporting of new data (no count has been made, so far as the writer knows) books share with articles the role of reporting research results and proposing new explanatory concepts, and it is really not possible to formulate criteria by which the content and purpose of one form may be clearly and consistently distinguished from that of the other.

In terms of the concept of a system of scientific communication, the fact that research may be reported in either article or book form is of little significance. The important observation is that the basic element of scientific literature, as of scientific knowledge, is the report of a detailed, systematic examination of a delimited, specifically defined problem. However, the existence of two principal formats for such reports may at times present some practical problems, since a number of tools affording access to the literature—for example, library card catalogs and periodical indexes—are limited to one form or the other. For this reason, it is perhaps useful to delineate a few gross characteristics that tend to distinguish books from articles, bearing in mind that such distinctions are necessarily clouded and inconsistent and can correspond only roughly to reality.

In general, the major difference between research projects and theoretical studies reported in articles and those appearing in book form is one of scope and perspective. Books are longer than most articles, of course, and consequently the investigations they report are likely to be more extensive. While journal articles, as noted earlier, generally focus on a single, very specifically defined problem, research projects reported as books may tackle somewhat larger questions, often by investigating simultaneously a number of interrelated aspects of the problem. Thus even though some books report very much the same sort of research as is published in articles, books tend to view the problem being investigated in broader terms.[6]

Unfortunately, there is no formula by which to identify "narrow" and "broad" subjects. As reflected in the choice of book or article format for publication of a given study, subjective and accidental factors may play as large a role as the "scope" of the work, however defined. Moreover, any objective distinction would depend largely on the state of research on the topic, and could not possibly remain stable through time. The first discussions of a new idea are likely to appear as articles, since the subject is unexplored and there is relatively little to be said about it. As research accumulates, new facets of the problem are revealed, each in turn generating further study, new knowledge, and recognition of additional questions. In time the subject comes to be seen as large and complex. At that stage, an article-length study will be able to encompass only one of the topic's now numerous aspects, and comprehensive treatment will be possible only at considerable length—i.e., in book form. For example, in 1958 one of the pioneers in the behavioral study of the judicial process—at that time a very new area of research—published an article "suggesting some of the kinds of hypotheses that may be worth looking into if we are willing to consider adding other strings to our bow, instead of limiting ourselves to the traditional workways in public law."[7] Five years later, a bibliographic review[8] of this subject identified four major areas of research interest, or subspecializations, each with its own burgeoning literature, and a volume designed to exemplify some of the major trends and accomplishments in this field contained ten essays by some dozen contributors and a bibliography roughly half the length of the 1958 article.[9] This is a rather dramatic illustration of a pattern of development which is quite common. A topic which is at first narrow and circumscribed grows into a broad research area possessing a large and varied literature as it attracts the interest and attention of scholars.

Such complications as the foregoing notwithstanding, it remains true that by far the largest portion of research in all areas of social science is reported in the form of journal articles, and that the journal is therefore the preeminent vehicle for introduction of new knowledge into a scholarly discipline. By reading current journals, the scholar keeps informed of research and new discoveries in his field. The accumulated journal literature of a discipline constitutes the prime source of the data and detailed reasoning underlying the field's established knowledge.

FOOTNOTES

1. Carl M. White, Sources of Information in the Social Sciences (Totowa, N.J.: Bedminster Press, 1964), p. ix.

2. Some journals do consist, either wholly or in part, of invited contributions, or differ in other respects from the "typical" research journal these paragraphs are intended to describe. See the list of "special purpose" journals in Appendix B.

3. For further discussion see the special issue of International Social Science Journal 19, (1967) entitled "The Social Science Press."

4. Literally understood, "book" means any publication issued between its own covers. In this discussion, "book" is used in a more limited sense to mean a publication which deals with a single, relatively closely defined problem, and which is not described by another generic term, such as textbook, handbook, or encyclopedia.

5. For example, John R. P. Friedman, "The Spatial Structure of Economic Development in the Tennessee Valley" (University of Chicago, Department of Geography, Research Paper no. 59, 1955). 104pp.

6. To illustrate, compare W. Buchanan, "An Inquiry into Purposive Voting," Journal of Politics 18, (1956): 281–296, a study that compares voting with several other forms of community participation in a Mississippi town of 5,000, with A. Campbell et al., The American Voter (New York: John Wiley, 1960) 573p., an investigation of the determinants of voting behavior throughout the United States, which reports survey data collected in three national campaigns. On the other hand, a direct ancestor of the Campbell study, P. Lazarsfeld et al., The People's Choice (New York: Duell, Sloan and Pearce, 1944) reports a study of the formation of voting decisions in a single county during a single election campaign, and was, as noted, published as a book.

7. Glendon Schubert, "The Study of Judicial Decision-Making as an Aspect of Political Behavior," American Political Science Review 52 (1958): 1007–1025.

8. Glendon Schubert, "Behavioral Research in Public Law," Ibid. 57 (1963): 433–445.

9. Glendon Schubert, ed., Judicial Decision-Making (N. Y., Free Press, 1963).

Appendix B

Selected List of
Social Science Journals

Listed below are some major English-language journals in the social sciences, with brief descriptions of their contents. The quoted statements in the annotations are, unless otherwise identified, from an editorial statement appearing in the journal, usually in conjunction with instructions regarding the submission of manuscripts.

The titles listed in the first group—"Representative Research Journals"—conform generally to the pattern described in the text. That is, their main purpose is dissemination of research reports and theoretical contributions within a field of study, and their principal content, accordingly, is the unsolicited, contributed article. This is often supplemented by other materials relating to current scholarship in the field, such as book reviews and announcements of meetings. The list that follows is a very small sample of such publications, chosen more or less at random to illustrate some typical characteristics of the genre. It may be noted that nearly all are published by academic societies or universities, and that, variations on specific points notwithstanding, their content is basically quite similar.

The journals in the second group—" 'Special purpose' journals"—do not have the reporting of research as their main function, but are designed for a variety of other purposes, as described in each instance. This list is of interest not only because the titles mentioned can be useful as sources of particular kinds of information, but also because it demonstrates that publications which look quite similar can vary substantially in their aims and the nature of their content.

REPRESENTATIVE RESEARCH JOURNALS

Anthropology

American Anthropologist. 1888 – . Washington, D.C., American Anthropological Association. bimonthly. GN1.A5

"Publishes scholarly articles of general interest to professional anthropologists, from all subdisciplines of anthropology. It also gives comprehensive review coverage to new publications of significance to the field." Alternate issues devoted to articles and book reviews. "Discussion and debate" section includes brief comments on previously published articles and other matters.

Ethnology: an International Journal of Cultural and Social Anthropology. 1962 – . Pittsburgh, University of Pittsburgh. quarterly. GN1.E86

"Ethnology welcomes articles by scientists of any country on any aspect of cultural anthropology. Theoretical or methodological discussions, however, will be published only if they specifically relate to some body of substantive data."

Economics

American Economic Review. 1911 – . Evanston, Ill. American Economic Association, quarterly. HB1.E26

Research and theoretical articles in all fields of economics; also briefer communications, and annual list of completed doctoral dissertations.

Economica. 1921 – . London, London School of Economics and Political Science. quarterly. HB1.E5

Articles and book reviews.

Quarterly Journal of Economics. 1886 – . Cambridge, Mass., Harvard University. HB1.Q3

Articles; notes and discussion.

Education

American Educational Research Journal. 1964 – . Washington, D.C., American Educational Research Association. quarterly. L11.A66

"Publishes original reports of experimental and theoretical studies in education"; also a small number of book reviews.

Harvard Educational Review. 1931 – . Cambridge, Mass., Harvard University. quarterly. L11.H3

". . . a journal of opinion and research in the field of education. Articles are selected, edited and published by an Editorial Board of graduate students in Harvard University. The Harvard Educational Review accepts contributions by teachers, scholars, research workers in education, and persons working in related fields." Articles and book reviews.

Geography

Association of American Geographers. Annals. 1911 – . Washington, D.C. quarterly. G3.A7

"The ANNALS was instituted . . . to stimulate scholarship and to provide for publication of significant contributions to knowledge in geography. Its volumes contain scholarly papers, presidential addresses, (book) reviews and review articles, maps of special interest, and occasional special items. The ANNALS welcomes article-length manuscripts on any geographical subject, without regard to the point of view represented or the manner of treatment, as long as these reflect sound scholarship, provide significant geographical information, or represent concepts and accomplishments of importance to geography and related disciplines." (Reproduced with permission from the Annals of the Association of American Geographers.)

Economic Geography. 1925 – . Worcester, Mass., Clark University. quarterly. HF1021.E4

Articles and book reviews, directed to "geographers, economists, urbanists, generalists in education and the professions, as well as all those interested in the intelligent utilization of the world's resources."

History

American Historical Review. 1895 – . Washington, D.C., American Historical Association. quarterly. E171.A57

Scholarly articles in all subfields of history; large number of book reviews, and lists of current articles.

History and Theory: Studies in the Philosophy of History. 1960 – . Middletown, Conn., Wesleyan University. three issues per year, plus supplements. D1.H8173

". . . publishes monographs, reviews, notes and also bibliographies, principally in four areas: theories of history, cause, law, explanation, generalization, determinism; historiography, studies of historians, historical philosophers, historical figures, and events which illuminate general historiographical problems; method of history, interpretation, selection of facts, objectivity, social and cultural implications of the historian's method; related disciplines, relationship of problems in historical theory and method to those of economic, psychological and other social sciences." (Copyright © Wesleyan University.)

Journal of American History. 1914 – . Bloomington, Ind., Organization of American Historians. quarterly. E171.J87

Articles, book reviews, professional news, classified list of current articles. Published 1914–1964 as Mississippi Valley Historical Review.

Political Science

American Political Science Review. 1906 – . Washington, D.C., American Political Science Association. quarterly. JA1.A6

Articles and book reviews.

Public Opinion Quarterly. 1937 – . New York, American Association for Public Opinion Research and Columbia University. HM261.A1P8

Articles; briefer comments on research in progress and current issues of professional interest; summaries of poll results; book reviews.

World Politics: a Quarterly Journal of International Relations. 1948 – . Princeton, Center of International Studies, Princeton University. D839.W57

Articles and book reviews.

Psychology

Developmental Psychology. 1969 – . Washington, D.C., American Psychological Association. bimonthly. BF699.D46

Research articles on problems relating to "broad range of growth, development, and their major associated variables."

Journal of Personality and Social Psychology. 1965 – . Washington, D.C., American Psychological Association. monthly. HM251.J56

". . . publishes original research reports in the areas of social psychology and personality dynamics."

Sociology

American Journal of Sociology. 1895 – . Chicago, University of Chicago. bimonthly. HM1.A7

Articles and book reviews.

American Sociological Review: Official Journal of the American Sociological Association. 1936 – . Washington, D.C. bimonthly. HM1.A75

Research and theoretical articles in all areas of sociology. Many book reviews prior to 1972, when they were discontinued with the inception, by the American Sociological Association, of Contemporary Sociology, a journal devoted entirely to book reviews.

Social Forces. 1922 – . Chapel Hill, University of North Carolina. quarterly. HN51.S5

Articles and book reviews.

"SPECIAL PURPOSE" JOURNALS

Professional Journals.   Primary concern not with incremental advancement of knowledge in a specialized field, but with broader issues in the professional life of the scholar. May occasionally publish research studies on topics touching many areas of specialization, but articles are more apt to deal with matters such as professional education and development, communication, organization, ethics. Large amounts of news of appointments, grants, meetings, etc.

American Psychologist. 1946 – . Washington, D.C., American Psychological Association. monthly. BF1.A55

"The American Psychologist is the official publication of the Association and contains archival documents, Comments, a Psychology in Action section, Announcements, Convention Calendars, and regular articles. Articles should be timely and of broad general interest to psychologists of all scientific and professional persuasions."

American Sociologist. 1965 – . Washington, D.C., American Sociological Association. quarterly.   HM9.A713

". . . an organ of information and discussion for the professional concerns of sociologists as a social collectivity." (Editorial statement, vol. 1, no. 1.)

Current Anthropology. 1960 – . Chicago, University of Chicago and Wenner-Gren Foundation for Anthropological Research. five issues per year.   GN1.C8

". . . serves as a clearinghouse for news and ideas, an indicator of trends and needs in the profession, and an instrument for acting on the latter as they emerge." (Note: This journal is devoted in part to professional news, and in part to reviews of the literature. See also "Review Journals" below.)

P.S. 1968 – . Washington, D.C., American Political Science Association. quarterly.

"P.S. is the Association's news journal with information on professional developments, research and study support, and professional as well as Association activities. Articles and reports on the discipline and profession are also included."

Interdisciplinary and International Journals.   Designed to promote communication among scholars normally separated by disciplinary and/or national boundaries. Tend to focus on topics of general concern in many areas of scholarship, and to emphasize invited (rather than individually generated) contributions.

American Behavioral Scientist. 1957 – . Beverly Hills, Calif., Sage Publications. bimonthly.   H1.A472

"Each issue . . . is prepared under the direction of a guest editor, and focuses on a specific theme (utilizing a variety of disciplinary approaches) selected from the emerging areas of cross-disciplinary interest in the social sciences."

Behavioral Science. 1956 – . Louisville, Ky., University of Lousiville. bimonthly.   BF1.B3

". . .publishes original articles concerning both living and nonliving systems. These include atoms, molecules, crystals, viruses, cells, organs, organisms, groups, organizations, societies, supranational systems, ecosystems, planets, solar systems, galaxies—as well as mechanical, conceptual and abstracted systems. The editors are especially interested in the submission of manuscripts with broad interdisciplinary approaches which would not normally be found in a journal devoted to a single discipline."

International Social Science Journal. 1949 –   . Paris, UNESCO. quarterly. H1.A2

Designed to facilitate cross-national and interdisciplinary communication among social scientists. Each issue is devoted to a single topic relevant to one or more of the social science disciplines, and consists of invited contributions from scholars in different countries together, usually, with an over-all review of the topic by the special issue editor. Extensive news of social science activity—institutes, conferences, new journals, etc.—around the world.

Public Issue and Popularizing Journals.   Focus on current social and political developments and problems. General, long-range aims are to bring scientific knowledge to bear on the problems of society and/or to educate and inform the general public. Some are primarily vehicles of scholarly discussion, and their articles have a fairly high degree of technical complexity; others are addressed mainly to the lay public and to the presentation of scientific knowledge in lay terms. Some journals of this type may include original research reports, but for the most part research is considered mainly in terms of its relation to issues of current social importance.

American Academy of Political and Social Science. Annals. 1890 –   . Philadelphia. bimonthly.   H1.A4

"Each issue contains articles on some prominent social or political problem, written at the invitation of the editors." Also brief reviews of a large number of books in all social science fields.

Daedalus: Journal of the American Academy of Arts and Sciences. 1846 – . Cambridge, Mass. quarterly.   Q11.B7

Each issue devoted to a topic of major contemporary significance, such as "The Future of the Black Colleges," "The Professions in America," and consists of invited papers by prominent scholars in several disciplines. Issues usually based on one or more conferences, at which the articles were presented and discussed. Many issues are later published separately as books.

Foreign Affairs. 1922 – . New York, Council on Foreign Relation. quarterly. D410.F6

Designed to inform the educated lay public, particularly "opinion leaders" such as businessmen and journalists, about foreign affairs. Articles concern the significant international concerns of the day, and are often written by political leaders and government officials, both American and foreign. Also contains extensive listing, with brief descriptive notes, of current books on international affairs.

Journal of Economic Issues. 1967 –   . East Lansing, Association for Evolutionary Economics and Michigan State University. quarterly.

". . . broadly concerned with major issues of public policy, of economic methodology, and of understanding the processes and problems of economic change. This general scope includes issues which have been made prominent by current economic changes. These issues are typically interdisciplinary in character; they pose problems of the relation between economic theory and economic policy; and they often bear on the changing role of government in the economy." (Editor's Notes, vol. 1, p. 137.)

Journal of Social Issues. 1945 – . Ann Arbor, Mich. Society for the Psychological Study of Social Issues. quarterly. HN51.J6

". . . the Society seeks to bring theory and practice into focus on human problems of the group, the community, and the nation as well as the increasingly important ones that have no national boundaries. This Journal has as its goal the communication of scientific findings and interpretations in a non-technical manner but without the sacrifice of professional standards." Some issues devoted to a single topic, with an introduction by an issue editor, and invited contributions. Others consist of single, contributed articles.

Law and Contemporary Problems. 1933 – . Durham, N.C., Duke University School of Law. quarterly.

Each issue devoted to a significant current issue (e.g., "Community Economic Development," "Consumer Credit Reform"). Contributions treat various aspects of the topic, with some emphasis on its implications for legal institutions and the legal profession.

Psychology Today: a Magazine about Psychology, Society and Human Behavior. 1967 – . Del Mar, Calif., Communications/Research&Machines, Inc. monthly.

Designed to inform the general public about developments in psychology. Most articles are accounts by academic psychologists describing research findings germane to topics of relatively broad public interest, such as social attitudes, child rearing, etc.

Public Interest. 1965 – . New York, National Affairs, Inc. quarterly. H1.P86

Articles commenting on current social and political issues, mainly written by academic social scientists.

Society: The Magazine of Social Science and Modern Society. 1963 – . New Brunswick, N.J., Rutgers, The State University. ten issues per year. H1.T72

Articles are often summaries or adaptations of research reports on topics of more or less widespread public interest, and are usually accompanied by brief lists of books recommended for further reading. A number of issues devoted to special topics have been reissued separately as books. Published 1963–1972 under the title Trans-Action.

Review Journals.   Consist of articles devoted to summary, analysis, and evaluation of research published elsewhere. See Chapter 4 for further discussion of these publications.

Current Anthropology. 1960 – . Chicago, University of Chicago and Wenner-Gren Foundation for Anthropological Research. five issues per year. GN1.C8

Current Sociology. 1952 – . London, Blackwell (for UNESCO). three issues per year. Z7161.C8

Journal of Economic Literature. 1963 – . Washington, D.C., American Economic Association. quarterly. HB1.J6

Psychological Bulletin. 1904 –   . Washington, D.C., American Psychological Association. monthly.   BF1.P75

Review of Education Research. 1931 –   . Washington, D.C., American Educational Research Association. five issues per year.   L11.R35

Bibliographic Journals.   Consist of book reviews and/or abstracts of current articles. For titles and descriptions see Chapters 7 and 8, Appendices G and I.

Chapter Four

Cumulating Publications (1):
Research Reviews and Handbooks

The publications discussed thus far, journal articles and some types of books, are means for bringing new information and new ideas into the literature. They report attempts to extend knowledge beyond its existing boundaries by raising new questions, devising new techniques of investigation, amassing new evidence. But the goal of developing, through research, a body of general concepts in social science requires that the disparate strands represented by independently conducted investigations be gathered together, sorted out and examined, so that their collective, cumulative meaning may be recognized and assessed.

If a question has been investigated by a number of researchers, do their results agree? Do the new findings confirm and extend what was already known, or do they suggest defects in existing theories? Is the total body of evidence that research has brought to bear on some point sufficiently consistent and convincing so that the question may be considered to have been answered, or are there conflicts and differences which can only be explained by more research? Have studies in one area of investigation yielded results which help to explain another set of problems? Or, conversely, do studies in related fields point to contradictory principles of behavior, so that the differences would need to be accounted for before either view could be accepted? In short, what has been learned? What does "science" (i.e., psychology, anthropology, etc.) know about the matter in question?

As noted earlier, the scientific system provides no final, definitive answer to questions such as these, and no scholar is obliged to accept anyone else's conclusion regarding what has or has not been demonstrated by research. Nonetheless, "scientific knowledge," the body of coherent principles presented to students, and to the world, as the content of a learned discipline means simply the answers to these questions as they would be given by a "consensus" of scientists, however defined.

It is thus evident that the process of collecting, assessing, comparing, organizing, and generalizing the concrete, piecemeal observations and propositions put forward by research studies is a critical aspect of the process of creating scientific knowledge. Several types of publications communicate this work. Some are quite close to the original research, intensively examining relatively narrow areas of study and attempting only limited generalization about what has been learned. Others formulate broader generalizations with less attention to detail, and still others concentrate on the common, widely accepted ideas held to be "established knowledge," with little or no notice of the potential innovations competing for recognition at the basic research level. The several publication forms belong to different levels of scientific discourse and represent different stages in the development of knowledge, but they share a common purpose and carry an essentially uniform message. All, in different ways and with different emphases, are vehicles for examining and assessing the results of research and for distilling out of unconnected studies and scattered information an interrelated body of observations and explanations.

RESEARCH REVIEWS

A research review (also called "review article," "review of the literature," or "bibliographic essay") is an analysis of the published research bearing on some problem, undertaken in an attempt to answer a question by examination of the total array of relevant data contained in the research literature. Such reviews are products of the individual, spontaneous efforts of scholars pursuing their scholarly interests, just as are research studies. For this reason the question posed by a review may be anything the author believes will be successfully illuminated by study and comparison of completed research. For example, if a matter is the subject of controversy, a detailed review of the data presented in support of both sides of the issue may reveal the sources of the conflicting explanations, or may indicate that the preponderance of evidence is on one side or the other. Or a scholar may review the research dealing with one set of problems in order to point out the relevance of its methods and results for other areas of investigation. Or he may wish to show that certain widely accepted concepts are contradicted by recent research, or that the research on which some idea was originally based adds up to a different conclusion when reexamined. These are some common reasons for undertaking a research review, but the possibilities are limited only by the author's ideas about the meaning and significance of some segment of the research literature.

Most research reviews are published as articles in journals, and they are sometimes (not always) distinguished from the more numerous research reports by the designation "review article" or "bibliographic essay." A few periodicals specialize in publication of review articles, or include them very frequently. Psychological Bulletin[1] is devoted entirely to research reviews of problems in psychology. The Review of Educational Research performs a similar function in education. The Journal of Economic Literature contains several review articles in each issue, as does Latin American Research Review. A review article appears in each issue of Crime and Delinquency Literature.[2]

Current Anthropology devotes a major portion of its content to review articles. In this journal each review article is accompanied by comments, solicited by the editors in advance of publication of the review, from authors whose work is discussed in the article and others who have done significant research on the problem. The intention is to present "in some sense an expression of the opinion of the profession"—in other words, a more explicit expression of consensus than can be conveyed by the review article alone. As the editors comment, "Whether this reveals a significant agreement on a particular matter or on the contrary, uncovers a controversy and indicates the kind of evidence required to bring about a consensus, a valuable stocktaking function is served."[3]

The foregoing are the principal social science periodicals in the English language specializing in review articles, but such articles appear with varying frequency in most of the scholarly journals. Another form of review publication is the periodic report of research trends and results in a discipline. These are also called research reviews, but they differ in several ways from the review articles discussed above.

The recurrent reviews result not from the independent interests and activities of individuals, but rather from a deliberate, institutionalized plan whereby a special review publication is established and an editor or editorial board selects the subjects to be reviewed and appoints the reviewers. The recurrent review publications typically summarize the research activities and accomplishments of an entire discipline (e.g., psychology) during a stated time period (usually one year). Given this framework, the reviews tend to be organized around the conventional divisions of the field rather than the individual outlook of the author, and hence are likely to be broader in scope than the individual review papers. The institutional reviews discuss the major developments represented by the research published since the previous review—the questions investigated, methods used, and general nature of the findings. They may note the existence of controversies and the appearance of new theories and approaches but, unlike the independent review articles, the recurrent reviews do not characteristically enter into the details of data and analysis presented in the research being reviewed, and do not focus extensively on explication or evaluation of particular substantive points. They are designed to provide a continuing description and assessment of the progress of research, and their emphasis is on major trends and significant accomplishments.

Periodic general reviews of the research literature have long been customary in most areas of natural science, and have more recently been instituted in some of the social sciences, such as psychology (Annual Review of Psychology, 1950-   ),[4] anthropology (Biennial Review of Anthropology, 1959-1971,[5] Annual Review of Anthropology, 1972-   [6]), political science (Political Science Annual, 1966-   ).[7] From its inception in 1931 until 1970, the Review of Educational Research reviewed each of fifteen major research areas in education at approximately three-year intervals. In mid-1970 this journal announced a change in content, from descriptive reviews of broad research areas to unsolicited review articles dealing with topics of the contributor's choosing, as described above. At the same time, the American Educational Research Association, sponsor of the journal, announced plans for an Annual Review of Educational Research to carry on the former function of the Review, but this had not yet appeared as of early 1973. Review articles of varying length and scope are commissioned by the Educational Resources Information Center (ERIC)[8] and issued from time to time as separate publications.

The Yearbook of World Affairs[9] includes a group of essays discussing the major books in the field of international relations which have appeared during the year. The Handbook of Latin American Studies (1936-   ) is primarily an annually issued annotated bibliography of research in the social sciences and humanities related to Latin America. (See Chapter 7.) However, each subject section is introduced by a discussion of major trends and accomplishments, and these prefaces give the publication some of the characteristics of an annual review.

Current Sociology is a review journal which resembles the recurrent reviews in purpose and content, but it is not recurrent. That is, there is no regular pattern or stated frequency governing the selection of subjects for review. Each issue consists of a single long article (called "trend report") describing the character, methods, and results of research studies on a particular topic of sociological interest. In similar fashion, the Journal of Economic Literature publishes invited reviews of the literature of major research topics in economics but, again, without a definite pattern for selection of subjects or systematic attempt to cover the entire field at some stated interval. A series of brief monographs published by the American Historical Association since 1971 under the title AHA Pamphlets reviews accrued scholarship and current thinking on major historical topics.[10]

Many issues of the Annals of the American Academy of Political and Social Science include, in a supplementary section, a fairly extensive account of trends and new developments in some area of social or historical research. Similar, though briefer, reviews appear with some regularity in several journals, notably International Social Science Journal, Journal of Social Issues, Daedalus, and (less frequently) American Behavioral Scientist. These publications typically devote each issue to a single topic, and one of the articles is usually a summary of trends in research on the subject.

HANDBOOKS

In the effort of the scholarly enterprise to synthesize a body of knowledge from the raw materials of research, it is sometimes useful to pause and take stock of the accomplishments of the past and the foreseeable tasks of the future. One way to do this is to divide the field of study into its principal component subjects and to set down for each an account of the status of research in the area. This would include the major findings of research and the conclusions which have been based on those findings, the concepts current in the field, and how and by whom they were developed, the over-all direction of research and its prospects. Such an undertaking is usually organized by an eminent scholar in the discipline, who calls on specialists in the various subdivisions to contribute accounts of research in their areas of specialization. The resulting publication is usually a book with the word "handbook" somewhere in its title (e.g., Handbook of Modern Sociology).

In everyday language, "handbook" conveys the idea of a compendium of facts, such as dates or statistics, collected from diverse sources and presented for convenient access and quick reference in summary form. This is exactly what the scholarly handbooks are for the scholarly community. They organize, summarize, and make readily accessible a body of basic information about a field of study.

The central focus of a handbook is the current substantive content of an area of research. The typical handbook article is primarily an exposition of the concepts which comprise the cumulated knowledge of its subject. This account is supported and amplified by mention of the essential elements of the underlying data, and references to the original studies in which the data were reported and the concepts formulated. For the scholar this material conveys concise but comprehensive information about work in a field of study broader than his particular area of specialization, and may furnish him with new ideas or with confirmation of his own findings from a new direction. For the student, a handbook is a repository of the content of a subject and a gateway to its literature.

The style and approach described here are generally characteristic, but handbooks vary in specific respects from one work to another, and even, to some extent, from one article to another within the same work. Several key elements—explanation of major concepts, summary of supporting data, and citation of the pertinent literature—are almost always present, but in varying proportions and with varying degrees of emphasis. For example, there may be detailed presentations of the main facts about the subject and their meaning, without much explicit consideration of the research which has generated the information, or detailed reference to the supporting literature. Or an author may concentrate on comparing and evaluating several approaches and points of view with regard to the subject, and give relatively less attention to detailed explication of the ideas and methods referred to. Overall, handbooks are probably inclined to emphasize the substance of a subject more than its history and trends in research, but there is no uniformity.

Handbooks vary also in their assumptions regarding the reader's prior knowledge of the subject. Some are aimed principally at specialists and advanced students, and focus mainly on currently important aspects of the field, assuming the reader's familiarity with underlying basic concepts. Others attempt a more comprehensive overview, giving attention to the subject's fundamentals as well as to issues of current research interest. A few works quite similar to hand-books—for example, Human Behavior: an Inventory of Scientific Findings, and American Negro Reference Book[11]—are expressly addressed to nonspecialists, and designed to convey to the lay public what scholars have learned. However, most handbooks are conceived as working tools in the research enterprise, and as such their principal aim is to illuminate significant questions of current interest, rather than to provide a basic introduction to the subject or a brief digest of well-established information.

A major and obvious defect of the handbook as a summarizing and stock-taking device is the appearance of these works as one-time publications without provision for updating. Some highly regarded and successful handbooks have been issued in successive editions, but such revisions are infrequent and the usefulness of the original work may decline, through age, almost to the vanishing point before a new edition is undertaken. There is really no way to state the useful life span of a handbook, as knowledge does not develop at a uniform rate and an account of one topic may remain substantially valid for years while another is quickly outdated by accumulating research. About all that can be said is that readers should always be aware of the date of any publication used, and bear in mind the possibility that the picture may have been significantly altered by more recent work. This problem will be further considered in the summary of the characteristics of scholarly literature in Chapter 6.

Appendix C lists handbooks and similar publications in a number of social science fields. In general, they resemble the pattern described above, with variations as noted in the annotations.

FOOTNOTES

1. Except where otherwise specified, bibliographic details for the review journals mentioned may be found in Appendix B.

2. This publication is further described in Appendix G.

3. Editorial foreword, published in each issue.

4. Stanford, Calif.: Annual Reviews. BF30.A56

5. Stanford, Calif.: Stanford University Press. Z5112.B56

6. Stanford, Calif.: Annual Reviews.

7. Indianapolis: Bobbs-Merrill. JA51.P6

8. See Chapter 7, for further description of the ERIC program.

9. London: Stevens, 1947– .JX21.Y4

10. Some representative titles are The Progressive Era 1900–20 by George E. Mowry (AHA Pamphlet 212, Washington, 1972); The Indian in American History by William T. Hagan (AHA Pamphlet 240, Washington, 1971). In most libraries the pamphlets are classed individually, according to their respective subjects, but the titles in the series will be listed in the library catalog under American Historical Association, AHA Pamphlets. This series updates an earlier one, the Publications of the Service Center for Teachers of History (an affiliate of the American Historical Association), published between 1956 and 1970.

11. See Appendix C for full description and bibliographic details.

Appendix C

Selected List of Handbooks and Similar Publications

American Geography: Inventory and Prospect. Edited by Preston E. James and Clarence F. Jones. Syracuse: Syracuse University Press for the Association of American Geographers, 1954. G73.3.U5J3

Essays presenting the content and concerns of the main subdivisions and methodological approaches in geography. As described in the foreword, the collection "brings together the experiences of modern American geographic research to provide guideposts for the decades ahead. It considers concepts or basic generalizations that have been used in professional geographic work, both those that have been found wanting and those that today steer our efforts; and the procedures or methods that have been found useful in geographic research." (p. v). (Reprinted with permission from the Association of American Geographers.)

American History: Retrospect and Prospect. Edited by George Athan Billias and Gerald N. Grob. New York: Free Press, 1971. E175.B49

Ten chapters describe the background and current perspectives of historical research dealing with six broad chronological periods and four major topical areas (economic, social, urban, and diplomatic history). Each contributor "was given a mandate by the editor to. . .deal with three questions. How had historians treated this subject in the past? How were contemporary scholars dealing with the same subject? What were the most fruitful lines of inquiry for the future?" (p. 2).

The American Negro Reference Book. Edited by John P. Davis. Englewood Cliffs, N.J.: Prentice-Hall, 1966. E185.D25

Essays on all aspects of Negro life in the U.S.: history, economic and social conditions, arts and literature. For the most part, the essays are presented as primary formulations by the contributors without specific mention of a body of underlying research or systematic citation of the pertinent literature. However, some of the articles are extensively footnoted and a number are accompanied by short bibliographies listing the major works on the topic.

American Sociology: Perspectives, Problems, Methods. Edited by Talcott Parsons. New York: Basic Books, 1968. HM51.P34

Relatively brief articles, addressed to laymen more than to sociologists, summarizing current issues and achievements in major areas of sociological study. Useful for general overview of the content of the discipline and descriptions of major works, but bibliographic references are minimal; the essays do not offer comprehensive surveys of the literature.

Anthropology Today: an Encyclopedic Inventory. Edited by Alfred L. Kroeber. Chicago: University of Chicago Press, 1953. GN4.I52

Fifty "inventory" papers presented to an International Symposium on Anthropology held in New York in 1952 in order "to assess the accomplishments of anthropological science...and to solicit answers on what direction future research would be likely to take" (Preface, p. v). Papers consider the prevailing concepts and outstanding issues in their subjects, with extensive citations to the literature.

Approaches to the Study of Political Science. Edited by Michael Haas and Henry S. Kariel. Scranton, Pa.: Chandler, 1970. JA71.A66

Seventeen contributions survey research directions, significant findings, and major organizing principles, and current issues in six major sub-areas of political science, with extensive citations to the literature. Introductory and concluding essays consider the impact and probable future consequences of the "behavioral revolution." Some of the essays are revised versions of earlier publications; others were written expressly for this volume.

Carmichael's Manual of Child Psychology. 3d ed., Edited by Paul Mussen. 2 vols. New York: John Wiley, 1970. BF721.C213

Latest edition of a manual originally edited by Leonard Carmichael, 1st ed., 1946, 2d ed. 1950. The preface to 3d ed. states as the intention of the work: "to provide a comprehensive and accurate picture of the current state of knowledge—the major systematic thinking and research—in the most important research areas of the psychology of human development." Vol. 1 contains nineteen contributions on topics pertaining to the biological basis of development, infancy and early experience, and cognitive development. Vol. 2 contains ten contributions dealing with socialization and psychopathology. Essays emphasize description and critical analysis of the research on each topic, with extensive citation of the literature.

The Columbia History of the World. Edited by John A. Garraty and Peter Gay. New York: Harper, 1972. D21.G28

Basic summaries of about 100 major topics in world history from pre-history to modern times, written by 40 eminent historians, all associated with

Columbia University. There are no direct citations to the literature, but a brief list of major works follows each chapter.

Culture: a Critical Review of Concepts and Definitions, by Alfred L. Kroeber and Clyde Kluckholn. Papers of the Peabody Museum, Harvard University, vol. 47, no. 1, 1952; reprinted New York: Vintage Books, 1963.

Systematic presentation and comparison of the concept of culture as formulated in various academic disciplines, and in several countries. Includes a general history of the word and its meaning and use; a comprehensive array of definitions ordered conceptually and chronologically; extensive quotation of major descriptive and analytical statements, with editorial comments. A concluding section sets forth the current status of the concept.

Encyclopedia of Educational Research. 4th ed. Edited by Robert L. Ebel. New York: Macmillan, 1969. LB 15.E48 1969

Covers a very comprehensive range of theoretical and applied topics that have received attention in the field of education. Articles generally summarize the nature of the problem, outstanding current questions, and the characteristics and main findings of research, with extensive citations to the literature. The first edition of this work appeared in 1941.

Encyclopedia of Military History From 3500 B.C. To the Present, by R. Ernest Dupuy and Trevor N. Dupuy. New York: Harper, 1971. D25.A2D8

"Chronologically and geographically organized narratives of wars, warfare and military affairs" (p. xiii). Brief summaries of specific battles and the like are imbedded within broader chapters introduced by an "assessment of the principal military trends of the period." There are no references to the literature for specific points, but an appended bibliography lists major books in the field.

Encyclopedia of Social Work. 16th issue. Edited by Robert Morris. 2 vols. New York: National Association of Social Workers, 1971. HV35.S6

Comprehensive articles and bibliographies dealing with all aspects of social work theory and practice, and biographical articles on prominent deceased persons in the field. Most articles consider the history and current status of research and practice. The current edition is the successor to fourteen editions of the Social Work Year Book, published between 1929 and 1960, and an earlier edition of the encyclopedia published in 1965. The transition from year book to encyclopedia has meant, generally, a shift in emphasis toward theory and research and away from descriptions of institutions and practices.

Essays on the Behavioral Study of Politics. Edited by Austin Ranney. Urbana: University of Illinois Press, 1962. JA66.R29

Papers presented at a round table conference convened by the International Political Science Association, intended to summarize and evaluate the nature of the behavioral approach in political science and its impact on the discipline. Contributions focus on the topics and research areas which have made significant use of behavioral concepts: for example, political participation, electoral behavior, legislative behavior. Compared with the typical handbook style, this work places somewhat greater emphasis on description of trends in research and somewhat less on exposition of the substance of the topic, but considerable substantive information is given.

Handbook of Marriage and the Family. Edited by Harold T. Christensen. Chicago: Rand-McNally, 1964. HQ728.C478

Twenty-four essays cover topics relating to theoretical orientations, methodological developments, societal influences, member roles, and a variety of applied problems. The stated aim is to focus on cumulation of empirical work on each topic, together with possible theoretical generalizations, the status of present knowledge, and the key current issues and apparent future directions of study.

Handbook of Mental Deficiency: Psychological Theory and Research. Edited by Norman R. Ellis. New York: McGraw-Hill, 1963. BF435.E55

The status of behavioral research and theory in mental deficiency. Ten essays in Part I examine a number of theoretical formulations (e.g., field theory, social learning) in relation to mental deficiency. Part II covers eleven major research areas (e.g., sensory processes, problem solving, language and communication).

Handbook of Modern Sociology. Edited by Robert E. Faris. Chicago: Rand-McNally, 1964. HM51.F3

Twenty-seven essays focused on a selection of topics considered to represent the research areas of greatest current interest and growth in sociology. Format and presentation follow the characteristic handbook style.

Handbook of Organizations. Edited by James G. March. Chicago: Rand-McNally, 1965. HM131.M335

Summary of "the present state of knowledge about human organizations" in the form of twenty-eight chapters encompassing theoretical formulations (e.g., influence, decision making, social structure), methodologies (e.g., field methods, simulation), theoretical-substantive areas (e.g., communications, interpersonal relations), specific institutions (e.g., unions, political parties) and problems of application (e.g., organizational change, systems analysis).

Handbook of Personality Theory and Research. Edited by Edgar F. Borgatta and William W. Lambert. Chicago: Rand-McNally, 1968. BF698.B623

Focus is "research conceptions of the problems of personality study." Contributions present critical summaries of current knowledge against the background of the topic's research history, with specific and detailed citation of the literature. Considerable emphasis is placed on current issues and promising directions for future explorations.

Handbook of Research on Teaching; a Project of the American Educational Research Association. Edited by N. L. Gage. Chicago: Rand-McNally, 1963. LB1028.G3

Summaries and analyses of research in a number of theoretical and applied areas relating to teaching. Included are teaching methods, instruments and media of teaching, personality variables in relation to teaching, social interaction in the classroom, the social background and context of teaching, factors relating to teaching various subjects and grade levels, and methodological and theoretical issues in research.

Handbook of Social Psychology. 2d ed., Edited by Gardner Lindzey. 6 vols. Reading, Mass.: Addison-Wesley, 1968.   HM251.L486

Consists of forty-five chapters in five volumes plus an index volume, organized as follows: volume 1, Historical Introduction and Systematic Positions; volume 2, Research Methods; volume 3, The Individual in a Social Context; volume 4, Group Psychology and Phenomena of Interaction; volume 5, Applied Social Psychology. Essays generally follow the characteristic handbook pattern. There is considerable emphasis on presentation of the substantive content of each topic, as well as the character and history of its research effort.

Handbook of Socialization Theory and Research. Edited by David A. Goslin. Chicago: Rand-McNally, 1968.   HM131.S59

Contains thirty contributions on topics pertaining to theoretical approaches to the socialization process and to content and stages of socialization, in society generally and in certain special contexts (e.g., mentally retarded). In general, follows the characteristic handbook pattern, combining systematic presentation of the subject's content with extensive citation of the literature. The editor states that the central aim was "to provide a fresh outlook on how existing ideas might contribute to an understanding of the socialization process and identify crucial issues for further research."

The Historiography of the British Empire-Commonwealth. Edited by Robin W. Winks. Durham, N. C.: Duke University Press, 1966.   DA1.W55

History, achievements, and current trends in research are set forth in twenty-one essays which divide the subject mainly along regional lines (i.e., Canada, British West Africa, etc.).

Horizons of Anthropology. Edited by Sol Tax. Chicago: Aldine, 1964. GN8.T3

Twenty-one essays, addressed to lay readers, describing the history, methods, and accomplishments of the various subfields of anthropological study. There are few specific references to the literature, but a brief bibliographical note accompanies each contribution.

Human Behavior: an Inventory of Scientific Findings, by Bernard Berelson and Gary A. Steiner. New York: Harcourt, 1964.   HM51.B42

A compilation of "important and verified generalizations" encompassing individual behavior, groups, institutions, and general societal characteristics. The book consists of a large number of propositions presented in a systematic order and expanded and supported by explanatory comments and summaries of the pertinent data. There are many references to the original literature, but not all statements are documented in detail.

Mental Measurements Yearbook. Edited by Oscar K. Buros. Highland Park, N. J.: Gryphon Press, 1938– .Z5814.P8B932

A compilation of critical reviews of psychological tests, with citations to the literature dealing with construction, use and validity of the tests, and excerpts from published reviews of test manuals and similar materials. The yearbooks have been revised at approximately six-year intervals; latest edition is the seventh, 1971. In addition, subject sections extracted from all the yearbooks have been issued separately with special indexes, as follows: Reading Tests and Reviews, 1968; Personality Tests and Reviews, 1970.

Psychology: a Study of a Science. Edited by Sigmund Koch. 7 vols. New York: McGraw-Hill, 1959- . (in progress). BF38.P8

An encyclopedic compilation sponsored by the American Psychological Association, covering trends, research findings, and the state of current knowledge in all the significant branches of investigation in psychology. About eighty lengthy contributions present detailed summaries, with extensive citation of the literature. Volumes 1–3 cover "major theoretical formulations of recent importance" (theories of sensory and perceptual processes, learning, personality, etc.); volumes 4–6 cover "the structure, mutual interrelations and associations with other sciences of the main empirical areas in which psychological research is pursued" (e.g., physiological psychology, personality and culture, social psychology). Volume 7 (in preparation) will be a summary by the general editor of the major trends and current issues emerging from the study as a whole.

Review of Child Development Research. Edited by Martin L. Hoffman and Lois W. Hoffman. 2 vols. New York: Russell Sage Foundation, 1964–66. HQ768.8.H6

Interpretive summaries of research pertinent to the interests of professionals serving children. Designed as a bridge from the discipline-centered and theory-centered research literature to the problem-centered orientation of the practitioner. Most chapters begin with a historical overview, and then discuss methodological considerations, the findings and meaning of the significant research in the area, and currently controversial questions or unsolved problems. The literature is cited in detail, and on many questions the relevant data are extensively summarized.

Social Systems and Family Patterns: a Propositional Inventory, William J. Goode, Elizabeth Hopkins and Helen M. McClure. Indianapolis: Bobbs-Merrill, 1971. HM17.G66

Compendium of the major propositions put forward in the research literature relating family variables to other social institutions. Based on extensive examination of the literatures of sociology, anthropology and psychology. Propositions are grouped in alphabetically arranged major categories, and more detailed sub-categories, with reference to the source.

The State of American History. Edited by Herbert J. Bass. Chicago: Quadrangle Books, 1970. E175.S7 1970.

Twenty essays, originally prepared for a conference of the Organization of American Historians, assess current achievements and trends in major subfields of American history. Some include extensive reviews of the literature.

The Study of Population; an Inventory and Appraisal. Edited by Phillip M. Hauser and Otis D. Duncan. Chicago: University of Chicago Press, 1959. HB871.H37

Thirty-three essays dealing with the nature and methods of demographic research, the development and status of demography as a field of scientific investigation in various countries, accumulated knowledge in the principal areas of demographic research, and the relation of demography to other disciplines.

Surveys of Economic Theory, by the American Economic Association and Royal Economic Society. 3 vols. London: Macmillan, 1965–66. HB34.A48

Comprehensive accounts of accumulated knowledge and current research trends in thirteen fields of economic research, divided among the three volumes as follows: vol. 1, Money, Interest, and Welfare; vol. 2, Growth and Development; vol. 3, Resource Allocation. The surveys were a joint project of the professional economic associations of the United States and Great Britain, and committees of the two organizations selected the topics and reviewers.

Chapter Five

Cumulating Publications (2): Essay Collections, Textbooks, Histories, Encyclopedias, and Dictionaries

ESSAY COLLECTIONS

Essay collections are volumes composed of scholarly papers written by a number of authors. Many such collections illustrate by example the nature, direction, and points of emphasis of research and theorizing in some field of scholarship, and in so doing they constitute a form of summary of the field's cumulated knowledge.

The type of collection that generally does this best is the volume consisting of papers reprinted from the research literature. In compiling such a work the editor selects from among the relevant research publications a group of studies that are, for one reason or another, particularly significant in relation to the subject of the collection. The papers may be chosen for their general excellence, or because they are characteristic examples of certain conceptual or methodological approaches, or because they had a marked influence on later work and are therefore considered to be landmarks in the field's development. The selections are arranged in sections or chapters that group related studies, and the editor adds his own comments to explain the ways in which the essays are related to the subject of the book and to each other.

It is apparent that the "summary" character of a work of this kind derives not from the essays themselves, but from the editor's work in selection, organization, and commentary. The individual papers make no statement about the cumulative accomplishments or current status of research. They are unrelated attempts to contribute new information and do not summarize or assess the efforts of the past. But in selecting certain writings as "significant" or "representative" and in arranging them into a set of categories, the compiler implicitly proposes certain ideas regarding the substance, dimensions, and determinants of the subject as demonstrated by its research. These ideas are made explicit in the editor's introduction and critical comments on the papers, which explain how reexamination of the reprinted studies can contribute to current understanding. Thus the scholar who compiles a collection of this kind undertakes to summarize and assess existing knowledge, using the reprinted essays as instruments by which to elaborate and illustrate his ideas and judgments.

An essay collection of this type is related to the handbook in basic conception, but differs from it in focus and emphasis. Handbooks summarize research accomplishment by describing and commenting upon a large number of studies. Essay collections tackle an essentially similar task by selecting a relatively small number of significant examples and presenting them in full. In consequence, the essay collection lacks the broad coverage and extensive citation of the literature provided by a handbook, but it presents a more extensive view of some central issues and concepts.

Collections of this kind are quite numerous, and it would be impractical here to attempt to do more than cite a few examples as illustrations of the summarizing and assessing functions of works in this format. A notable collection, which encompasses landmark works pertinent to an entire discipline, is Theories of Society, edited by Talcott Parsons and others.[1] This contains almost 200 essays, ranging from Machiavelli and Hobbes to sociologists of the mid-twentieth century, collected to illustrate the background and ramifications of sociological theory as it has developed to the present time. Somewhat similar, though on a more limited scale, is Theories of History, edited by Patrick Gardiner.[2] American History and the Social Sciences, edited by Edward N. Saveth,[3] attempts to illustrate various aspects of the relationship between concepts and methods in the social sciences and in history. Some of the contributions discuss the subject directly; others are examples of the use of social science concepts (e.g., motivation, subconscious) in historical study. Politics and Social Life: an Introduction to Political Behavior, edited by Nelson Polsby, Robert A. Dentler, and Paul A. Smith[4] is another broadly gauged collection, designed to set forth the methods, problem areas, and epistemological and philosophical foundations of behaviorally-oriented political studies. A Source Book in the History of Psychology, edited by Richard J. Herrnstein and Edwin G. Boring[5] presents a group of writings, mostly pre-1900, which were important in shaping fifteen major areas of psychological research. Understanding Negro History, edited by Dwight W. Hoover[6] and Black History: a Reappraisal, edited by Melvin Drimmer[7] are two collections designed to offer new perspectives in a field of study by means of reexamination of a body of selected writings of the past. The Reinterpretation of the American Revolution 1763-1789, edited by Jack P. Greene[8] collects a number of recent studies of the revolutionary period to illustrate the current thrust of scholarship on the subject.

Selections from the research literature of a subject are frequently published in collections designed to be used as instructional material in college courses. The main purpose here is to give large groups of students convenient access to writings which are widely dispersed or unavailable in their original form; it is not particularly to employ these writings as a vehicle for a general statement about the subject. Accordingly, the usefulness of such works as cumulative summaries of knowledge is largely dependent on the extent to which editorial additions are included or absent. Some volumes of this type are virtually indistinguishable from the more deliberate attempts at summary and assessment discussed above. Others contain little or nothing in addition to the papers themselves, the assumption being, more or less, that criticism, explanation, interpretation, and summary will be furnished by the course instructor.

In actuality, there can be no clear-cut categorization of essay collections as "summaries and assessments" or "instructional aids." Any collection is almost inevitably some combination of both, as the following statement, from the preface to an early volume in a series of reprinted papers in economics published for many years by the American Economic Association, clearly indicates:

> Primarily the Series is oriented toward the senior and graduate university student; but there is also the hope that professional economists will find it a useful means of keeping abreast of developments in other fields than their own. . .(The) editorial committees desire. . .to acquaint the reader with doctrines common to many or all of the scholars in the field, with the contentious issues, and with the more interesting idiosyncracies of certain writers.[9]

The American Economic Association's "Series of Republished Articles on Economics" series is noteworthy in that the subjects of the volumes and the papers included are selected by committees of the association. This means that the presentation of "doctrines common to the field" and other matters reflects some sort of consensus among prominent specialists in the subject rather than the judgment of a single editor. In the volumes themselves, explanation of the basis for selection and the current significance of the essays ranges from quite extensive to almost nil. For many years it was the practice to include in each volume an extensive bibliography of works on the subject of each reprinted study. In recent collections the detailed, unannotated bibliographies have been replaced by more general discussions of the body of literature from which the papers have been selected, a change which, though instituted for other reasons, enhances the value of these volumes as summaries and assessments of knowledge in economics.

Volumes consisting of original papers contributed by an invited group of scholars, or a combination of original and reprinted studies, appear with some frequency in social science. Although these are usually designed to illustrate in some way the concepts and research approaches representative of a field of study, they are generally less useful in this regard than collections of reprinted papers, since retrospective assessment of the impact and significance of the component papers is, of course, not possible. A number of collections of this type have been issued by the Society for the Psychological Study of Social Issues (e.g., Herbert C. Kelman, ed., International Behavior, a Social-Psychological Analysis, N. Y., 1965) and under the series title "International Yearbooks of Political Behavior Research" by the Free Press, a commercial publisher (e.g., Morris Janowitz, ed., Community Political Systems, 1961).

A special type of original-paper collection is the Festschrift. This is a volume published to honor a distinguished scholar (the term literally means, approximately, "festival writing") consisting of writings contributed for the occasion by his students or colleagues. Such books pay homage to an individual, and while they may illustrate in some measure the breadth of his influence and the ramifications of his work, there is no direct intention to summarize the accomplishments or status of research in a particular subject.

TEXTBOOKS

Earlier in this discussion, the textbook was charged with misleading students about the nature of scientific knowledge by presenting as a body of stable, orderly principles what is in reality a dynamic, contentious, inherently disorderly, and unstable process of assertion and challenge (see Chapter 1, p. 11). Nonetheless it is precisely by producing an appearance of order and consistency, inconvenient and illusory though this may be in some respects, that the textbook makes a real and significant contribution to the creation and development of scientific knowledge.

Textbooks usually attempt to convey to the student certain fundamentals of a subject in a readily accessible, portable form. It is important to recognize, however, that the author of a text has not simply recorded a body of "basic principles" already in existence, but has himself to a large extent formulated these principles and defined them as basic. The textbook presents its author's conclusions concerning the essential points that can be derived from the total array of research results, theoretical propositions, and cumulative efforts put forward in the field up to the time the text is written. It is a statement of what is known about the subject, addressed not only to students, but also, and often primarily, to the author's colleagues in the discipline.

The role of the textbook in the scholarly communication system is thus to propose a systematic, relatively brief and general summary of existing knowledge. If the formulation is one that many scholars accept, the text will be widely adopted for classroom use, appear in successive editions, acquire a good deal of prestige, and come to be referred to as a "standard work" in its field. It may be observed again, that "standard work" does not mean one which contains "standard" information, but rather one that itself defines and establishes certain information as "standard" by virtue of its widespread acceptance and generally conceded authority.

This general characterization of the communication role of textbooks should not be misconstrued. While many textbooks can shape a systematic body of principles from the raw material of the subject's total literature, not all works in this form are equally good performers in the role nor are all such works equally intent on performing it. There are many more textbooks than there are authoritative summaries of their subjects, and while a similar stricture applies as a matter of course to all forms of publication, the existence of a large and lucrative market for textbooks results in proliferation of those works. A textbook that is essentially derivative in content may comment itself to teachers, and therefore to a publisher, on the ground of literary style, illustrations, or a multitude of other factors. The number of useful textbooks is too large, and their scope too varied, for a listing here to be practical. Reliable introductory works on many subjects may be identified by consulting the introductory bibliographies cited in Appendix J and the guides to the literature in Appendix K.

HISTORIES

One way of arriving at "what is known" about a subject is through examination of its current concepts and their foundations in research. This is the approach generally characteristic of review articles, handbooks, textbooks, and many essay collections. Another way is to consider the course of development through which current knowledge has evolved. When and under what circumstances did interest in the matter arise? How has the subject been investigated, and by whom? How have earlier ideas been changed or modified, and what brought about the changes? Where does the matter stand now? On a limited, short-term basis, this is the focus of the descriptive review. With a longer, more evaluative perspective it is the avenue of approach to current knowledge represented by the history of a discipline.

An account of the history of a field of research can be a useful device for summarizing and assessing its current content as a result of the cumulative character of scientific work. Since research, the attempt to add new knowledge, is generally an attempt to build on an existing foundation and is in its turn significant as it becomes a part of the foundation and the jumping-off place for further investigation, "current knowledge" can only mean (as has been noted several times previously) this endless process arrested for examination and contemplation at a given point in time, or the current, transitory product of an ongoing series of developments. Thus a history of a discipline or area of research is an attempt to summarize and assess the current product against the background of the developments which have produced it. This idea is reflected in the following comment by E. G. Boring, an eminent psychologist and author of a history of experimental psychology.

> The experimental psychologist, so it has always seemed to me, needs historical sophistication within his own sphere of expertness. Without such knowledge he sees the present in distorted perspective, he mistakes old facts and old views for new, and he remains unable to evaluate the significance of new movements and methods.[10]

For reasons suggested by the above, a history of a field of study is not infrequently also a vehicle for discussion and definition of the scope, methods, and general outlook of the subject (What is history? What is anthropology?) since to ask what the field is and where it is going leads almost inevitably to consideration of how it arrived at its present condition.

A history of a field of study is usually the independent undertaking of an individual scholar, and its focus, emphasis, and point of view are therefore whatever the author considers useful for his purpose. Three general approaches are encountered in histories of social science with sufficient frequency to be considered characteristic, though they in no sense exhaust the possibilities.

One approach, which is perhaps the most common, is the straight historical account which focuses on the subject. This traces the development of the field from its origins, noting the significant developments, the most influential contributors, and the ramifications of their work, and the outcome of all this as manifested in current knowledge and current concerns. Examples of this genre, mentioned here for illustrative purposes from among a large number of possibilities, are Gardner Murphy's Historical Introduction to Modern Psychology, and Roscoe Hinkle's Development of Modern Sociology.[11]

A second approach to the history of a discipline is one that focuses not on the subject as a whole, but on the work of particular scholars. The central concern here is to trace the influence of certain individuals on the character and direction of research, and to assess their contributions in the light of subsequent developments. An outstanding and very well-known study of this type is History and Historians in the Nineteenth Century by George P. Gooch, first published in 1913 and frequently reprinted. Other examples are They Studied Man by Abraham Kardiner and Edward Preble, and Ten Great Economists from Marx to Keynes by Joseph Schumpeter.

An interesting variant of this method is found in A History of Psychology in Autobiography. This work consists of autobiographical essays by a number of distinguished psychologists, in which each author discusses his own work, the influences which were significant in its development, and his general assessment of the area of psychology to which he has contributed.

A type of work that often employs a historical approach, though it may not always do so, is the account of the development and content of several "schools of thought" or distinct theoretical positions in some area. Examples are Theories of Economic Growth edited by Bert F. Hoselitz, and Contemporary Schools of Psychology, by Robert S. Woodworth. This represents the least specifically "historical" of the three general approaches outlined here, but historical factors are nearly always quite important in the development of "schools," and influential theories of the past as well as currently important positions generally enter the discussion. Again, the close relation between investigation of the past and understanding of the present is apparent.

Among the social sciences there is considerable variation in the extent to which scholars have given attention to study of the development of their disciplines. In history, perhaps because historians are habituated to thinking in developmental terms, this work is significant enough to constitute a sub-discipline of the field—historiography—in which the philosophy, scope, method, and history of historical research are the subjects of continuing study and a very substantial literature. At the other end of the spectrum, there are very few general histories of political science and economics.[12]

Evidence of increasing interest in the history of research may be seen in the recent inception of two journals devoted to the subject. The Journal of the History of the Behavioral Sciences has been published since 1965. A large proportion of its articles are concerned with the fields of psychology and psychiatry, but there has been growing attention to other social science areas, particularly sociology and anthropology. History of Political Economy, published since 1969, is concerned with the history of economic research. As would be expected, articles in these journals usually report new research on rather narrowly limited questions, and they are relatively unlikely to consider the broad, long-term trends which are characteristically treated in book-length histories. However, the book review section of the Journal of the History of the Behavioral Sciences (reviews are not published in History of Political Economy) is a good source of information about the appearance of new books in this field.

A selective list of histories of the social science disciplines, with emphasis on fairly recent publications, appears in Appendix D. A good general source of historical information is A Reader's Guide to the Social Sciences, edited by Bert F. Hoselitz (rev. ed., New York, Free Press, 1970). This contains brief accounts of the development of sociology, anthropology, psychology, political science, economics, and geography, with emphasis on their landmark works. Historical accounts are included in several (but not all) of the articles pertaining to the various disciplines in International Encyclopedia of the Social Sciences (see below), and in some instances the bibliographies accompanying the articles cite the major historical studies of the field.

ENCYCLOPEDIAS

The term "encyclopedia," as generally used, suggests an all-embracing compilation of information, and in the structure of scientific literature the specialized scholarly encyclopedia is likewise a vehicle of broad and inclusive summary. Although, as will be seen presently, the term is applied to several dissimilar types of publications, their common quality is comprehensiveness. In general, there are two ways in which encyclopedic compilations extend the processes of cumulation and generalization beyond what has been described up to this point. One involves breadth of subject matter, which in the case of encyclopedic works may transcend the disciplinary boundaries that normally divide the scholarly discussion into separate arenas. In addition, the approach to the subject tends to be multi-faceted, encompassing both current and developmental perspectives, in contrast to the emphasis on one or the other characteristic of other forms of summary. These distinctions may be clarified by recapitulating some observations made in the preceding discussion.

The structure of scholarly literature as outlined in the preceding pages suggests a forum called "social science" in which a number of conversations proceed simultaneously. At the level of the research literature, the discussion centers on very limited and specific questions and mainly concerns the details of data, method, and inference reported in single investigations. Succeeding phases of the colloquy, as conveyed by research reviews, handbooks, and the other "cumulating" publications, gradually broaden the focus, so that attention moves from direct observation of specific phenomena toward the generalizations to be drawn from the cumulative investigative effort. Thus by the time the discussion reaches the textbook it centers on the broad, widely accepted picture, and the contradictory, nonconforming details have largely dropped from view. This does not mean, of course, that all unanswered questions have been resolved and controversial issues eliminated. These continue to generate active discussion in the research literature, but are largely disregarded for purposes of summary and generalization.

Once again it may be observed that a "body of knowledge" does not really exist, except hypothetically. Instead, a continuing effort to generalize and systematize gives rise to a number of propositions ("cumulated knowledge") which, simultaneously with their creation, are being eroded and altered by the pressure of new information and ideas coming from the rivulets of research to battle for a place in the mainstream. To state "what is known" is to assume a halt in this process.

In principle, this can be done at any point in the scientific discussion, from the detailed analysis of a specific research problem to the enunciation of the broadest and most widely applicable concepts and relationships. In principle also, formulation of "what is known" can encompass any range of subject matter. As the patterns of science have evolved, the academic disciplines have come to form the boundaries of the scientific forum for most purposes,[13] so that the processes of summary and generalization tend to be carried on within each discipline as largely self-contained and autonomous discussions. Reflecting this, each field possesses its own array of cumulating publications—review journals, handbooks, etc.—which are the vehicles of the various phases of its discussion. These publications, in turn, tend to employ either of two major approaches or perspectives. One concerns itself with the substance of accumulated knowledge: such matters as the prevailing conceptualizations of the subject and the evidence on which they are based, alternative hypotheses, and the arguments on various sides of a given issue. At differing levels of generality, this is the perspective characteristic of review articles, handbooks, and textbooks. The other approach looks at accumulated knowledge mainly in developmental terms, tracing the growth and modification of ideas and the impact of seminal contributions. In essence, this is the point of view of the recurrent, descriptive reviews of the literature, and of histories. (Essay collections may be, and are, constructed on either pattern, as governed by the compiler's purpose in each instance.)

In contrast, then, to the more limited forms of summary and synthesis discussed up to now, encyclopedias are efforts to convey a body of knowledge very inclusively, and to bring together within a unified organizational framework what are otherwise separate realms of discussion. They are the vehicles for the most comprehensive and generalized statements of "what is known" produced by the scholarly system.

Before proceeding to closer examination of scholarly encyclopedias, it may be useful to distinguish these specialized works from the more familiar general encyclopedia, which is designed to serve a somewhat different purpose. In many respects the prototype for the modern universal encyclopedia, embracing all subjects, is Encyclopedia Britannica, first published in Edinburgh in 1768. At that time, and for many years thereafter, the universal encyclopedia was viewed as a summary of knowledge for the learned world. However, the specialization and professionalization of scholarship have made the concept of a single compendium of knowledge at a scholarly level unrealistic, and the spread of literacy and extension of education have created a "general" market for information. The universal encyclopedia, in consequence, is now largely a work of popularization, transmitting the results of scholarship to the general public, and providing a convenient, comprehensive source of well-known, generally available information. Eminent authorities sometimes contribute to general encyclopedias, but scholars do not, as a rule, regard these writings as scientific communications addressed to a professional audience, i.e., as part of "their" literature.

Summaries of information relating to a single subject or field of study are sometimes entitled "encyclopedia" as in the Encyclopedia of Social Work and the Encyclopedia of Educational Research.[14] In their essential features of style and purpose, such works can be quite similar to handbooks, and it is difficult to draw a clear line of distinction between the two forms. In general, handbooks are perhaps more apt to emphasize a current perspective, geared to the interests and concerns of ongoing work, while "encyclopedia" implies a longer-range and more inclusive overview. By this standard, some of the larger and more elaborate single-subject compilations, listed earlier as handbooks, have some notably encyclopedic characteristics. An example is Psychology; a Study of a Science,[15] issued under the auspices of the American Psychological Association and covering all the significant research areas in psychology in very comprehensive terms. The broad scope of its subject matter, its organizational sponsorship, and the eminence of its contributors all impart to this work qualities of "authority" and "representativeness" often associated with encyclopedias. On the other hand, as the product of a single discipline addressed primarily to scholars of that field, it does not specifically attempt to relate the findings and concerns of psychology to wider areas of knowledge.

Another approach to encyclopedic summary of a single field is exemplified by the Encyclopedia of Education.[16] This work was designed as a comprehensive source of information for practitioners, administrators, and school-board members. Some of its articles are descriptive accounts of institutions and practices, but others summarize, at a very general level and with basic bibliographies, activities and accomplishments in various areas of educational research. Comparable in some respects is the Encyclopedia of Psychology.[17] This contains many brief, dictionary-type definitions of psychological concepts, but also some longer articles written at a fairly basic level.

In the field of history, a unique form of publication known as the "encyclopedic set" is used as a vehicle of comprehensive summary. Encyclopedic sets are multi-volume, multi-authored studies of large historical subjects. Some examples, whose titles are indicative of their scope, are The University of Michigan History of the Modern World (nineteen volumes), The Rise of Modern Europe (twenty volumes), Cambridge Economic History of Europe (six volumes).[18] Works of this kind have sometimes been sponsored by universities and learned societies. In other instances, individual scholars, acting on their own initiative or at the invitation of commercial publishers, have undertaken to produce them. The over-all design is laid out by a general editor or editorial committee, and scholars who are specialists in the topics to be covered are invited to contribute individual volumes or chapters. These works do not, ordinarily, report new research. Instead, the aim is to construct a comprehensive account of cumulated results of historical scholarship, in greater detail and with more attention to the problems and contentious issues in research than is usual in textbooks. Usually these sets include extensive bibliographies or essays on the relevant literature, although there are instances in which the literature is not cited in detail and the account rests mainly on the authority of its author.

Appendix E describes selected encyclopedic sets in history and notes some sources of additional titles.

The most comprehensive form of scholarly publication is the multi-disciplinary encyclopedia. Works of this type represent efforts to create channels of communication among adjacent disciplines, and to set forth as fully as possible "what is known" across a broad field of interrelated subject matter. Since the number of such encyclopedias is very small, there is little to be said about their "typical" content or communications role, and a more realistic procedure is to consider individual titles.

At present there is one modern social science encyclopedia in English: International Encyclopedia of the Social Sciences.[19] This massive compilation is the work of more than 1,000 social scientists from all over the world, including many of the most eminent and respected scholars. In a number of respects, the International Encyclopedia of the Social Sciences (referred to hereafter as IESS) illustrates the idea of an encyclopedia as outlined above. Its subject matter encompasses all of the social science disciplines.[20] The articles treat significant concepts and research areas in social science, as well as methodological problems and techniques, and the lives and contributions of important social scientists. Each article includes a bibliography of substantial length. Many major topics are covered by a series of articles, in an effort to bring together all the aspects of the topic toward which scholarly investigation has been directed. Thus there are nine articles on the topic "communication," ranging from social and psychological analysis of animal communication to international political communication. A number of topics are the subject of multiple articles, reflecting an effort to juxtapose the concepts and research findings of several disciplines in relation to one subject, such as, for example, "Leadership: Psychological Aspects; Sociological Aspects; Political Aspects."

IESS also exemplifies an effort to combine the two approaches to summary and synthesis found in other parts of the literature: the conceptual, emphasizing what is known, and the developmental, emphasizing how it came to be known. For the most part, the articles dealing with substantive concepts and research areas in social science tend to place their greatest stress on exposition and explanation of the main ideas currently held about the subject. Quite often, however, there is also some discussion of the landmarks and turning points underlying the current situation. In addition, the research histories of broad fields of study and of many specific topics are given extensive consideration in the biographical articles and the articles devoted to the various disciplines. Similarly, a number of articles include consideration of the methods used in study of the topic, and methodological topics receive more extensive treatment in separate articles.

The foregoing are characteristics of IESS as a whole, but are not necessarily typical of all its articles or its treatment of all subjects. Rather, the encyclopedia manifests considerable diversity in its mode of discussion and in the relative emphasis likely to be accorded the various aspects of a topic.[21] This point warrants some further consideration, not only because of its pertinence to the specific qualities of IESS, but also because it illuminates some important characteristics of present-day social science.

Some authors in IESS employ a consciously scientific pattern in organizing and presenting their subjects. That is, "knowledge" of the subject it assumed to mean the transitory, cumulated output of the research enterprise, and the validity of any proposition is regarded as derived from its standing in the scientific community. Accordingly, the discussion centers on the questions scholars have raised concerning the topic, the various interpretations and points of view that have found support among its investigators, and the degree of agreement or contention surrounding currently held conclusions. Specific citations to the literature buttress or illustrate the points made in the article. The style resembles that of a handbook or review article, although in keeping with the broad, generalized focus of the encyclopedia, there tends to be more emphasis on basic principles and major issues than on the pointed examination of narrower questions characteristic of the more detailed levels of summary.

A number of articles in IESS follow a strikingly different pattern. In these, the summary of knowledge takes the form of an ordered presentation of facts and conclusions, without specific reference to a body of research as the point of origin or confirmation of the author's statements. Significant works on the subject are listed in the bibliographies, but not necessarily discussed or cited in the texts of the articles. These contributions employ a style and tone generally suggestive of an elementary textbook, in which the subject matter is set forth as a body of "known" information, certified as "correct" by the author's standing as an expert. This is likewise the usual approach of the general encyclopedia, whose nonspecialist reader is assumed to be more interested in, and better served by, a set of relatively firm conclusions, unambiguously stated, than by a chronicle of hypotheses, evidence, and competing judgments.

It would appear that there is some lack of agreement among social scientists as to the appropriate content and emphasis of an encyclopedia article and, by extension, the role of an encyclopedia as an instrument for the summary and synthesis of scholarship. Both types of articles described above summarize "what is known" about their subjects, but in different terms and from different points of view.

These differences may in part be rooted in differing views of the function of an encyclopedia. Some authors may see the encyclopedia as primarily a tool for communicating with scholars in adjacent fields, who would perhaps consult it to gain a broader perspective on matters germane to their own studies. This view would tend toward the production of articles centering on research, since the scholarly reader is likely to be at least as interested in the methods and theoretical concepts employed to investigate a subject as in the substantive conclusions. Other authors may view the encyclopedia as a means for communicating knowledge of social science to the lay public. These would be inclined to present their subjects in substantive terms only, since the nonprofessional reader may be interested in learning the social scientists' conclusions and opinions, but does not seek to explore related questions.

The variability of the content of IESS may also stem from differing conceptions of the nature of knowledge in social science and the character of scientific activity. The research-oriented approach clearly reflects a view of science as a collective venture in which new ideas are proffered and considered in direct relation to previous work and the cumulation of earlier ideas; knowledge is defined as the concepts accepted by a consensus of scientists. Articles which set forth a subject without explicit reference to its research context may or may not be based on similar assumptions; the manner of presentation tends to obscure these considerations. It seems likely that authors employing the former approach are apt to be more interested in, and influenced by, a conception of scholarly activity which stresses cumulativeness and the detailed spelling-out of the theoretical and methodological assumptions on which conclusions rest, than are those whose articles fall into the latter category.

From this point of view, IESS would appear to reflect the transition, still underway in social science, from an older orientation centered on description and normative judgment, to the model derived from the natural sciences, with its emphasis on explicit methodology and cumulative theory building. Evidence of the substantial growth in influence of the "scientific" model during recent years may be seen in a comparison of IESS with a similar work produced by an earlier generation of social scientists, the Encyclopedia of the Social Sciences.[22]

The older encyclopedia (ESS) contains many articles which describe concrete social entities; for example, "Automobile Industry," "Continuation Schools," "Suez Canal." Topics such as these have been almost entirely omitted from IESS, whose content runs in much greater proportion to abstract topics such as competition or concept formation. Similarly, ESS contains many biographical articles about major historical figures, such as Alexander the Great and Napoleon I, while biographical inclusions in IESS are limited to people who have figured significantly in the study of society, such as Jean-Jacques Rousseau or Max Weber. Articles dealing with research methodology occupy a much larger share of space in IESS than in its predecessor. All these changes mirror a narrowing and sharpening of perspective regarding social science; an altered view of the subject from one that encompasses all matters important in social life, to one which defines its subject matter on the basis of the research activity and output of social scientists. The changes also suggest increased concern with the precise meaning and derivation of "knowledge" in science and heightened sensitivity to methodological and epistemological problems. Thus the impact of the natural science model on the scope, methods, and concerns of social science is very much in evidence in the International Encyclopedia, as is also the lack of unanimity among social scientists on these matters.

DICTIONARIES

A dictionary of the terminology of a field is a highly compressed account of its cumulated knowledge. Dictionaries are not always seen in this light,[23] but are often regarded as utilitarian tools that translate difficult words into language the reader can understand. However, the terms included in the dictionary delineate the scope and boundaries of the field of study the dictionary represents, and the definitions encapsulate the field's knowledge.

From this point of view, there are some noteworthy differences between a general dictionary of a language and a specialized work intended to define the terminology of a field of scholarship. An unabridged dictionary containing all the words in the language is designed to encompass the technical terminology of specialized fields and ordinarily will define words in both their general and specialized uses. However, it does not thereby perform the same function as the specialized dictionary.

The difference is that the general dictionary aims to report the meanings that a word has in use. The basis for the definition is whatever meaning the people who use the word intend to convey. A specialized dictionary, by contrast, considers the meaning of terms in relation to a larger body of knowledge. It not only reports what speakers and writers mean by a given word, but also attempts to assess the suitability of such usage. The distinction is well expressed in the following passage, from the preface to a psychological dictionary:

> It is a common opinion that a dictionary is merely a record of frequently used meanings. This is wrong on two counts. In the first place, since every use of a term in a new context gives it a new meaning, there are as many meanings as there are contexts. The task of the dictionary is thus to be representative, to set forth nuclear definitions that stand for the myriad individual meanings. . .
>
> In the second place, goodness of terminology is not merely statistical. . .it is psychological and social. Our goals are clarity of thinking and effectiveness of communication. Misleading terminology does not become better by being widely diffused; it merely does greater damage.[24]

Accordingly, specialized dictionaries are apt to consider the internal consistency of the various definitions and uses of a term, and their consonance with each other and with broader concepts in the field.[25] Not infrequently there are references to the writers, schools of thought, or general theoretical orientations associated with the various definitions. In this way the specialized dictionary may be regarded as a cumulative distillation of knowledge, providing, albeit in very compressed form, an overview of the concepts and areas of investigation in a discipline.

Appendix F lists selected dictionaries of social science terminology. The quality of summarizing and compressing a body of knowledge is more clearly evident in some of these works than in others, as the annotations attempt to indicate.

FOOTNOTES

1.   New York: Free Press, 1961, 2 vols. HM15.P33

2.   Glencoe, Ill.: Free Press, 1959. D16.G33

3.   New York: Free Press, 1959. E175.S36

4.   Boston: Houghton Mifflin, 1963. JA71.P67

5.   Cambridge, Mass.: Harvard University Press, 1965. BF81.H4

6.   Chicago: Quadrangle Books, 1968. E175.H75

7.   New York: Doubleday, 1968. E185.D7

8.   New York: Harper, 1969. E210.G7

9.   American Economic Association, Readings in Business Cycle Theory, (Philadelphia, 1944), p. vii.

10. Edwin G. Boring, A History of Experimental Psychology. 2d ed. (New York: Appleton-Century-Crofts, 1957), p. ix, copyright, 1929, The Century Company, copyright, 1950, Appleton-Century-Crofts, Inc.

11. See Appendix D for additional information about the works cited in the discussion.

12. There are many historical accounts of speculative political and economic philosophy, such as George Sabine, A History of Political Theory (3d ed., New York, 1961) or Robert Heilbroner, The Worldly Philosophers (rev. ed., New York, 1961) but these are not histories of research and the development of knowledge in a discipline, the kind of work being discussed here.

13. See Chapter 1, pp. 13–18 for discussion of the meaning of disciplinary specialization and some of the reasons underlying the importance of this phenomenon.

14. See Appendix C.

15. Ibid.

16. Lee C. Deighton, ed. (New York: Macmillan, 1971), 10 vols. LB15.E47.

17. H. J. Eyesnck, ed. (New York: Herder and Herder, 1972), 3 vols. BF31.E522

18. See Appendix E for additional description and full bibliographic information.

19. New York: Macmillan, 1968, 18 vols. H40.A215. A comparable foreign publication is Handwörterbuch der Sozialwissenschaften, (Stuttgart, Fischer 1952–68), 13 vols. H45.H18

20. History is included in the form of articles on historical concepts and theories, but the encyclopedia does not cover specific historical periods or events.

21. For a detailed analysis of IESS, including extended discussion of this point, see the review by the Reference and Subscription Books Review Committee of the American Library Association in Booklist and Subscription Books Bulletin, 65 (1969):1085–1094.

22. New York: Macmillan, 1930–35, 15 vols. H41.E4

23. The writer is indebted to Charles Bunge for the suggestion that dictionaries function as devices for cumulation and synthesis of knowledge.

24. Horace B. English and Ava Champney English, A Comprehensive Dictionary of Psychological and Psychoanalytic Terms (New York: Longmans Green, 1958), p. v.

25. For example, the definition of "intelligence" in English's Comprehensive Dictionary of Psychological and Psychoanalytic Terms, cited above, begins "There is more agreement on the behaviors referred to by the term than there is on how to interpret or categorize them. Three concepts recur frequently in attempts to state its connotations." In contrast, Webster's Third New International Dictionary simply lists, without comment or comparison, a series of current and older meanings which the term has been used to convey.

Appendix D

Selected List of Histories
of the Social Sciences

Anthropology

Brew, J. O., ed. One Hundred Years of Anthropology. Cambridge, Mass.: Harvard University Press, 1968. GN17.05

Five lectures given in 1966 commemorating the 100th anniversary of the founding of the Peabody Museum of Archeology and Ethnology at Harvard. The lectures, each by a distinguished scholar, concern developments in five major areas of anthropology during the past century: American archeology, old world prehistory, biological anthropology, ethnology and social anthropology, anthropological linguistics.

Harris, Marvin. The Rise of Anthropological Theory: a History of Theories of Culture. New York: Thomas Y. Crowell, 1968. GN320.H33

Critical discussion of the development of theory in anthropology from the eighteenth century to the present, oriented toward a search for general historical laws of culture.

Hays, H. R. From Ape to Angel; an Informal History of Social Anthropology. London: Methuen & Co. Ltd., 1959. GN405.H34

The history of social anthropology presented mainly in terms of description of the work of about fifty major scholars, with some consideration of more general topics (e.g., anthropology and experimental psychology).

Kardiner, Abram and Edward Preble. They Studied Man. Cleveland: World, 1961. GN405.K3

Accounts of the lives and work of ten major figures in the history of anthropology, each having "invented either a seminal hypothesis or a new technique for the study of man." The central aim is "to relate the seminal hypotheses of the few great innovators in the development of a 'science of man' to the ethos of the times and to the specific lives of these innovators." (Introduction, p. 13).

Economics

Fusfeld, Daniel R. The Age of the Economist; the Development of Modern Economic Thought. Chicago: Scott, Foresman, 1966. HB75.F87

    History of economic thinking in Europe and America from the beginning of the market economy in the fifteenth century. Some attention to development of economics as a field of scientific investigation, but emphasizes exposition of the positions of various school of thought, and the relation between economic ideas and the public policies of the time.

Hoselitz, Berthod, ed. Theories of Economic Growth, Glencoe, Ill.: Free Press, 1960. HD82.H62

    Seven essays by individual contributors deal with the idea of economic growth, as developed in major schools of economic thought from the mercantilists and physiocrats to the present.

Rima, I. H. Development of Economic Analysis. Homewood, Ill.: Richard D. Irwin, 1967. HB75.R46

    "Traces the development of the analytical tools and concepts which comprise the body of economic theory." Some consideration of economic philosophy but "selects only individuals and schools whose works have a predominantly theoretical content, and notes only in passing those aspects of their work that are not contributions to economic theory." (preface).

Roll, Eric. A History of Economic Thought. 3d ed. Englewood Cliffs, N. J.: Prentice-Hall, 1956. HB75.R64   1956

    Mainly a history of economic doctrines, with emphasis on economists "whose contributions to economic thought appear to have significance in relation to present day theory and controversy in the wider field of political economy, rather than in the narrowly technical branches of economic science." (p. 16).

Schumpeter, Joseph A. History of Economic Analysis. New York: Oxford University Press, 1954. HB75.S456

    An extensive, detailed account, written at the level of the professional or advanced student, of the history of scientific analysis in economics. The author carefully distinguishes between his subject and the history of economic thought: "We are not so much interested in what (an economic theorist) argued for as we are in how he argued and what tools of analysis he used in doing so." (p. 38).

Schumpeter, Joseph A. Ten Great Economists from Marx to Keynes. New York: Oxford University Press, 1961. HB85.S35

    Lengthy essays on ten economic giants (Marx, Walras, Menger, Marshall, Pareto, Böhm-Bawerk, Taussig, Fisher, Mitchell, and Keynes) originally published as articles at various times between 1910 and 1950. The book is thus not a coherent history of economics, and much of it is written from the perspective of the economics of fifty years ago, but it is mentioned here for its detailed exposition and analysis of some of the most highly significant contributions to economics.

Whittaker, Edmund. Schools and Streams of Economic Thought. Chicago: Rand McNally, 1960. HB75.W584

Presents the development of economic ideas from ancient times to the present. Some consideration of the evolution of economics as a field of study, but most attention to the conclusions and policy positions put forward by economic philosophers, rather than to the nature of their analyses.

Education

Brubacher, John S. A History of the Problems of Education. 2d ed. New York: McGraw-Hill, 1966. LA11.B7 1966

Historically oriented consideration of major issues in education—aims, philosophy, methods of instruction, etc. Purpose is to present the history of education in terms of its relevance to current knowledge and practices in the field.

Geography

Freeman, T. W. A Hundred Years of Geography. Chicago: Aldine, 1961. G99.F7 1962

History of the growth of geography as a modern academic discipline, with discussion of the development and characteristics of branches and subfields.

History

Barnes, Harry E. A History of Historical Writing. 2d rev. ed. New York: Dover, 1963.

Relatively brief comprehensive survey of historical writing from the ancient Greeks and Romans to the twentieth century. Originally published in 1937, the text has been little changed for the second edition, but some brief comments on recent trends have been added and the bibliographic references have been updated.

Butterfield, Herbert. Man on His Past: the Study of the History of Historical Scholarship. Cambridge: At the University Press, 1955. D13.B79

The nature of historiography and its place in historical scholarship, considered by means of an examination of "the modern historical movement" from mid-eighteenth to early twentieth century.

Gooch, George P. History and Historians in the Nineteenth Century. 2d ed., London: Longman, 1952. D13.G7 1952

A pioneering history of historical writing, first published in 1913, offers detailed analysis of major trends and writers of the development of scientific history. The 1952 edition contains some revision of the original text and updated bibliographic references.

Higham, John, with Leonard Krieger and Felix Gilbert. History. Englewood Cliffs, N. J.: Prentice-Hall, 1965. D13.H43

Account by John Higham of the development of historical study in America, from its professionalization in the latter part of the nineteenth century, to the present. Essays by Krieger and Gilbert deal respectively with "European History in America" and "European and American Historiography."

Higham's account is carried forward in his essay "American Historiography in the 1960's," a chapter in his American History; Essays on Modern Scholarship (Bloomington: Indiana University Press, 1970). E175.E654

Kraus, Michael. The Writing of American History. Norman, Oklahoma: University of Oklahoma Press, 1953. E175.K75

Comprehensive survey of American historiography from the accounts of explorations and first settlement to the mid-twentieth century.

Smith, Page. The Historian and History. New York: Knopf, 1964. D13.S57

Brief account of the development of the concept of history in western civilization, from the ancient Hebrews and Greeks to the present, followed by critical discussion of modern conceptions of history.

Wish, Harvey. The American Historian; a Social Intellectual History of the Writing of the American Past. New York: Oxford University Press, 1960. E175.W5

Survey of American historical writings, with emphasis on fairly extensive consideration of the work of selected leading figures, particularly in terms of the social context surrounding their work.

Political Science

Crick, Bernard. The American Science of Politics: its Origins and Foundations. Berkeley: University of California Press, 1959. JA84.U5C7

A critical account of the development of the scientific perspective in political studies in the U.S. "It seeks to explain the special plausibility to American students of politics of the view that politics can be understood (and perhaps practiced) by the method of the natural sciences." Examines the main trend and writers in American political science from this point of view, from the founding of the Republic to the mid-1950s.

Hacker, Andrew. Political Theory: Philosophy, Ideology, Science. New York: Macmillan Co., 1961. JA81.H23

Discusses the ideas of fifteen major political theorists, from Plato to John Stuart Mill. As history of political writing, it is history of political philosophy more than political science in the modern sense. However, the ideas of the classic, speculative writers are presented and considered in relation to a number of current problems of political research. "One of the major aims of this book will be to show the systematic theorists that the historical texts contain just the sort of analysis which is central to their studies." (p. viii).

Sabine, George H. A History of Political Theory. 3d ed. New York: Holt, Rinehart, Winston, 1961. JA81.S3 1961

Well-known and widely used text covering speculative political philosophies from the ancient Greeks to twentieth-century liberalism, socialism, communism, and facism. Extensive and detailed analysis of major ideas and trends in terms of their internal logic and consistency, their connections to the political and social conditions of their time, and their impact on other writers.

Somit, Albert and Joseph Tanenhaus. The Development of American Political Science: from Burgess to Behavioralism. Boston: Allyn and Bacon, 1967. JA84.U5S63

Account of the development of political science as a profession in the United States, with emphasis on the changing views of political scientists concerning the "scope and method" of the field, from the late nineteenth century to the present. The aim is to illuminate the current state of the discipline, particularly as it emerged from the major methodological controversies of the 1940s and 1950s, by examination of its history.

Psychology

Boring, Edwin G. A History of Experimental Psychology. 2d. ed. New York: Appleton-Century-Crofts, 1957.

Account of the development of modern experimental psychology, mainly in the past 100 years, from its roots in philosophy and experimental physiology.

A History of Psychology in Autobiography. vols. 1–3, edited by Carl Murchison. Worcester, Mass.: Clark University Press, 1930–1936; vol. 4, edited by E. G. Boring and others, Clark University Press, 1952; vol. 5, edited by E. G. Boring and Gardner Lindzey. New York: Appleton-Century-Crofts, 1967. BF105.H5

Autobiographical essays by eminent psychologists in which they discuss their work, the influences that have shaped it, and their ideas about psychology and their role in its development. The five volumes published so far contain seventy-three contributions, and it is planned that the series will continue.

Murphy, Gardner. Historical Introduction to Modern Psychology. rev. ed. New York: Harcourt, 1951. BF95.M8

A survey of the history of psychology from its antecedents in Greek philosophy to the major contemporary "schools of thought" and research areas.

Neel, Ann. Theories of Psychology; a Handbook. Cambridge, Mass.: Schenkman Publishing Co., Inc. 1969.

Chronologically oriented account of important theories and theoretical positions. Presents the main points of each theory, the social and intellectual milieu in which it developed, the criticisms that have been levelled against it, and its current standing and influence. The whole is summarized in relation to current concerns in the final chapter, "An Overview of Psychology at Mid-century."

Schultz, Duane P. A History of Modern Psychology. New York: Academic Press, 1969. BF95.S35

Comprehensive historical account emphasizing the past 100 years. Designed as a course text; each chapter lists suggested further readings.

Watson, Robert I. The Great Psychologists: from Aristotle to Freud. Philadelphia: J. B. Lippincott Co., 1963.   BF81.W35

Discussion of the history of psychology, to 1930, in terms of the contributions of about thirty highly significant scholars.

Wolman, Benjamin B., ed. Historical Roots of Contemporary Psychology. New York: Harper, 1968.   BF103.W6

Analysis of three main concepts in psychological thought important as background for contemporary work: associationism, animal psychology, and conditioning; critical philosophy, personalistic and cultural currents; studies of unconscious and psychoanalysis. Consists of sixteen chapters by separate authors, each dealing with a specialized aspect of the topic.

Woodworth, Robert S. in collaboration with Mary R. Sheehan. Contemporary Schools of Psychology. 3d ed. New York: Ronald Press, 1964.   BF105.W6 1964

Presents the outlook, methods, and accomplishments of about twelve major and minor "schools of thought" in psychology that have been important during the twentieth century.

Sociology

Abel, Theodore. The Foundation of Sociological Theory. New York: Random House, 1970.   HM24.A23

A study of the development of systematic theory in sociology. Examines the work of Durkheim, Simmel, and Weber in laying the foundation of modern sociological theory, and the threads of continuity between the foundations and newer analytical approaches.

Aron, Raymond. Main Currents in Sociological Thought. 2 vols. New York: Basic Books, vol. 1, 1965, vol. 2, 1967.   HM19.A73

Analysis of the work of some important sociological theorists from the eighteenth to the early twentieth century. Aim is to trace the connections between modern analytic sociology and its forerunners in philosophic system-building. Volume 1 treats Montesquieu, Comte, Marx, and Toqueville; volume 2 Durkheim, Pareto, and Weber.

Becker, Howard, and Harry E. Barnes. Social Thought from Lore to Science. 3d ed. 3 vols. New York: Dover, 1961.   HM19.B27   1961

Extensive and detailed account of social theorizing, from the social thought of preliterate peoples and ancient cultures, to sociology around the world in the twentieth century. Emphasis is on the content and societal context of basic social philosophies, but some attention is given also to methodological considerations and evolving conceptions of social science. The third edition is basically the text of the second, published in 1952 (1st ed. 1938) with additional comments appended to each chapter and updated bibliographies. An appendix dealing with contemporary sociological trends, 1937–1960, is a year-by-year account originally written for the yearbook of Encyclopedia Britannica.

Hinkle, Roscoe C. and Gisela J. Hinkle. The Development of Modern Sociology: its Nature and Growth in the United States. New York: Doubleday, 1954. HM22.U5H5

A brief (seventy-five pages) introduction to the history of sociology, designed for students.

Madge, John. The Origins of Scientific Sociology. New York: Free Press of Glencoe, 1962. HM24.M22

Analysis of about fifteen studies that made important theoretical and methodological contributions to the development of sociology as an empirical science. A good source for extended analysis of classic works (e.g., Durkeim's Suicide: Whyte's Street Corner Society) from a modern perspective.

Mitchell, G. Duncan. A Hundred Years of Sociology. London: Gerald Duckworth, 1968. HM19.M56

Summarizes the development of sociology from the mid-nineteenth to the mid-twentieth century. Gives attention to the development of two major traditions—speculative and descriptive—and contains fairly detailed, critical consideration of major personalities and landmark works.

Sorokin, Pitirim A. Contemporary Sociological Theories. New York: Harper, 1928. HM19.S6. Sociological Theories of Today. New York: Harper, 1966. HM51.S674

Contemporary Sociological Theories is a detailed analytic survey of the data, methodology, and reasoning underlying the principal sociological theories prevalent from the mid-nineteenth century onward, "to find to what extent they are scientifically valid" (p. xviii). Sociological Theories of Today is a continuation, covering the main currents from the 1920s to mid-century.

Appendix E

Selected List of Encyclopedic Sets in History

Listed below are some well-known and relatively recent series in the English language. Additional works of this type are listed in Carl M. White ed., Sources of Information in the Social Sciences and in the various guides to historical literature (see Appendix K). The titles of individual works comprising a series can be found in most libraries by consulting the card catalog. This information is also given in the bibliography Titles in Series, compiled by Eleanora A. Baer (2d ed. New York: Scarecrow Press, 1964, and supplements. AI3.B3 1964).

Cambridge Economic History of Europe. 2d ed. General editors, M. M. Postan and J. J. Habakkuk. Cambridge, Eng.: At the University Press, 1966– , 6 vols. HC240.C312

Encompasses European economic history from the Middle Ages to the mid-twentieth century, in chronological divisions. Volumes consist of separately written chapters, and each includes a bibliography of major writings on each topic covered.

Europe in the 20th Century. Edited by J. M. Roberts. 4 vols. New York: Taplinger, 1970– . D424.E9

Relatively brief introductory essays by well-known historians on major topics in twentieth century European history. There are no direct references to the literature, but short lists of major books are appended to the chapters.

Michigan. University. The University of Michigan History of the Modern World. 19 vols. Ann Arbor: University of Michigan Press, 1958– .

Comprehensive, summary accounts of the histories of countries and regions in modern times. There are few footnotes or other detailed references to sources.

Each volume has a section headed "suggested readings," which cites, with brief comments, the major literature of the subject and, in some instances, recommended basic sources such as bibliographies, atlases, and encyclopedias to aid further study. The series is still in progress, and several of the volumes have been revised and issued in second editions since their original publication.

New American Nation Series. Edited by Henry Steele Commager and Richard B. Morris. 43 vols. New York: Harper, 1954– .

An extensive series of volumes, each presenting an overview of a major theme or period in American history. The total series is designed to constitute ". . .a comprehensive cooperative survey of the history of the area now embraced in the United States from the days of discovery to the late twentieth century" (editor's introduction). Each volume includes an extensive bibliographic essay on the major sources for its topic. The series is modelled on an earlier, very highly regarded effort: the American Nation Series edited by Albert Bushnell Hart and published by Harper in twenty-seven volumes from 1904 to 1918.

New Cambridge Modern History. Edited by George N. Clark. 14 vols. Cambridge, Eng.: At the University Press, 1961– . D208.N4

As stated by the editor's "General Introduction" (vol. 1) the aim of the series is "to set out the ascertained results of research into the history of that 'civilization' which, from the fifteenth century, spread from its original European homes, assimilating extraneous elements as it expanded, until it was more or less firmly planted in all parts of the world. The civilization is. . .treated in all its aspects, political, economic, social, 'cultural' and religious." The volumes follow a chronological order, from the Renaissance (1493) to the mid-twentieth century. A number of the volumes consist of chapters separately written by several contributors. There are very few footnotes, following as the editor states, "well-established practice in works which give brief surveys of very wide fields" (Vol. I, Renaissance, xxxv. Used with permission of Cambridge University Press.) No bibliographies are included in the volumes, but A Bibliography of Modern History by John Roach (Cambridge, 1968) was published separately to supplement the series. (See Appendix J for further description of the bibliography.)

The New Cambridge Modern History is one of a group of well-known and highly regarded "Cambridge histories." Others, now somewhat out-of-date are Cambridge Ancient History (New York: Macmillan, 1923–39, 17 vols.), Cambridge Medieval History (New York: Macmillan, 1911–36, 8 vols.), Cambridge Modern History (New York: Macmillan, 1902–26, 14 vols.). New editions of the ancient and medieval histories are in progress.

Oxford History of England. Edited by George N. Clark. 15 vols. Oxford Clarendon Press, 1936–1965.

Encompasses English history from Roman Britain to 1945, in chronological divisions. Each volume includes a bibliographical essay discussing the main pertinent literature. Several of the earlier volumes have been reissued in second editions.

The Rise of Modern Europe. Edited by William L. Langer. 20 vols. New York: Harper, 1945– .

A series "designed primarily to give the general reader and student a reliable survey of European history written by experts in various branches of that vast subject." The intention is to focus on "larger forces common to the whole of European civilization" as distinguished from separate national histories (Introduction). The divisions are mainly chronological, and encompass the period from about 1250 to the Second World War. Each volume contains an extensive bibliographical essay.

Appendix F

Selected List of Social Science Dictionaries

Social Science (all disciplines)

Gould, Julius and William L. Kolb, eds., A Dictionary of the Social Sciences. New York: Free Press, 1964. H41.G6

Includes about 1,000 terms used in the social sciences, with emphasis on terms considered "general and/or in some way basic to the disciplines concerned" and omitting "terms about whose meaning there was little to dispute and concerning which little need be, or could be, added to a standard dictionary definition." The definitions were written by specialists in the topic concerned, and the contributions are signed. The definitions include the "core meaning" of the term as used in one or more of the social sciences, and also consider the historical background of the term and variations in its meaning and use. There are many bibliographic references. The dictionary was compiled under the auspices of UNESCO, with the assistance of an international advisory committee.

Anthropology

Winick, Charles, Dictionary of Anthropology. New York: Philosophical Library, 1956. GN11.W5

Brief definitions of terms encountered in anthropological writing. Specific bibliographical references are not given, but names of anthropologists associated with major concepts are sometimes mentioned.

Economics

McGraw-Hill Dictionary of Modern Economics. Compiled by Douglas Greenwald et. al. New York: McGraw-Hill, 1965. HB61.M16

Defines about 1,300 terms used in economics and ancillary fields such as accounting and statistics. The aim is to make technical terminology comprehensible to readers with little prior knowledge of economics. Many definitions include simplified examples of the relevant mathematics, and there are usually citations to the major writings that have employed or developed the concept.

Seldon, Arthur and F. G. Pennance. Everyman's Dictionary of Economics. London: J. M. Dent, 1965. HB61.S39

Includes important concepts in economics, plus some business terminology and names of people and institutions. Definitions are fairly extensive, but do not cite specific works or discuss controversial meanings or usages. Each entry is keyed to a subject classification designed to identify and to group related terms. A brief bibliography is given for each of thirteen major subject categories.

Education

Good, Carter V., ed. Dictionary of Education. 2d ed. New York: McGraw-Hill, 1959. LB15.G6

Brief definitions of about 25,000 terms used in the professional literature of education, contributed by a group of several hundred education specialists. The aim is to set forth authoritative, generally accepted definitions; there are no bibliographic citations or discussions of alternate or disputed meanings.

Geography

British Association for the Advancement of Science. A Glossary of Geographical Terms. 2d ed. Edited by L. Dudley Stamp. New York: John Wiley, 1966. G108.A2B7

Terms used in current geographic literature, as defined and used in authoritative sources, which are cited in detail. For each term, definitions are extracted from standard English language dictionaries and from major geographical writings. Editorial comment discusses points of similarity and difference among the various meanings, and characteristics of current usage.

Political Science

Dunner, Joseph, ed. Dictionary of Political Science. New York: Philosophical Library, 1964. JA61.D8

Brief definitions of terminology used in political science; also many personal names, organizations and institutions, and historical events. The definitions were written by some 200 contributors, and each entry is signed. Usually there are no bibliographic references or discussion of alternate or controversial meanings.

Psychology

English, Horace B. and Ava Champney English. <u>A Comprehensive Dictionary of Psychological and Psychoanalytic Terms</u>. New York: Longmans Green, 1958. BF31.E58

Intended to encompass "all terms frequently used in a special or technical sense by psychologists." Reports the various meanings a term has been given, with attention to points of convergence and difference, and editoral comment on the clarity, consistency, and suitability of the various meanings and usages. "Sources are not routinely identified but the specialized terms or usages of a branch of science, a school, or an individual are so labelled" (preface).

Sociology

Mitchell, G. Duncan, ed. <u>A Dictionary of Sociology</u>. Chicago: Aldine, 1968. HM17.M56 1968

About 300 terms central to sociology are defined and discussed at some length. Most definitions include an account of the history and development of the term in sociological discourse, with bibliographic citations. Words considered to have much the same meaning in sociological and nonsociological contexts are excluded, or given only brief treatment. Biographical sketches of a small number of significant sociologists are included.

Chapter Six

Organization of the Literature: Summary

The preceding chapters have attempted to show how the system of scholarly communication operates, and how the aims, the organization, and the customary practices of scholarship in the social science disciplines shape the literature of the social sciences. The central idea is that scientific knowledge is the product of the communication process within a scientific community, in which discussion starts with the detailed reporting of reserach findings, then progresses from discrete observations to increasingly broad statements. This same progression from specific to general is reflected in the structure of the literature.

Over all, scholarly literature addresses itself to the question, "what is known"; meaning the questions scholars have raised about a subject, the manner in which it has been investigated, and the outcome of the investigations. Each of the various publication forms comprising the literature "has its job to do"[1], communicating what is known from a distinctive perspective and at a distinct level of generality. The sources and their jobs may thus be structured in an array that parallels the progression of the scholarly discussion, from the reporting of specific research findings to the formulation of broad explanatory principles. This is the framework within which the literature has been described in the preceding chapters.

Learning about a subject through its literature is a matter of "tuning in" on the scholarly community's discussion by reading that portion of the literature which addresses itself to the problem under investigation. This involves locating publications that deal not only with relevant subject matter, but also approach the subject from the point of view and at the level of generality that correspond to the problem the reader has in mind. In most instances, an investigator searching the literature tends to move from the general to the specific. That is, the most generalized and firmly established principles are sought out first, and these provide the necessary background for consideration of more detailed and unsettled matters, closer to the advancing frontiers of knowledge. This progression derives logically from the cumulative quality of science, in which new ideas build on what has gone before.

With this in mind, a brief review here of some central characteristics of scholarly publications can point up the contribution of each form of publication to the over-all picture of "what is known," and therefore the kinds of questions each is best suited to answer. This will serve to summarize what has been said so far and will set the stage for what is to follow.

The most comprehensive, generalized, and many-sided account of a subject is apt to be that presented by a scholarly encyclopedia, which will generally summarize current knowledge as well as the background and developmental history of a subject. In addition, a multi-disciplinary work such as the International Encyclopedia of the Social Sciences can show the ways in which a particular topic has been studied in several disciplines, and thus guide the reader to the literature of that field whose approach best suits his requirements.

The history of a discipline conveys "what is known" at another level. From the historical perspective, existing knowledge is viewed as the outcome of the scholarly effort as it has developed over time. Attention is directed toward the origins of study of the subject, the evolution of current knowledge out of earlier conceptions, the major investigative trends and schools of thought, and the impact of the principal contributors and landmark works.

The textbook represents yet another approach to synthesis. It formulates a systematic body of explanations and definitions derived from past research effort. A similar function is performed by the essay collection consisting of papers selected from the literature and annotated to convey a particular view of a topic or field of research.

All of the above focus on "what is known" in the form of solid, well-recognized, and widely accepted ideas. Another group of works convey the scholarly discussion with closer attention to the outer boundaries of existing knowledge and the ongoing research effort.

The handbook is characteristically a vehicle for summarizing current activity in a research field, and for examining the status of questions of current interest. In consequence, its approach to a topic is apt to be more fragmented than that of a textbook or encyclopedia. On the other hand, handbooks give more attention to the specifics of data and methodology and to the unsolved problems and contentious issues engaging the interest of researchers and advanced students.

Similarly, the periodic, stock-taking review considers the ongoing research effort, outlining its directions and accomplishments and the issues of major current interest. It tends to focus on the subject as it has developed within the limited time period covered by the review, on the assumption that the reader is generally acquainted with the basic principles and research patterns involved.

The review article represents a more limited and detailed level of approach to "what is known." It examines and weighs the evidence from a body of research in quite specific terms and proposes conclusions that may be drawn. Very frequently such reviews reveal gaps in available knowledge and suggest directions for future research.

Finally, the reports of individual studies view "what is known" with emphasis on newly acquired knowledge proposed for addition to the existing stock. The research report and detailed theoretical paper are the gateways through which new information and ideas enter the system, to combine and interact with what is already there and, potentially, to produce changes in what has been set forth all the way back up the line to the generalized formulations of textbooks and encyclopedias.

This route, from the generalized, comprehensive account of what is known about a subject to the detailed studies of single instances, is the basic pattern of information seeking in scholarly literature. This is the case for the advanced scholar as well as the novice, for the exhaustive study and brief course paper alike. This is not to say that every search must traverse the full gamut of publications, from encyclopedias to research journals, with all intermediate stops. Only a portion of the sequence may be involved on any particular occasion, even though the basic pattern and direction are essentially unvarying.

The portion of literature to be traversed in a given instance represents the distance from where the searcher is, in terms of his prior knowledge, to where he wants to go. A reader for whom the subject is new will find in the generalized account presented by an encyclopedia or textbook the background he needs to comprehend the discussion at the more specific and contentious research level, while a reader who is already familiar with the fundamentals can move directly to consideration of the specific point with which he is concerned, at more detailed levels of the literature. Likewise, a reader relatively unfamiliar with the subject may be unaware of specific questions that can be raised about it. Comprehensive, generalized accounts may suggest these questions, opening the way to more detailed and intensive investigation.

It may be noted that the progression from a generalized broad view, to detailed discussions of a subject may occur at one time, as is the case when a reader begins with a basic text or encyclopedia article and works his way down to more detailed publications, or occur through study over an extended period. The essential point is that the investigation of any problem through the literature has a more or less "natural" course, from relatively broad concepts to more specific points, and the starting point for each reader along this continuum is determined by "where he is," or the extent of his prior knowledge of the subject.

The point at which a literature search ends is determined by what the searcher wants to know. That is, the reader proceeds along the continuum from more general to more specific publication forms until he reaches the level of detail and specificity corresponding to the question he has in mind. For example, a reader interested in the development of political attitudes could learn from an encyclopedia's generalized account of the subject that direct personal influence appears to play a larger role than mass communications, and that the most important direct influence appears to be the family.[2] From the more detailed article in an annual review he could learn that the nature and strength of family influence have been differentiated by such factors as the character of the family structure and relationships, the nature of the political system, and the means by which political information and values are transmitted within a given family.[3] From the same source he would also learn that little is known about the actual processes of transmission of political values, and that the generalizations set forth in the review are based on studies of the political attitudes of adults and the family circumstances and experiences reported by them, rather than of the processes of transmission per se. To find whether subsequent research has attempted to deal with this problem, the reader would have to go to the research literature. Thus the search continues until it reaches the level of detail corresponding to what the reader wishes to know.

In theory, this sequence from more generalized to more detailed accounts can be matched to a corresponding sequence of publications forms, from encyclopedias to journals, as outlined above. The difficulty in practice is that while the array thus presented describes scholarly literature as a whole, each component is not necessarily found in relation to every question. Over all, there are many fewer cumulating publications than would be optimally desirable. Despite the evident importance of such works in a system of scientific communication, scientists, for a variety of reasons, have tended to place more emphasis on undertaking new research than on assessment and synthesis of what has already been found.

As one commentator vividly expresses it,

> The little teams burrowing away along their separate tunnels seldom pause to clear the seams that lie between them. The emphasis in research is so greatly on changing or contributing to the consensus that the task of defining and expounding it often lags far behind. The scientific literature is strewn with half-finished work, more or less correct but not completed with such care and generality as to settle the matter once and for all.

The tidy comprehensiveness of undergraduate Science, marshalled by the brisk pens of the latest complacent generation of textbook writers, gives way to a nondescript land, of bits and pieces and yawning gaps, vast fruitless edifices and tiny elegant masterpieces. . .The consensus may exist chiefly in the knowledge and wisdom of experienced scholars in the field and only by implication in the published literature.[4]

A Presidential advisory committee investigated the problem of information transmission in science and reported in a similar vein:

We shall cope with the information explosion, in the long run, only if some scientists and engineers are prepared to commit themselves deeply to the job of sifting, reviewing, and synthesizing information; i.e., to handling information with sophistication and meaning, not merely mechanically. Such scientists must create new science, not just shuffle documents: their activities of reviewing, writing books, criticizing, and synthesizing are as much a part of science as is traditional research. We urge the technical community to accord such individuals the esteem that matches the importance of their jobs and to reward them well for their efforts.[5]

Both statements quoted here have reference mainly to conditions in natural science and technology, but they apply with even greater force to the social sciences. Thus, only relatively few fields in social science have specialized review publications, with the result that review articles tend to be buried indistinguishably amid the research reports in the general journals and are very difficult to locate. Similarly, handbooks exist for only a relatively small number of research areas, and are too seldom revised. In most disciplines, study of the history of the field does not receive a large share of attention. Although steady improvement may be noted, there are many inadequacies.

Within the social sciences there are substantial differences among the disciplines with regard to the extent to which the tools of cumulation and summary have been developed. Without attempting to enumerate here all the relevant resources of each discipline, or to assess their adequacy in any precise way, it may be useful to recapitulate briefly the main elements of the cumulating apparatus in the various fields.[6]

The literature of psychology offers the fullest array of cumulating resources to be found among the social science disciplines, a circumstance which doubtless reflects the relatively early development of empirical methods in psychology and the strong influence of the natural sciences on its styles of operation and communication. A specialized journal, Psychological Bulletin, is devoted to review articles. The Annual Review of Psychology publishes stock-taking reports of research trends and results in major subdivisions of the discipline on a regular, rotating schedule. Handbooks are frequently used to convey the essential points of current research interest in specialized areas. The history of the field has received substantial attention in the form of historical texts, contributions to the Journal of the History of the Behavioral Sciences, and the unique publication, History of Psychology in Autobiography. The multi-volume, collaborative work, Psychology: a Study of a Science is an exhaustive effort to compile the cumulated knowledge and current concerns of the field. Gaps in this picture could be pointed to as well, but, on the whole, no other area of social science is as well equipped for systematic, progressive ordering of its content.

Sociology lacks a specialized journal for publication of review articles; these contributions make up an incidental part of the content of the research journals of the field. More generalized trend reports, summarizing and assessing the scholarly effort in broad areas of research, are published in the review journal Current Sociology. There are several handbooks pertinent to areas of sociological interest; the most generally significant are probably the Handbook of Modern Sociology and Handbook of Social Psychology. Another notable work of summary is Theories of Society, a collection of writings on sociological theory selected and arranged to trace the development of ideas on this subject from classical to modern times.

In anthropology, the journal Current Anthropology publishes many review articles treating specific aspects of the research literature. Major segments of the field are reviewed on a continuing and more generalized basis in Annual Review of Anthropology. The handbook format is relatively little used; a few titles pertinent to anthropology are cited in Appendix C, but the only one really central to the field is Anthropology Today (1953), now quite seriously outdated. At broader levels of summary there are several histories and, of course, textbooks, but no large-scale, comprehensive compilations have been published recently.

The Review of Educational Research publishes review articles in the field of education. More generalized assessments of relatively broad areas of study are issued from time to time as separate publications by the ERIC clearinghouses, but without any regular pattern of subject treatment or attempt to cover systematically all areas of the field. Reviews and handbooks pertaining to child development and child psychology often include topics of interest in education, but the principal comprehensive compilation for the field as such is the Encyclopedia of Educational Research, which has been issued in a new edition every few years since 1941.

Economics has recently developed a vehicle for analytic review articles on specific topics, the Journal of Economic Literature. However, there is as yet no publication that regularly reviews all the research areas of economics from a descriptive, stock-taking perspective. Likewise, the handbook format tends to be infrequently used. The "Republished Articles" series of the American Economic Association is a major project that uses the device of the essay collection to convey cumulated knowledge in a number of areas of economic research. Histories of economics are often accounts of speculative economic philosophy and ideology, rather than histories of the development of an economic science, but the journal History of Political Economy is a vehicle for detailed historical studies of the discipline.

In political science, about the only recurrent summary vehicle is Political Science Annual which has not, as yet, achieved regular, annual publication or established a stable pattern for recurrent reviewing of the sub-areas of the field. There are some handbooks and essay collections pertinent to this discipline, but on the whole these forms are not highly developed or frequently used as communication devices. As in the case of economics, histories of the field more often treat the significant speculative philosophical positions of the past than the history of research, though more works in the latter perspective have begun to appear recently.

In history the major vehicles for commentary on historical theories or "schools of thought," and assessment of their current status, tend to be books in the field of historiography, or the history of historical writing. The multi-volume, multi-authored encyclopedic set is important as a means of presenting comprehensive accounts of broad areas of historical knowledge. However, as the earlier discussion of this form of publication pointed out, these works vary a good deal in their style and approach. While all present authoritative summaries of what is known, all do not give explicit consideration to the data from which the summarized account is derived and the ongoing controversies and debates among historians. Not infrequently, only the final historical narrative is conveyed, without reference to its underpinnings. At more specific levels there is little by way of review publications or handbooks. The AHA Pamphlets are very general reviews of the literature of major topics. In the absence of better alternatives they are a useful resource for students, but they do not approach the level of detail characteristic of scholarly reviews.

All the disciplines are represented in the International Encyclopedia of the Social Sciences, which is the single most important cumulating publication in social science at the present time. This statement perhaps applies somewhat less to psychology and history than to the other disciplines: to psychology because its relatively full array of summarizing works affords a number of alternatives to IESS; to history because the concerns of that field are covered to only a limited extent by the encyclopedia.

The essential aim of all of the foregoing was to convey a picture of the literature that would enable a reader to approach it with something more in mind than an undifferentiated conception of "information about" a subject. Using the metaphor of "tuning in" on the scholarly forum, the searcher can assess the relevance to his problem of the several phases of the discussion, and thus the probable utility of the several publication forms: encyclopedias, text-books, research journals, and so forth. Still unconsidered, for the most part, is the problem of identifying and locating specific works in any given category. This aspect of the scholarly communication system—the location devices, or "bibliographic tools"—will be the focus of the chapters which follow.

FOOTNOTES

1. See p. 53.

2. Fred Greenstein, "Political Socialization," International Encyclopedia of the Social Sciences vol. 14 (New York: Macmillan, 1968), p. 554.

3. Richard E. Dawson, "Political Socialization," Political Science Annual vol. 1 (Indianapolis: Bobbs-Merrill, 1966), p. 47.

4. John Ziman, Public Knowledge (Cambridge, Eng.: At the University Press, 1968). p. 73.

5. U.S. President's Science Advisory Committee, Science, Government, and Information: The Responsibilities of the Technical Community and the Government in the Transfer of Information. (Washington, D.C.: Government Printing Office, 1963), p. 2.

6. See the preceding chapters for details concerning the titles mentioned.

PART III

Literature Retrieval and the System of Bibliographic Records

Several methods are commonly employed by students and researchers to identify the literature relating to a subject in which they are interested. One familiar procedure is to follow up references cited in the works that the reader has already seen. Since practically all scholarly publications contain references to related materials it is possible for the reader to follow the leads thus provided from his first encounter with the topic, in a textbook or encyclopedia, for example, to increasingly specific and detailed accounts. This method is likely to turn up publications that focus directly on the problem under consideration. By the same token, however, the problem will be defined by the particular chain of writings reached in this way, and it is possible that additional dimensions or alternate approaches that may have been introduced by other writers will not be uncovered. Moreover, the following up of citations can take the reader only backward through time; he will not locate any materials more recent than the work with which he began.

A second means of finding information in the literature relies on the searcher's memory and personal familiarity with what has been written on a subject. This approach is employed quite often by scholars, who typically devote considerable time and effort to keeping up with the literature of their areas of special interest. By regular reading or scanning of a number of journals, and by attendance at professional meetings where information and ideas are exchanged on a face-to-face basis, the scholar develops a rather thorough knowledge of the literature of his field and can frequently recall from memory the works that can provide the information he seeks. Many researchers buttress their memories by devising personal systems for recording and organizing their notes pertaining to materials encountered in their reading that they may want to consult again.

Personal familiarity with the literature is a tool which can be used to only a very limited extent by students and other readers who are not deeply immersed in the subject, and the scholar, too, encounters many situations that require him to give consideration to a broader range of literature than that which he regularly monitors. This is likely to be the case when exhaustive and detailed analysis of the background and status of a question is required, or when the scholar's investigations lead him to an unfamiliar line of inquiry and thus oblige him to acquaint himself with a new body of literature.

A third method of locating information in the literature is through the use of bibliographies, or "bibliographic tools." Both these terms can have several specialized and more or less restrictive meanings, but in the present discussion they are used interchangeably and in the broadest sense to refer to any publication that is intended primarily to point out where to go for information, rather than to convey information directly. Instruments of this type are very numerous and varied, and the ability to use them effectively as aids in literature searching requires a basic understanding of their diverse purposes and characteristics.

A bibliography is essentially a representation of a body of literature in a compressed, abbreviated form. As such, it is much like a map, in that both maps and bibliographies are ways of representing complex realities that encompass a great many variables of potential interest. The information needs of geographers and other map users have led to the development of a number of styles of map-making, each suited to the presentation of particular types of information. Thus, for example, there are globes to show the shape of the earth and the distribution of land masses and bodies of water, relief maps to depict the contours of a terrain, navigational charts which show currents, tides, winds, reefs and the like, and many types of maps designed to indicate the distribution of some factor, such as soil types, or vegetation, or population, within an area. In analogous fashion the various ways in which the processes of study and research draw on the scholarly literature have given rise to several more or less distinctive modes and patterns of recording the literature in bibliographies, each constituting a characteristic means for conveying certain types of information about the literature. These will be described and discussed in some detail in the sections that follow, but a preliminary overview at this point can set forth the basic characteristics of bibliographic tools and the factors that differentiate one from another.

A type of bibliography significant in scientific communication is the inclusive, periodically issued inventory of current contributions to the literature of a discipline or field of study. Bibliographies of this character have been described as vacuum cleaners, because their purpose is to sweep up everything in their paths. That is, the inventory-type bibliographies attempt to encompass all publications relevant to their subjects, irrespective of form or origin and without evaluation of relative merit or importance. Unlike vacuum cleaners, however, the bibliographies do not simply collect materials and dump them. On the contrary, the comprehensive bibliographies typically sort out their contents in a detailed and systematic fashion, employing a classification scheme which reflects the basic and relatively stable dimensions and subdivisions of the field. In this way, comprehensive bibliographies serve as inclusive, permanent repositories of the records of scholarship and are able to provide access to the total scholarly effort in their respective subject areas.

The scholar's task of keeping up with the literature of his subject is facilitated by another type of bibliographic tool, here termed the "current awareness list." The major goal of these publications is to announce new materials, and particularly those likely to be of more than routine interest, as rapidly as possible following their appearance; exhaustive coverage of the literature and the detailed, systematic organization of the listings that are required for the permanent record are of lesser importance. Traditionally the announcement of new publications has been an ancillary function of the research journals, accomplished by publication of book reviews and lists of articles appearing in other journals of the field. As the volume of scientific literature has grown, inclusion in journals of current bibliographic lists has become increasingly impractical and special bibliographies have been instituted to disseminate news of current publications likely to be of greatest immediate interest.

The comprehensive recurrent bibliographies create basic bibliographic records of the scholarly literature by adding new publications to the existing stock as they are issued. Another type of bibliographic compilation, retro-spective bibliographies, results from a reexamination of some portion of the accumulated literature. This is undertaken, generally speaking, in order to identify materials in terms of a dimension or point of view not revealed by the existing bibliographic records. The scientific process is not static, but constantly generates new concepts and relationships and hence new interpreta-tions and evaluations of the work of the past. Thus the bibliographic descriptions and classifications made at the time of a publication's appearance may not be relevant to subsequent developments or to the new significance or implications the work may acquire at some future time. This circumstance provides the impetus for compilation of retrospective bibliographies. Some works in this category derive from attempts to define and explain a new concept or approach, a process that often entails identification of the connections between the new line of inquiry and its antecedents. Somewhat similarly, when research that has originated in several disciplines or subject areas begins to develop interrelated ideas and points of common concern, a bibliography bringing together all of the relevant literature, otherwise dispersed among the bibliographic records of the separate disciplines, may serve to lay out a common foundation for further study. There are also many retrospective bibliographies designed to identify the outstanding books in a field or the introductory materials most suitable for first explorations of the subject.

A type of bibliographic publication called "guide to the literature" presents a general overview and description of the literature and bibliographic arrangements of an area of study. Guides frequently identify the field's landmark works and major journals, in which respect they resemble the introductory retrospective bibliographies mentioned above, but the guides tend to place their greatest emphasis on the methods and bibliographic tools that may be used to search the literature of the subject. Thus the essential purpose of guides is less to identify the specific publications appropriate to the reader's problem than to instruct him in how to go about finding relevant materials. The present work is an example, not necessarily typical, of the genre.

A basic resemblance may be observed between the categories of bibliographic tools, as described above, and the categories of the scholarly literature discussed earlier. The several types of bibliographies tend to focus on particular segments of the literature in somewhat the same way as the various forms of publication tend to convey particular phases of the scholarly discussion. While the correspondence is not precise, some parallels are worthy of notice.

The comprehensive, recurrent bibliography is the counterpart, in bibliographic form, of the total, undifferentiated literature of each field of study. Retrospective bibliographies, as the products of reexamination of past writings from a current perspective, perform a task with regard to description and evaluation of the literature of a subject comparable to that of the cumulating publications in organizing and assessing the subject's content. The substantive and bibliographic approaches reflect substantial differences in emphasis, but not in basic purpose. Those retrospective bibliographies that identify and classify the literature in terms of its relation to a specific concept or line of inquiry, set forth in bibliographic terms an idea quite similar to that conveyed by review articles and handbooks. In the handbook or review article, the substance of the topic is dealt with directly and the citations to the literature are adjuncts and supports of the author's message. The bibliographies focus on the citations and communicate the compiler's interpretation and assessment of the subject obliquely, by means of subject headings, annotations, or, perhaps, brief introductory comments. Similarly, retrospective bibliographies designed to point out a basic core of writings on a subject are closely related in their function to textbooks. The textbook may be regarded, from this point of view, as an organized, systematized summation of the content of the materials identified by the introductory bibliography. Finally, the general overview of a field's bibliographic organization provided by the guide to the literature is analogous to the overview of its content presented by an encyclopedia.

All of this suggests that the bibliographic tools of scholarship may be viewed as comprising a system whose structure and organization parallels that of the scholarly literature. The description quoted earlier (p. 53) to introduce the systematic conceptualization of the literature may thus be applied to bibliographies as well: "each type of source has its job to do," and the job is to provide a route to an identifiable segment of the literature and thereby to the phase or aspect of the scholarly discussion appropriate to the problem at hand. This is not to assert, any more than was done with regard to the literature, that the system is intrinsic to the materials or that the bibliographic tools have been designed to function in systematic, complementary fashion. Largely to the contrary, bibliographies have tended to develop independently of each other, in response to specific needs and possibilities as these were perceived at various times by particular groups and individuals. There have been few coordinated efforts to assess the total range of bibliographic requirements and to design the appropriate instruments. As a result, the system seldom functions as smoothly as might be desired and it is possible to identify a fair number of literature-searching jobs in social science for which no effective tool is available. Despite this, the concept of a system is very useful as a device for comprehending and differentiating among the bibliographies pertaining to a given range of subject matter and thus for making the most effective use of the existing bibliographic arrangements.

Fundamentally, three characteristics or dimensions of a bibliography determine its functioning as an identification tool, or the "job" it is able to do. These are: scope, or the range of publications included in the bibliography; description, or the information which the bibliography provides about the listed materials; and organization, or the way in which the listings are arranged and identified within the bibliography. Another look at the similarity between bibliographies and maps may help to clarify the point. To be of use in a given situation, a map must encompass the area in which the user is interested, must show the facts about the area—highways, political boundaries, topography or whatever—that the user wishes to know, and must organize the information in some readily distinguishable form, as is done by the use of color, shading, symbols, and the like. Applying similar considerations to bibliographies and the literature they represent, one may say that a bibliography, to serve effectively as an identification tool for a given purpose, must include the appropriate segment of literature and must describe and organize its materials in ways relevant to the problem at hand.

The principal ways in which the basic factors of scope, description, and organization tend to vary in bibliographies, and the impact of such variations on the functioning of bibliographies, may be briefly summarized as follows.

Scope.   Clearly the access to a subject's literature afforded by a given bibliography is limited ultimately by the range of materials included since, irrespective of other considerations, the searcher will not find what is not there. Thus the obvious first question to be asked regarding any bibliographic tool is: what range of materials is included; what portion of the total output one can find there? It may be somewhat less obvious that considerably more is likely to be involved here than a simple statement of the bibliography's subject. However, the compilation of any bibliography entails a process of selection. Even if the aim is to include all works known to exist on a subject, decisions must be made regarding what pertains to the subject and what does not. If, as is more typical, the bibliography is designed to include only a portion of the extant materials in some area, it is necessary to consider how the portion is defined. What standards were employed in choosing the listed works; what distinguishes the materials included from those omitted? If the selection criteria employed in compilation of a bibliography correspond to the dimensions of the searcher's problem, the bibliography's selective coverage is an asset, since material of lesser relevance will have been screened out in advance. For example, a reader interested in the major steps in the evolution of a current theory would be better served by a recent bibliography including only those older works still considered important than by a publication that listed all materials on the subject as they appeared. On the other hand, if a problem requires consideration of all previous efforts to study the question, or if a reader wishes to ascertain whether a given approach or technique has been attempted in the past, a bibliography whose coverage is limited to "major" works or publications in a single language will leave an indeterminate portion of the needed materials out of reach.

Description.   Inclusion of a given publication in a bibliography makes the work accessible to the user of the bibliography, but the user will seek out the publication only if the relevance of the publication to the user's need is made evident by the bibliographic entry. The scope of the bibliography should be considered, since, as outlined above, any criterion employed in the selection of materials is also a descriptive statement about each item selected. Thus, for example, if a bibliography purports to list all scientifically valuable works on a topic, the reader is informed that each work listed has been judged to be scientifically valuable. In addition, almost all bibliographies provide some indication of the subject of each listed item, along with such basic identifying data as author, title, and place and date of issuance. Yet more information than this may be required to identify the materials suited to the reader's need. Most questions are most satisfactorily answered at a particular level of analysis—research report, review of the literature, textbook, historical account, etc.—but subject designation alone does not distinguish among these. Some problems require identification of publications in other terms. A reader may be interested in locating studies that employed a particular methodology, or that relate to a specified theoretical concept, or that were carried out in a particular setting. In such circumstances the subject of a publication, defined as the specific problem investigated or considered, may be quite unimportant, and the usefulness of the bibliography will depend on the extent to which its entries supply information regarding the other dimensions of the listed materials.

Organization.   Organization and classification of a bibliography's entries are intended to permit selection of appropriate items without the necessity of inspecting the entire list. This is possible to the extent that the bibliography's organization and identification of its materials correspond to the reader's definition of his problem. The various dimensions of a publication mentioned above—level of analysis, methodology, theoretical orientation, etc.—may be indicated in the entries, as is likely to be the case, for example, when the listings include abstracts, but for the publications to be readily accessible in these terms it is necessary that these elements also be reflected in the bibliography's classification or indexing scheme. The selection of materials in terms of subject matter is also affected by the way in which subjects are related within the bibliography. For example, some bibliographies divide their entries into specific subject categories, alphabetically arranged, while others utilize a system of broader, conceptually related groupings. Generally speaking, the former is an efficient way of pinpointing materials on a clearly delimited topic, such as the events of a particular election of the operation of a specific legislative body, but the relation of specific topics to more general concepts—for example, the relevance of studies of particular elections or legislative bodies to consideration of an abstract idea such as representation—is likely to be made more evident by a conceptually ordered arrangement.

Because of their determining effect on the kind of route to the literature that a bibliography is able to provide, and thus on the usefulness of a given bibliography for a given literature-searching task, the basic dimensions of scope, description, and organization are the essential facts to be noted with regard to any bibliographic work. They are, therefore, the central focus of the following discussion of the major bibliographic tools in social science.

Chapter Seven

Comprehensive Recurrent Bibliographies: The Foundation of the Bibliographic Structure

An inclusive, continuing record of all contributions to the literature is a basic component of a system of scholarly communication. The idea of science as a collective enterprise whose work is cumulative implicitly assumes the existence of such a record. Since scientific questions are never regarded as definitively and finally answered, the work of the past is never totally superceded or discarded. Instead, it is always assumed that the continuous flow of research and theorizing may at any time suggest new meanings for information and ideas put forward in the past, or alter existing views of the validity and implications of current knowledge. The entire stock of extant literature thus forms the basis on which study proceeds, requiring the existence of an inclusive, continuously updated inventory of the scholarly output. Such inventories generally take the form of bibliographies that are issued at regular intervals and record systematically and inclusively the current contributions to the literature of a field of study. Publications of this type are here termed "comprehensive recurrent bibliographies."

It may seem that the availability of a total record of the literature of a field is of greater theoretical than practical interest, since the need to identify everything which has been written in relation to some topic, while perhaps pertinent to the work of advanced scholars, will not arise for most students most of the time. However, this is not necessarily the case. It is true that a student or researcher whose aim is to familiarize himself with the main outlines of a topic on which there is a copious and well-developed literature—say, for example, leadership in small groups—will ordinarily not find it necessary, or even helpful, to be able to locate everything that has been published on the subject. For issues of this scope the exhaustive literature survey is likely to be of interest mainly to the scholar working at the frontiers of existing knowledge, whose explorations of previously uncharted territory require acquaintance with all previous relevant work. On the other hand, any reader wishing to locate information on a specific point that may not have been extensively investigated—say, for example, the effect of Big Brother programs on juvenile delinquency—will need to cast his net as widely as possible over the potentially relevant material. Though all questions are ultimately connected to broader issues, "everything" dealing directly with a specific, concrete point may mean only one or two articles, and the chances of finding them are clearly better in an exhaustive bibliography than in a limited or selective one. Thus, access to the total literature of a field is not a need that arises only rarely and for very advanced and specialized researchers. It is a fundamental requirement of both the cumulative development of knowledge and the systematic study of what has been learned, and the comprehensive recurrent bibliography is, therefore, an essential instrument for several aspects of scientific communication.

Notwithstanding their evident importance, comprehensive recurrent bibliographies are not very well developed in the social sciences. Many have been instituted only recently, so that systematic records of the literature are lacking for long periods in a number of areas. In several disciplines, the most inclusive of the available bibliographic publications are not truly comprehensive in their coverage and leave out significant segments of the literature. And in nearly all instances the description of the publications and the organization and indexing of the listings fall short of the optimum for scholarly purposes. This seemingly paradoxical situation is explainable if one considers the role of comprehensive bibliographies in scientific communication in relation to the history of the social sciences as fields of scientific investigation.

The comprehensive bibliography is not only a tool for identification of publications. In some very significant ways such bibliographies also serve to define a field of study and its content. The publications selected for listing in the bibliography become, by virtue of their inclusion, "the literature" of the field. To the extent that scholars rely on the bibliography as a literature-searching tool, the materials it lists come to delineate the range of investigation and deliberation in the field. Thus the basic idea, stated above, of the inclusive bibliographic record as a critical component of the communication system of a field of scholarship rests heavily on the assumption that the scholarly "forum" in that field is indeed a forum; that its participants are addressing each other on a common range of concerns and within a commonly understood and accepted framework of discussion, and that their publications, in consequence, constitute an identifiable body of materials, readily distinguishable among the general output of the printing presses. In other words, the model of science as a collective and cumulative enterprise, and of the social sciences as sciences—the underlying premises employed throughout the present work—are assumed. Yet, as has repeatedly been seen, this model is only partially and imperfectly applicable to the social sciences, where the institutions and practices characteristic of the scientific system are in some instances quite new and undeveloped.

In this light, it can readily be understood that comprehensive, recurrent bibliographies are longest established in the branches of social science that have relatively long traditions of a distinct scholarly identity, and hence a distinctive, identifiable literature. In history, geography, and psychology there are bibliographic records extending back to the turn of the century and earlier. The most generally satisfactory inventory of the literature is found in psychology, a field that has many points of contact with biological science and has been the social science discipline most strongly influenced by the natural science model. On the other hand, continuing, comprehensive records of the scholarly literature have been slowest to develop in sociology, political science, and economics, the fields in which the subjects of scholarly inquiry most often impinge upon matters of general public concern, and in which the meaning and utility of the scientific model has been the subject of much uncertainty and debate. The point is well illustrated by the following statement, which appeared less than twenty years ago in the preface to what was then a new annual inventory of the political science literature:

> It is hoped that the bibliographical work of the international association may lead to a better understanding of the concepts involved, and thus help to secure some degree of unification in the field of political science. But as matters stand at present, the chief difficulty that faced the editor of this bibliography was the lack of uniformity on the international scale.
>
> Two outstanding—and closely related—aspects of that difficulty may be mentioned here: the selection of material for the bibliography, which raised the problem of the boundaries of political science, and the classification of the material collected, which raised the problem of its general composition.[1]

To a large extent, the development of comprehensive recurrent bibliographies in the social sciences has mirrored and paralleled the development of a scientific identity and model for scholarly work, and as recognition of the relevance and importance of the customs and practices of science has grown, so has attention to creation of the requisite bibliographic facilities. At the present time, there is in each of the social sciences at least one bibliographic publication that at least approximates an inclusive, regularly updated inventory of publications in the field. These works vary a great deal in the length of time they have existed and in the comprehensiveness and effectiveness of their coverage, but all contribute to creating an inclusive, continuing record of the literature. Before proceeding to consideration of the individual tools, it may be helpful to note some general characteristics of comprehensive recurrent bibliographies as a species, in order to set down some points to serve as framework and guidelines for the details that follow.

Most comprehensive, recurrent bibliographies are focused on the literature of an academic discipline since, as noted earlier, the discipline generally represents the area of broadest common interest in scholarship, and thus tends to mark the boundaries of the scholarly discussion. However, some bibliographies are records of inter-disciplinary research fields, such as area studies, or of subdivisions of larger fields, such as American history or demography. A relatively recent phenomenon is the "mission-oriented" bibliography, encompassing the literature relevant to a specialized field closely tied to some aspect of social policy, such as poverty or arms control. Any field of study that regards itself as a distinct and more or less autonomous segment of the scientific community is apt to institute a continuing record of its literature since, as suggested above, such records are, like professional organizations and journals, a means by which an area of scholarship defines and identifies itself.

A bibliography designed for comprehensive coverage would be expected to encompass all scholarly writings within its subject range, irrespective of the form of publication, the country of origin, or the language in which the work is written. Most of the comprehensive recurrent bibliographies in the social sciences include publications in all forms, though a few are limited to journal articles only, usually for reasons of economy. The matter of world-wide coverage and inclusion of materials in all languages presents some serious dilemmas. The idea of science recognizes no national or linguistic boundaries, and it is clearly desirable that a scholar investigating a problem have access to the relevant foreign literature as well as to works produced in his own country. However, this implies greater linguistic versatility than most scholars in fact possess, and compilation of world-wide bibliographies poses a number of problems, ranging from difficulties of obtaining foreign publications to the question of the language or languages to be used for subject classifications and abstracts. Most of the comprehensive bibliographies attempt some degree of international coverage, but practice and accomplishment along these lines vary. Some bibliographies are specifically international, produced through the cooperative efforts of scholars in many countries. They typically adopt either French or English, or sometimes both, as "international" languages to be used for subject headings, annotations, and other editorial matter, and list the titles of works in other languages both in the original and in French or English translation. Bibliographies produced by national academic groups generally list foreign as well as domestic publications, but are likely to give most thorough coverage to the literature of their own country. In consequence, there is a certain amount of duplication of bibliographic effort, with similar types of bibliographies being produced in several countries. The works to be described below are mainly international and American bibliographies, but some foreign works that include substantial coverage of English language publications and are widely available in American research libraries will also be considered.

Abstracts are the most generally satisfactory form for presentation of the bibliographic listings, since they permit the searcher to identify useful materials more precisely than can be done on the basis of title and subject designation alone. However, an abstracting publication is relatively difficult and expensive to produce, and sponsors of bibliographies have sometimes had to choose between extensive coverage of the literature with minimal description, and fuller description of a more limited range of materials. In such cases the most frequent choice has been the first alternative. In several fields, there is an unannotated bibliography affording the most inclusive coverage of the literature, and also an abstracting publication encompassing a smaller number of "core" publications.

The bibliographies are most frequently organized in terms of a subject classification corresponding to the pattern of research specialization in the field, with subdivisions reflecting the relationships of the topics and subtopics to each other and to the subject as a whole. In addition, there is usually a detailed alphabetical subject index, and an author index. Typically the subject indexing focuses on only one dimension of the work, the subject matter of the data, but there have been a few attempts at construction of multi-faceted indexes capable of identifying such additional variables as methodology or research setting. Computers offer greatly increased possibilities in this direction, but such innovations are still in the very earliest stages of development. The major comprehensive, recurrent bibliographies covering the social science literature are described below in three categories: inventories of the various disciplines; bibliographies of interdisciplinary or applied research areas; library catalogs and indexes. The last group are not, strictly speaking, part of the scholarly communication system, but are generated by other needs and designed to serve distinctive purposes of their own. However, they also function as searching tools for the social science literature, and not infrequently help compensate for gaps and deficiencies in the scholarly bibliographies.

DISCIPLINARY BIBLIOGRAPHIES

Although all the comprehensive bibliographies that chronicle the literatures of the various disciplines have basically similar functions and therefore a number of common characteristics, they are the result of separate efforts carried on, for the most part, without central planning or control. In consequence there is little uniformity in the details of content and organization of these bibliographies. In some fields a single bibliography encompasses all segments of the literature to form a coherent, unified record. In other fields, several publications may contribute to the task, with varying amounts of duplication, overlapping, and omission. In general, each bibliography is a response to the particular bibliographic circumstances prevailing in its field at the time of its inception: the characteristics of the field's literature, the bibliographic facilities already in existence, the practices and achievements of neighboring disciplines. The individual tools are therefore best understood from an evolutionary perspective, as elements of a developmental process, and what follows is mainly a chronological account of the development of comprehensive bibliographies in the social science disciplines.[2]

The first recurrent bibliographies in the social sciences were annual accounts of the publications of the preceding year. Perhaps the earliest was Jahresberichte der Geschichtswissenschaft, an annual review and inventory of historical writings published in Berlin under the auspices of the Historical Society beginning in 1880. The annual volumes consisted of chapters devoted to the various periods and topics of historical study, each written by a specialist in the area, who commented on many of the titles enumerated. Thirty-six volumes were issued, covering the literature from 1878 to 1913. Publication was interrupted by the First World War and not resumed afterward but, having demonstrated to historians the usefulness and importance of comprehensive bibliographic recording on an international scale, the Jahresberichte was an important precedent for later efforts.

Another pioneering work was Psychological Index, an annual list of psychological publications instituted in 1890 as a supplement to the journal Psychological Review.[3] The Index was an unannotated list, classified by subject, of books and articles in psychology published anywhere in the world. It appeared regularly until 1935, when it was discontinued because Psychological Abstracts (see below), instituted in 1927, had rendered it superfluous.

Bibliographie Géographique Internationale has the longest publication history of the social science bibliographies currently in existence. It was instituted in Paris in 1891 under the sponsorship of the Association de Géographes Francais, and is still being issued. In 1923, the Association of American Geographers undertook cosponsorship of the bibliography, and the professional geographical organizations of several other countries associated themselves with the venture in subsequent years. At present the Bibliographie appears under the auspices of L'Union Géographique Internationale, a federation of national societies. It is an annual list intended to include all geographical articles and monographs of scholarly interest published anywhere in the world. Some of the entries are accompanied by brief, descriptive annotations (in French) but for most of the items only bibliographic data are given. As is characteristic of annual lists, the lapse of time between the appearance of a publication and its listing in the bibliography is ordinarily about two years.

Since 1906 the American Historical Association has produced an annual inventory of publications in the field of American history, entitled Writings on American History. As an illustration of the relationship, discussed above, between a discipline's professional identity and the character of its bibliographic tools, it is of interest to note that inception of this bibliography coincided with a general transition from amateurism to professionalism in American historical scholarship, which took place around the turn of the century. Until the latter nineteenth century, American historians were mainly gentlemen-scholars of independent means, who saw their work as essentially a form of literary endeavor. From their perspective, a comprehensive record of the historical output was of no special importance. In the words of a modern historiographer:

> The amateur historian expected his work to survive or perish on its individual merits; he was little concerned about its status as a "contribution" to some continuing collective inquiry. Having no feeling of corporate identity (except in a local or ethnic sense) the amateur historian did not write primarily for other historians. He chose his subject for its intrinsic interest and wrote either for his own satisfaction or for a public that would accept him on his own terms.[4]

But toward the end of the nineteenth century, as all the social science disciplines became increasingly professionalized, the dominant influence of the "patrician amateurs" began to be displaced by growing numbers of professionally trained and employed historians. These men regarded historical literature as the internal communications of members of a scholarly community, and "made war on the disconnected nature of amateur scholarship."[5] In Europe, where many of the emerging group of professional, science-oriented American historians had studied, and where the idea of history as science had strongly influenced the outlook and communication patterns of historians, some of the national historical associations had instituted recurrent bibliographies.[6] These were designed as definitive listings of the national historical literature, more complete than the accounts available through the world-wide Jahresberichte der Geschichtswissenschaft. In undertaking publication of Writings on American

History, the American Historical Association, itself a manifestation and instrument of the new professionalism, assumed responsibility for the record of the historical output relating to America and thus contributed to the efforts of an international community of historians.[7]

Writings on American History "is designed to cite every book and article published during (the year) that has any considerable value for study and research pertaining to the history of the United States from primitive times to the present."[8] This includes not only historical scholarship per se, but a considerable amount of factual and descriptive writing judged to contain data of interest to historians. The listings provide bibliographic data only, without abstracts, but very brief descriptive annotations are sometimes added to amplify the meaning of a title. The usefulness of the bibliography is impaired by chronic publication delays. Recently issued volumes have appeared as much as twelve years later than the year covered by the volume, due to severe financial difficulties, and the future of the publication is uncertain.

Bibliographie der Sozialwissenschaften, a recurrent bibliography touching on several areas of social science was begun in Berlin in 1905 and has continued to the present except for interruption from 1943 to 1950 due to the Second World War. Before the war the bibliography concentrated on political science and economics, and listed books, articles and, occasionally, government documents published in Europe and America. When publication was resumed in 1950, the scope was broadened to include sociology and anthropology in addition to the two original fields. However, economics has always been most heavily emphasized, and this continues to be the case. The listings are unannotated.

Bibliographie der Sozialwissenschaften is valuable for the long span of its coverage. It is the most comprehensive record available to American scholars of the writings of European social scientists during the first half of the century. On the other hand, its usefulness in American libraries is limited, primarily, of course, because of the high proportion of foreign language publications and the classification and indexing in German, but also because it employs a very general subject classification, which does not readily lend itself to identifying materials in terms of specific problems and research interests.

During the 1920s there were efforts to create systematic bibliographic records for several fields of the social sciences. In 1926 an International Committee of Historical Sciences was organized, composed of representatives of the national historical associations of a number of countries. The stated purpose of the committee was "the advancement of the historical sciences through international cooperation"[9] and one of its first concerns was establishment of a continuing record of historical scholarship. The Jahresberichte der Geschichtswissenschaft had ceased publication some ten years earlier, during the war, and this was felt to have left a significant void in historical communication.

Several national bibliographies comparable to Writings on American History were being published, but there was no unified bibliographic record to support the concept of a general science of history, transcending the specific events of a particular time and place. To meet this need the International Committee instituted the International Bibliography of Historical Sciences, an annual inventory of the world's historical literature that began in 1926 and is still being published.

The International Bibliography of Historical Sciences was never intended to be a totally inclusive record of historical publications. The assumption of its founders was that the historians of each country had created, or would create, a national bibliography as an exhaustive record of the historical writings pertaining to the country. The International Bibliography was designed to make available to the world-wide historical community the literature of more than strictly local interest. This was understood to mean, roughly, writings likely to be of interest to historians outside the confines of the country concerned, because of their relation to general historical concepts or to a comparative approach in historical study.[10]

The task of distinguishing between the universal and the parochial in historical literature is obviously a difficult one, and it has never been accomplished to the entire satisfaction of all concerned.[11] Nonetheless, the International Bibliography is the only ongoing record of historical writing that is world-wide in scope and encompasses all the chronological and topical specializations within the historical discipline. The selection of works to be listed is made, in the first instance, by committees of historians in each country who screen their national output, and a further, final selection is made by an over-all editorial committee. The bibliography has a unique linguistic arrangement in which five "official" languages (English, French, German, Spanish, and Italian) are used in rotation for the editorial content (subject headings, etc.). Titles of works in languages other than one of the five are translated into the language of the particular volume in which they are listed. Writings in oriental languages are not included.

Entries consist of bibliographic data only. In planning the bibliography, the International Committee recognized the utility of some form of summary of the contents of the listed works, but decided against such an attempt. The decision was governed in part by economic factors but an additional consideration of some importance was a fear that annotations might be regarded as subjective and biased, and hinder international acceptance of the bibliography.[12] This would appear to suggest that historians, at least at that time, did not feel that there was sufficient agreement in their discipline with regard to the rules of inquiry and argument to protect its scholarship from the effects of personal bias and political commitment. It is not unlikely that the atmosphere of heightened national sensitivity and suspicion generated by the First World War was a factor in this, but in any case the matter affords yet another illustration of the connection between a discipline's outlook regarding the nature of its work and the character of its bibliographic tools. As a kind of compromise on the abstracts question, it was decided to include in the bibliography, wherever possible, citations to reviews along with the listings for books.

A record of the research literature of education was instituted by the United States Office of Education in 1927 under the title Bibliography of Research Studies in Education. This bibliography differed from the general pattern of the literature inventories of the other disciplines. It listed only research reports, excluding other types of contributions to the literature. Moreover, most of the reports listed were not in the form of journal articles or books, but were separate documents issued by school systems, state education departments, or other agencies conducting or sponsoring research, or unpublished dissertations and theses. The reporting of research through separate papers circulated among people in contact with the author or connected with the project tends to be somewhat more customary in education than in the other social science disciplines, where such reports, generally speaking, are not numerous and tend not to be regarded as significant components of the literature.[13] The Bibliography of Research Studies in Education was an effort to facilitate dissemination of these reports, which otherwise were quite difficult for scholars to learn about and acquire, and thus to bring the information they contained into the general stream of communication in the discipline. Copies of reports listed in the bibliography were made available on loan from the Office of Education Library, an arrangement which foreshadowed the much more elaborate and technologically advanced ERIC system for disseminating education research, to be described below.

The Bibliography of Research Studies in Education was limited to American research; no foreign reports were included. Annual issues appeared from 1926 to 1940, following which the bibliography was discontinued in the interests of governmental economy.

Psychological Abstracts was instituted by the American Psychological Association in 1927. In several respects this was a significant advance over previous bibliographic efforts in the social sciences. It included abstracts, and was therefore vastly more informative than the earlier bibliographies, and it appeared monthly rather than annually. The basic pattern of Psychological Abstracts has not changed in any fundamental way during its nearly fifty years of publication, and, in the opinion of many, its format and organization constitute the most generally satisfactory form of disciplinary bibliographic record developed so far in the social sciences.

Psychological Abstracts encompasses the world-wide psychological literature in all forms: books, journal articles, as well as many doctoral dissertations and occasional reports issued separately by various research agencies. In addition to psychological publications as such, there is substantial coverage of materials germane to the interests of psychologists appearing in the literatures of adjacent disciplines such as sociology, psychiatry, and physiology. Originally the abstracting was done by psychologists who volunteered for the work, but in recent years it has become increasingly customary for journals to require that authors include abstracts with manuscripts submitted for publication. Transmission of these abstracts to Psychological Abstracts when the article is published has the effect of reducing the delay in appearance of the abstracts, and items are usually listed within a few months following publication.

The organization of Psychological Abstracts is characteristic of abstracting journals, and a similar pattern was followed by abstracting publications instituted subsequently in other fields. Listings are classified according to the generally prevailing pattern of research specialization in the field. These are supplemented by author and subject indexes.

The American Psychological Association now offers computerized access to Psychological Abstracts on a fee basis. The service is called PASAR (Psychological Abstracts Search and Retrieval Service) and it offers the possibility of identifying publications in terms of a combination of desired characteristics, relating to several aspects of subject matter as well as other qualities, such as the setting in which the research was done. This is designed to permit more detailed and precise identification of the literature pertaining to a problem than is ordinarily afforded by manual searches of an index.

In 1928 the Social Science Research Council established a bibliography called Social Science Abstracts with the aim of supplying a bibliographical service comparable to Psychological Abstracts for the other social science disciplines. The Social Science Research Council, it will be recalled, was formed in 1923 by representatives of the various disciplinary associations who were especially concerned to advance the growing scientific orientation of the social sciences and to promote the "scientific" model as the general pattern of scholarship. For all the reasons discussed earlier, the absence of a comprehensive bibliographic record was clearly an impediment to the council's goals and Social Science Abstracts was instituted to overcome this deficiency.

The abstracts were issued monthly for five years and attempted to list the world's output of scientific literature in the social sciences. The main fields of concentration were economics, political science, sociology, statistics, and history but materials in such additional areas as cultural anthropology, psychology, and human geography were included if they were judged pertinent to the interests of scholars in the "core" disciplines. Both factual reports and contributions to theory were listed, but great attention was given to limiting the inclusions to scientifically valuable materials, screening out the popular, the purely descriptive, and the polemical. Thus a major task and function of Social Science Abstracts was that of defining and identifying "the literature" of social science.[14] It was the intention of the editors of Social Science Abstracts to include eventually publications in all forms, but its content during its rather short life consisted of journal articles only. Articles from about 4,000 journals, American and foreign, were abstracted.

Social Science Abstracts was discontinued at the end of 1932, after the Social Science Research Council determined that the use of the bibliography as a research tool was too small to justify the expense of its publication. The council concluded nonetheless that the abstracts had made a definite contribution by "breaking down the isolation of the different disciplines. . .emphasizing the mutuality of research problems and. . .advancing the conception of the essential unity of science."[15] Whether this was actually the case is hard to judge. As will be seen presently, more recent efforts to establish bibliographic records in the social sciences have not followed the interdisciplinary model of Social Science Abstracts, but have tended to focus instead on delineating the distinctive literature of each discipline in its own terms. However, the abstracts made a very definite contribution in selecting and organizing the scientifically useful materials in a broad range of fields, and in developing concepts and terminology for summarizing the scientifically relevant content of publications. Both of these represented considerable achievements for that time and were of undoubted importance as models for bibliographic services in the social sciences established during the 1950s and 1960s. As to its current utility as a literature-searching tool, Social Science Abstracts is a good record of the scholarly output of its period, but its brief existence limits its value today to rather specialized purposes.

Following the demise of Social Science Abstracts, the disciplines of sociology, economics, and political science remained without comprehensive bibliographic coverage until the 1950s. One specialized research area, demography, succeeded in establishing its own abstracting publication during the intervening years. Population Index was instituted by the Population Association of America in 1935 and has continued to the present. It is a quarterly publication abstracting the population literature and reports and documents that are sources of population data, published in occidental languages in all formats.

The foregoing summarizes the development of the bibliographic records in the social sciences up to the 1940s, when the outbreak of the Second World War halted further consideration of bibliographic problems. Following the war, the creation of adequate bibliographic tools became a subject of intensified concern. Interest in the social sciences, the number of social scientists and the volume of social science publications were all growing rapidly. In a number of ways, the war, and the massive social upheavals and changes which preceded, accompanied, and followed it, had heightened social scientists' awareness of both the importance of a science of society and the great lacunae in existing knowledge. Several of the disciplines were locked in vigorous internal debate over the meaning and implications of "science" in relation to their subject matter, but a conviction regarding the importance of a collective and cumulative approach was widespread and growing. In this atmosphere, the handicap to communication imposed by the lack of adequate bibliographic tools was acutely felt. In a thorough study of social science bibliographic facilities sponsored by the Carnegie Corporation it was reported that the bibliographical situation was "recognized as unsatisfactory by a large majority of the present-day users of social science literature."[16] Observations of a similar nature were made at about the same time by an international study group sponsored by UNESCO.[17]

The only disciplines without critical bibliographic problems were psychology and demography, which were reasonably well served by Psychological Abstracts and Population Index. The annual inventories in history and geography were less satisfactory, being slow to appear, minimally informative about the publications they listed and, in the case of history at least, somewhat uncertain in scope and comprehensiveness. The situation was worst of all in political science, economics, sociology, and anthropology, where there were virtually no arrangements for systematic, comprehensive recording of the literature on a continuing basis. Literature searching in those fields relied on library catalogs and on general indexes such as International Index and the Bulletin of the Public Affairs Information Service. These will be considered in further detail in the discussion below of library-oriented bibliographic tools, but it may be noted here that while they afford access to some social science publications, they are not intended to be comprehensive records of the literature of any discipline, and do not perform the functions for which the disciplinary bibliographies are instituted.

In 1950 an International Committee for Social Sciences Documentation was organized under the sponsorship of UNESCO. Composed of representatives of eight international academic societies,[18] the committee's task was "to supply each social science discipline with the basic bibliographic instruments essential to it"[19] where these were not already in existence. In accordance with the idea that the first bibliographic requirement is a complete listing of what has been published, the principal outcome of the committee's work was a group of annual world-wide inventories covering the literatures of political science, economics, sociology, and social and cultural anthropology.

Issued under the series title International Bibliography of the Social Sciences, the titles and starting dates of the four bibliographies are as follows: International Bibliography of Sociology, 1951 – , International Bibliography of Political Science, 1952 – , International Bibliography of Economics, 1952 – , International Bibliography of Social and Cultural Anthropology, 1955 – . They are all quite similar in content and format, and basically resemble the annual inventories in history and geography that preceded them. Each is a listing, as complete as the editors are able to make it, of scholarly books and journal articles that have appeared during a given year. The entries are not annotated, but reviews of books are often cited. Issues of the bibliographies ordinarily appear about eighteen months to two years following the end of the year covered.

The UNESCO-sponsored inventories aim for maximum comprehensiveness in their coverage, but provide minimal information about the works listed and, as annual publications, are very slow to appear. Several abstracting journals established around the same time or since reflect an alternate approach to the problem of bibliographic recording, providing fuller and more frequent information about a smaller number of works selected as the "core" literature of the discipline. Most of the abstracting publications began with very limited coverage and have expanded as their resources permitted. Thus their selectiveness is the result of economic limitations, and is not a matter of intent, as is the case with the purposefully selective bibliographies to be discussed later. The eventual goal is maximum coverage of the literature relevant to scholarship in the field. The abstracting journals are issued at least quarterly.[20]

International Political Science Abstracts was instituted by the International Committee for Social Sciences Documentation in 1951, to abstract articles from the world's leading political science journals. The first issues, listing publications of 1950, abstracted articles from about seventy journals, ten completely and the remainder selectively. By 1972 coverage had been extended to approximately 500 journals. While still more extensive coverage may be desirable,[21] this would appear to indicate the direction in which the bibliography is moving.

During the first two years of its existence, International Political Science Abstracts published English-language abstracts of articles written in languages other than English, and French-language abstracts of articles originally in English. This meant that most of the abstracts were in French, as a result of the predominance of English in the political science literature. Beginning with the third volume, the system was changed so that English-language articles are abstracted in English and all others in French. The change is of interest not only because it increases the utility of the bibliography to American readers, but also because it suggests a changed conception of the function of abstracts.

Under the original scheme the abstract was, in effect, a substitute for the original publication: readers unable to read English were provided with French summaries of English articles, and vice versa. The revised system reflects the more usual concept of the abstract as a device for identification and selection of material to be read in full.

Sociological Abstracts has been published since 1953 under the sponsorship of the American Sociological Association in cooperation with several other learned societies in sociology. This publication strongly resembles Psychological Abstracts in its format and organization, and is coming increasingly to achieve a comparable inclusiveness in its coverage of the literature. In recent years, Sociological Abstracts has listed about 5,000 items annually, which is close to the number appearing in the International Bibliography of Sociology. While it is not unlikely that the Abstracts are more exhaustive in coverage of the American literature, and the International Bibliography more internationally comprehensive, there is clearly a substantial amount of overlap between the two. An interesting innovation in Sociological Abstracts is publication of supplementary issues containing abstracts of unpublished papers read at sociological conferences.

Historical Abstracts was instituted in 1955 by Eric Boehm, an historian and bibliographer. Its coverage is limited to periodical articles, and occasional books that are collections of articles, dealing with the modern period, from 1775 to the present. Listings are selected from about 2,000 periodicals published all over the world. These include, in addition to historical journals, publications in other social sciences whose contents are apt to be of interest to historians. Particularly for the period since 1914, journals in international affairs, sociology, and economics receive attention.

For some years, Historical Abstracts used a classification system incorporating an unusual feature. The basic divisions were rather broad topical and regional categories. Within these, each listing was further identified by a line of "cues," or identifying terms, preceding the entry. The cues represent a finer breakdown of the subject, area, and period to which the article pertains. (For example, such added designation as "imperialism" or "nationalism," plus the country and years concerned might occur in conjunction with the general heading "International Relations.") The system was abandoned in 1970, apparently because of lack of user interest, but it is worthy of note as an attempt to achieve greater flexibility in the description and identification of publications than is permitted by the more familiar type of classification scheme, in which there is a fixed hierarchy of topics and subtopics ordered in a predetermined relationship to each other. As presently constituted, Historical Abstracts uses a conventional classification scheme consisting mainly of geographical categories.

Geographical Abstracts, covering the world-wide geographic literature has been published in England since 1966. At present, its coverage is somewhat less than that of Bibliographie Géographique Internationale (about 7,000 entries per year in the Abstracts, compared with something over 10,000 in the Bibliographie) but the Abstracts, issued bimonthly, are much quicker to appear and, of course, offer much more information about the materials listed.

Two significant bibliographic publications have been produced in recent years by the American Economic Association. In 1961 the Association began publication of Index of Economic Journals, a record of the English-language journal literature from the late nineteenth century to the present. The index begins with 1886, or roughly the beginning of economics as an academic discipline in the United States. Current volumes index English-language articles in about 150 major journals published all over the world. From 1960 onward the index has included articles in collective books, such as conference reports, Festschriften and collections of readings, as well as journals, and the title is now Index of Economic Articles in Journals and Collective Volumes. The indexing scheme is very detailed, but listings provide bibliographic information only, without any form of annotation or abstracting.

The Journal of Economic Literature, published quarterly since 1969, combines fairly extensive listings of publications in economics with fuller description and discussion of a more restricted range of "core" literature. Issues consist of a classified list of current books, with brief annotations, and a listing of the articles appearing in about 150 journals, both English-language and foreign, arranged by journal and also by subject classification. There are also critical reviews of the more significant books (about fifty per issue) and author-written abstracts of some of the articles appearing in a selected group of journals. Each issue also contains one or more review articles. Thus the Journal of Economic Literature combines within itself several distinct communication and bibliographic functions that are more typically the province of separate publications. It is a comprehensive, permanent record of the economics literature, a current awareness and book review publication comparable to those to be considered below in Chapter 8, and a review journal for summary and cumulative assessment of the results of economic investigations.

Another abstracting service in economics, Economic Abstracts, has been published at The Hague since 1953 by the Library of the Netherlands Ministry of Economic Affairs in collaboration with the Ministry of Social Affairs and the Netherlands School of Economics. This publication differs somewhat in scope from the American Economic Association's bibliographies. Reflecting its connection with a government agency, Economic Abstracts is oriented toward applied, rather than theoretical, aspects of economics. Much of the material abstracted deals with production, trade, and business, and many publications are primarily sources of economic data, such as government documents and bank letters. In the more strictly defined category of economics, there is much emphasis on such topics as national and international finance, labor problems, economic development, and other matters impinging closely on problems of economic policy and administration.[22]

An important French bibliography of scientific literature in all disciplines, the Bulletin Signaletique of the Centre National de la Recherche Scientifique in Paris, has included sections devoted to psychology and education, sociology, and ethnology since 1961. Each part is issued quarterly. The listings encompass books and journal articles published all over the world, and supply bibliographic data only except for brief abstracts (in French) for some items.

Since 1963, the Library of the Royal Anthropological Institute, a research institution located in London, has published Anthropological Index, covering about 500 anthropological journals received in its library. Although its coverage is more restricted than that of the International Bibliography of Social and Cultural Anthropology, which also lists books, Anthropological Index extends to all areas of anthropology (the International Bibliography of Social and Cultural Anthropology excludes physical anthropology) and, appearing quarterly, it is considerably more up-to-date than the annual International Bibliography.

Abstracts in Anthropology was begun in 1970 by a group of American anthropologists working independently, without official sponsorship. It is a quarterly publication abstracting anthropological literature in all forms without restrictions as to language or place of publication. In other words, the aim is to produce a comprehensive abstracting journal comparable to those in psychology and sociology. Coverage is still much more limited, however, and tends to be uneven because the journal depends heavily on abstracts submitted by authors and editors. At present about 1,500 items are abstracted annually, compared with about 4,000 in the International Bibliography of Social and Cultural Anthropology and about 6,000 items listed each year in the Royal Anthropological Institute's Anthropological Index.

A bibliographic record for the field of social work was begun in 1965 with the inception of Abstracts for Social Workers by the National Association of Social Workers. This publication encompasses "all aspects of social work knowledge as well as any material from other fields that lends itself to improving social work practice"[23] and on this basis it includes not only contributions to the social work literature as such, but also numerous articles from journals in such adjacent fields as sociology, psychology, law, economics, and political science. The first issue contains an editorial comment that is of interest here as an unusually explicit statement of the relationship, described earlier, between the development of a discipline as an identifiable branch of knowledge and the creation of a bibliographic record.

The inauguration of Social Work Abstracts. . .represents a milestone in the development of a knowledge base for the social work profession. The abstracts will not in themselves produce knowledge, but they should help overcome certain obstacles which have limited the development of knowledge in the past.

Prior to 1955, social work practice was developed in several fields and fragmented among seven separate organizations. . . .In spite of creative contributions from many individuals, the thinking and writing about practice reflected in social work literature were not cumulative because most of the writers tended to start fresh from their own experience and to limit their analysis to single instances.

. . .The abstracts service makes possible two new developments in the field. First, social work practitioners and teachers will be able to follow quickly innovations in the diagnosis and treatment of social problems. Second, the formulation of a classification scheme should help break the barrier, hitherto insurmountable, of codifying social work literature.[24]

A unique system of records of the education literature was instituted by the U.S. Office of Education during the early 1960s. Called ERIC (Educational Resources Information Center), this project is in part an outgrowth of the Education Office's various programs for funding educational research, which have been conducted on a relatively large scale since about 1956. Allocation of federal funds to education research stimulated a substantial increase in research activity and reporting. Many of the reports, however, never found their way into the published literature, but were simply submitted to the sponsoring agency and perhaps circulated among a small number of people who were acquainted with the project. It was quite difficult for the general community of education scholars to learn of or acquire these studies. The first activities of ERIC centered on collection and dissemination of separately issued research reports, but the program has progressively expanded to embrace all aspects of the education literature.

ERIC consists of twenty "clearinghouses" located in educational research institutions (chiefly colleges of education) around the United States. Each clearinghouse specializes in a particular research area, such as counseling or early childhood education, and carries on a number of activities aimed at regularizing and systematizing the flow of communication in that field. The clearinghouses screen the writings in their respective areas of interest as comprehensively as possible and attempt to collect all materials of scholarly interest for recording and dissemination through the ERIC system. Reports issued as separate papers, or published in journals of very small or specialized circulation are reproduced and made available for general, low cost distribution in microprint or "hard copy" (i.e., paper). Two recurrent bibliographies are produced:

Research in Education, for separate reports, and Current Index to Journals in Education, for journal articles. In addition, the clearinghouses sponsor and produce a variety of occasional publications such as reviews of the literature, bibliographies on special topics, and guides to instructional materials.

Research in Education has been issued monthly since 1966.[25] It is a listing of all the research documents collected and reproduced for distribution by the ERIC system. Most of these documents are reports of American studies, but English-language reports of foreign projects are also included. The listings include, in addition to standard bibliographic identification, a detailed abstract of the report and an extensive list of descriptors, or identifying terms. The descriptors are the "tags" by which the documents are classified and identified in the over-all ERIC collection. They represent mainly a detailed analysis of the subject matter covered in the reports, but also may include additional variables such as the methodology or research techniques employed, the setting of the research, and so forth. The descriptors are the basis for the subject indexes published in each issue of Research in Education, but the published indexes include only the "most important" terms entered for each report. This means that the ERIC files, which are computer-produced, are potentially accessible to more detailed and complex searches, than can be carried on by means of the published indexes. Several organizations offer computerized searches of the ERIC file on a fee basis.[26]

Current Index to Journals in Education encompasses about 700 journals, including a number of foreign titles. Brief abstracts of the articles are included. The Current Index uses the descriptors and indexing scheme developed by ERIC and employed also in Research in Education, so that a reader may search a problem in both the journal and the report literature, utilizing the same concepts and terminology.[27]

Most of the growth and development of comprehensive bibliographies in the social sciences has centered on expansion of the bibliographic record to encompass the literature more fully. The concepts governing the content and organization of the record have been stable. The characteristic organization scheme, consisting of subject classification supplemented by detailed subject indexing, with "subject" referring to the substance of the data presented in the work, has been employed from the earliest bibliographies to the present without substantial change. The use of abstracts to convey the essential facts about the listed works dates from the 1920s. There have been a few additional experiments and innovations, such as the "cue" system developed by Historical Abstracts and the use of multiple descriptors in the ERIC system, but on the whole there has been more attention to extending the range of the bibliographic record than to developing and improving the techniques employed in compiling and organizing the record.

The latter aspect of the bibliographic problem is the main concern of a political science bibliography instituted in 1966 under the title Universal Reference System: Political Science, Government and Public Policy Series. Its aim is not to extend bibliographic coverage to previously unrecorded literature, but to introduce a new system for classification and indexing of the literature. The series consists of ten parts, nine encompassing research areas within political science (international affairs, legislative process, administrative management, current events and problems of modern society, public opinion, law, economic regulation, public policy, comparative government and cultures) and one devoted to bibliographies in all branches of the discipline. For each part there is a basic volume, or "codex" intended to encompass the core literature of the field from its origins to the present. New literature is listed in annual supplements consisting of two or three volumes that cover all the divisions of the basic bibliography.

Each volume contains a basic list, with abstracts, of the publications included. This is followed by an extensive multi-faceted index, which is the chief innovation and raison d'etre of the bibliography. The index is called the Grazian index because it is the invention of Alfred de Grazia, a political scientist with a strong interest in problems of scientific communication.[28] It is based on logical analysis of the possible content of a scientific publication.

The basic premise of the Grazian index is that the question "Who says, 'Who does what with whom, where and when, by what means, why' and how does he know so?" encompasses all significant dimensions of a scholarly publication in the behavioral sciences. The possible answers to the question yield twenty-eight topical and methodological categories relating to the people who are the subject of the study and their time, culture, institutions, values, relationships, and actions as considered or represented in the publication, and to the assumptions, theories, and methods of inquiry and argument employed by the author. In each category are listed the terms selected to represent the range of possibilities, and those are the descriptors used in the index. For example, the topical category "processes and practices" ("who does what") has nine divisions, among them "choosing," which includes the descriptors "apportionment," "election," "representation," and "suffrage." The methodological ("how does he know so") category "analysis of temporal sequences" lists as possible descriptors "biography," "chronology and genetic series of men, institutions, processes, etc.," "projection of trends," "prediction of future events." The indexing process tags each item with the appropriate descriptors from all the categories judged applicable. This results in a much more detailed display of the publication's content in the index than is accomplished by conventional procedures.

The difference may be illustrated by comparison of the listings for the same work in the Universal Reference System and the traditionally organized

International Bibliography of Political Science. An article entitled "The Demography of the Congressional Vote on Foreign Aid, 1939-1958"[29] is listed in the International Bibliography in the general category "Government and Public Administration–Political Systems" under the subdivision for national legislative studies, and is identified in the index by the terms "legislative power," "U.S.–foreign aid," "U.S.–foreign relations," and "U.S.–legislative power." The listing for the same article in the Universal Reference System Legislative Process, Representation and Decision Making codex includes approximately equivalent descriptors, but the article is also identified as pertaining to ethics of public policies, political parties, and formation and existence of consensus, and as employing demographic and geographic variables, statistics, and quantitative content analysis.

In the Universal Reference System index, each of the descriptors is listed in turn, followed by the relevant entries listed in abbreviated form with the most important of the other descriptors assigned to each entry. The searcher is thus able to define the materials he is seeking in terms of a combination of characteristics representing subject matter, methodology, research population, theoretical orientation, or whatever is desired, and to identify through the index the works possessing that combination.

It is not universally agreed that this represents an advantage. Many would argue that the conceptual precision and sophistication of the Universal Reference System index outruns that of the literature it represents and that the impressionistic and speculative writings that comprise much of the political science literature cannot be meaningfully described in terms of a system of categories based on the logic of scientific inquiry.[30] Thus an index entry such as "consensus" (as a "condition or measure of activities being discussed") might yield an array of disparate items whose interconnections, while logically tenable, are remote and unilluminating in terms of specific research problems. Countering this view is the argument that articulation of meaningful categories is itself an impetus to systematic and rigorous conceptualization of the discipline's subject matter, and that the absence of bibliographic tools capable of identifying the literature in scientifically relevant terms can only act as a brake on the field's advancement. (Note the similar observation in the introduction to Abstracts for Social Workers, quoted above on page 156.)

Whatever the merits of the Grazian indexing scheme, it is applied in the Universal Reference System to a somewhat limited body of materials. The basic codex volumes, whose listings are selected out of all the past literature of political science, contain 2,000-3,000 entries each. The number of journals cited ranges between 100 and 300, nearly all in English. This is unfortunate, since the detailed, multi-faceted indexing that is the real contribution of these bibliographies is likely to be most useful for the very specific and theoretically advanced type of research question, which by its nature entails consideration of the broadest possible range of related efforts and contributions. The annual supplements for recent years list about 600 periodicals as having been screened for the selections. These include journals in a broad range of theoretical and applied areas of social science, though political science predominates. There are some foreign titles, but the emphasis is strongly American and English language. There is also a substantial admixture of popular political magazines, and it is doubtful that their content is appropriate to the distinctly technical and scholarly focus of the URS index.

The Universal Reference System is still relatively new. Its scope and organization have been altered in several ways since its inception, and the pattern described here may undergo further change. So far, the bibliography suffers from too limited scope and lack of clarity in its choice of literature appropriate to its highly sophisticated analysis, but, on the other hand, the concept of multi-faceted indexing has much promise.

Citation indexing is another innovative retrieval concept, which has recently been introduced into the social sciences. This is a system for identifying later writings that refer to an earlier work. The entries in the index are the works cited as references in a body of literature; for example, a group of current journals. Under each entry are listed the articles (in the journals covered by the index) that have cited that publication. Thus a searcher who knows of one publication dealing with his problem can identify later works which have referred to it, and in this way trace the further development of the subject.

The advantage offered by citation indexing is that the system works independently of any predetermined classification or subject heading scheme. Publications are connected by any facet regarded as relevant by an author who cites another work; the connection may involve subject matter, research technique, or theoretical framework. A concomitant disadvantage may be that the group of publications listed as citing a given work may relate to that work in a variety of ways, and the searcher has no way to distinguish the citations pertinent to his interests from others. Since citation indexing has barely begun to be used in social science, its impact or usefulness relative to other techniques cannot be assessed, but it clearly represents a new form of access to the literature, unlike anything available heretofore.

The concept of citation indexing of scientific literature has been developed by Eugene Garfield and the firm he founded, the Institute for Scientific Information, in Philadelphia. Science Citation Index, published since 1964, indexes citations in over 2,000 natural science journals, and in recent years has covered about 150 titles in the behavioral and social sciences, principally psychology. Social Sciences Citation Index is to begin in 1973 with coverage of about 1,000 journals in all social science fields.

INTERDISCIPLINARY AND MISSION-ORIENTED BIBLIOGRAPHIES

The preceding section has summarized the evolution of comprehensive bibliographic records in the basic social science disciplines and in some specialized research areas within disciplines. Bibliographic records have also been established for the literature of fields that cross the boundaries of traditional disciplines and whose work, therefore, is not adequately identified and organized by bibliographies constructed along disciplinary lines.

Bibliographies for Interdisciplinary Fields and Area Studies

An early example of a comprehensive bibliography in an interdisciplinary field is Child Development Abstracts and Bibliography, instituted in 1927 by the Committee on Child Development of the National Research Council, and now published by the Society for Research in Child Development. This publication resembles Psychological Abstracts in its content and arrangement, and duplicates to some extent the listing of child development literature in Psychological Abstracts. However, Child Development Abstracts gives much more extensive coverage to the child development literature originating in such disciplines as pediatrics and physical medicine than does Psychological Abstracts.

Recent Publications in the Social and Behavioral Sciences draws on all the social science disciplines to list publications that employ an empirical approach or manifest a distinctly "behavioral" orientation.[31] This bibliography is issued annually, cumulating a list that appears bimonthly in the journal American Behavioral Scientist.[32] It is in some respects inaccurate to describe this publication as a "comprehensive recurrent bibliography," since it does not aim for exhaustiveness but attempts instead to select the works of somewhat more than routine interest or significance. However, while this can be done from a current perspective for the bimonthly lists in which the bibliography originates, the meaning and validity of the bibliography's selectiveness is inevitably vitiated by the passage of time. On this basis the annual cumulations may be regarded as the most comprehensive record available of the behaviorally oriented literature in all fields of social science. The record is not exhaustive and the question of whether it represents the "best" literature is moot.

Several interdisciplinary bibliographies focus on the literature of one of another branch of "area studies"; that is, fields of study in which the subject matter of a broad range of disciplines in the social sciences and humanities are brought to bear on a particular geographic area. Such bibliographies are now being issued for scholarly work pertaining to Latin America, Asia, Africa, Russia and Eastern Europe, and North America. These works vary in comprehensiveness, descriptive content, frequency, and so forth. For particulars see Handbook of Latin American Studies, Bibliography of Asian Studies, African Abstracts, American Bibliography of Russian and East European Studies, and America: History and Life in Appendix G.

The field of Black Studies, or Afro-American Studies is logically related to the area studies concept. Relatively new as a separate branch of study, Black Studies has not yet developed and stabilized a system of bibliographic records, but there have been some undertakings in that direction. Black Information Index was instituted in 1970 by a group of librarians in predominately black academic institutions "to disseminate information by and about black people and their environment."[33] The index covers both general and scholarly publications in all subject areas relating to blacks in the United States and abroad, and to the general topics of minorities and race relations. Other bibliographic publications pertinent to the Black Studies field are Index to Periodical Articles By and About Negroes and Dictionary Catalog of the Schomburg Collection of Negro Literature and History, discussed below under library-oriented searching tools.

Mission-Oriented Bibliographies

The term "mission-oriented" refers to fields of study, often interdisciplinary, which are built around areas of practical social concern or action, rather than the traditional academic divisions. Bibliographies in these fields tend to differ somewhat from the more strictly academic tools, in ways reflecting the closer connections of the applied fields to issues of policy determination and program administration. In contrast to the academic bibliographies' concentration on research and analysis conveyed through scholarly books and journals, the mission-oriented tools generally included substantial proportions of factual and descriptive materials, such as government reports, as well as current policy discussions appearing in the general public press, and, not infrequently, unpublished reports issued separately by operating agencies, and accounts of research in progress.

The number of bibliographies in specialized, applied fields related to the social sciences is fairly large, since it is not unusual for government agencies and other groups active in a particular field to issue recurrent lists of publications pertinent to their work. Mentioned here are some mission-oriented bibliographies that are significant records of a portion of the social science literature. Additional details regarding each title will be found in Appendix G.

Mental Retardation Abstracts is issued by the National Institute of Mental Health, a unit of the U.S. Department of Health, Education and Welfare, and abstracts articles from about 1,000 journals in the fields of psychiatry, psychology, education, medicine, social work, and sociology.

Abstracts on Criminology and Penology is issued by the Criminological Foundation of the Netherlands, in cooperation with the University of Leiden and the Netherlands Ministry of Justice and National Bureau for Child Protection. The abstracts cover the world literature relating to "the etiology of crime and juvenile delinquency, the control and treatment of offenders, criminal procedure and the administration of justice,"[34] More limited coverage of approximately the same subject area is offered by Crime and Delinquency Literature, published in New York by the National Council on Crime and Delinquency, which abstracts from about 150 journals in the fields of law, social work, and criminology.

Arms Control and Disarmament: a Quarterly Bibliography with Abstracts and Annotations is prepared by the Library of Congress, with the support of the U.S. Arms Control and Disarmament Agency. Most of the publications listed are from the research and theoretical literature of international relations, but there is also a fair amount of journalistic commentary on current political issues.

Poverty and Human Resources: Abstracts and Survey of Current Literature was founded by the University of Michigan-Wayne State University Institute of Labor and Industrial Relations, and records publications relating to "research and action programs, legislative and community developments and policy trends"[35] in its subject. Listings include books, journal articles, and some separate reports issued by government agencies and research institutions. In addition to the abstracts, most issues contain an interpretative or review article on some topic within the scope of the bibliography (e.g., "the Hard-Core Unemployed, Myth and Reality"[36]).

LIBRARY-GENERATED BIBLIOGRAPHIC TOOLS: PERIODICAL INDEXES AND LIBRARY CATALOGS

Libraries and library-connected organizations produce several types of bibliographic tools that can function as searching aids for the social science literature. The library catalog is familiar as a locator of the books available in a particular library. The catalogs of libraries that have extensive collections on particular subjects are in many respects the equivalent of comprehensive bibliographies of these subjects, and a number of these are in book form and available outside the particular institutions whose collections they represent. Another type of library-generated tool, the periodical index, locates periodical articles, since articles are not ordinarily listed in library catalogs. The Reader's Guide to Periodical Literature is a well-known index to general magazines. Similar indexes are published for periodicals in specialized fields, and these often take in the scholarly journals that are also covered by the bibliographies of the various disciplines. While there is thus some overlap between the library-generated and discipline-generated bibliographic records, there are also noteworthy differences stemming from the differing aims and orientations characteristic of the library and academic enterprises.

Most academic bibliographies have been created by scholars who had their own needs in mind. This means that the bibliographies are designed to serve the relatively limited and well-defined purpose of placing the literature of the past at the service of the field's continuing research and discussion. The library tools, in contrast, are intended to identify the contents of libraries for library users, a diverse group whose needs and interests in consulting the literature are presumed to be extremely varied. The producers of the library tools are not themselves participants in the communication system represented by the literature and the reader is generally assumed to be likewise outside the system. This difference in perspective affects the scope, content, and organization of the two groups of bibliographies.[37]

The academic bibliographies are records of the contributions to the literature of a field. As such, selection of the publications belonging to the scientific literature, and inclusiveness in coverage of such publications, are important considerations. The library tools do not share these concerns. Their central purpose is to make accessible a body of library materials. A library catalog is an inventory of the books in a library's collection. Periodical indexes serve to extend the coverage of the inventory to encompass a category of materials—periodical articles—normally omitted from the catalog. In consequence, the scope of library-generated bibliographic tools tends to reflect the actual or expected range of library holdings pertinent to a subject, which is not the same thing as the literature of a field of scholarship. Library tools typically include popular and descriptive materials as well as writings pertaining to research and theory, but they do not strive particularly for comprehensive coverage of the latter. Many library-generated periodical indexes cover a preselected group of periodicals in their entirety, indexing all the articles without exception. This contrasts with the usual practice of academic bibliographies, which are apt to be more selective in their coverage of a given journal and to omit materials judged to fall outside the range of the bibliography. One way to characterize these contrasting approaches might be to say that the academic bibliographies focus on a field of study and ask which publications are pertinent to it, while the library tools focus on an array of materials and ask which subjects each is related to.[38]

The library tools provide bibliographic identification only, without abstracts or annotations. Many factors may underlie this difference, but assumptions regarding the characteristics and interests of users are undoubtedly relevant. As was observed repeatedly in the account of the development of the disciplinary bibliographies, above, abstracting requires a measure of unity in the presumed aims and interests of users, as a basis for selecting the aspects of the publication to be brought out in the abstract. The academically oriented bibliographies assume the reader's involvement in the stream of investigation and discussion of which each publication is a part. The concerns and patterns of discourse in the field thus furnish a framework for summarizing the content of publications that is lacking when the nature of the reader's orientation to the material cannot be assumed. Accordingly, the library tools simply note the existence of the publication with minimal specification of its character.

The library tools characteristically employ a "dictionary" arrangement, which is an array of specific, mutually independent categories arranged in alphabetical order, in contrast to the classed ordering of conceptually interrelated categories characteristic of the academic tools.[39] Several related factors can account for this difference, which is quite striking in its consistency. The academic bibliographies are constructed with the needs of scholars primarily in mind, and the classified arrangement permits the specialist to peruse in a general, "browsing" way the writings in his area of interest, something that cannot be done very conveniently in an alphabetically arranged list. Moreover, the scholar is likely to be aware that the research question for which he consults the bibliography relates to an identifiable line of inquiry or well-defined subdivision of the field, and a classified arrangement tends, in general, to group together the entries likely to bear on a particular problem. In the case of the library tools there is no real basis for determining what goes with what, since such connections depend ultimately on the point of view of the reader, which is assumed to be essentially unpredictable. Finally, the classified arrangement, in bringing together specific topics in terms of their relation to more general concepts, is congruent with a view of science as explanation, and scientific literature as the medium for presenting and discussing explanatory propositions. The alphabetical arrangement, in its emphasis on the specific subject matter treated by the publication, suggests a view of the literature as primarily a means for conveying specific, concrete information.[40]

Along the same lines, it may be noted that the classifications employed in the academic bibliographies quite often reflect specific aspects of research and discussion in the field. Examples are categories such as "Demographic and Economic Interrelations," in Population Index, or "Tension Areas" and "International Political Environment" in Arms Control and Disarmament. The library tools, on the other hand, aiming for broader and more "neutral" applicability, tend toward more concrete terminology—for example, "migration," "natural resources," or names of places and events—whose meaning is less closely tied to the theoretical assumptions and lines of inquiry prevailing in a particular discipline.

To summarize, the library tools are most likely to be useful as alternatives to the scholarly bibliographies in situations in which the information sought is relatively concrete and specific, and scrutiny of the total range of potentially relevant literature is not required. On the other hand, the library tools have longer publication histories than the disciplinary bibliographies in many instances, and may therefore constitute the only route to certain segments of the literature for particular periods. Some periodical indexes and library catalogs that are significant as searching tools for the social sciences are briefly described below. Additional details may be found in Appendix G.

Periodical Indexes

The Social Sciences and Humanities Index is perhaps the most widely used means of access to scholarly literature in American libraries. It indexes about 100 major English language journals in sociology, anthropology, political science, economics, history, and geography, and about the same number in literature, religion, and other fields of the humanities. The character of this index is best understood in the light of its history. Under the title International Index to Periodicals, it was instituted in 1907 by the H. W. Wilson Company, which also publishes the Reader's Guide, to index the specialized and foreign periodicals held by larger libraries but not by many of the institutions that subscribed to Reader's Guide and to the popular American magazines that it indexes. Accordingly the International Index covered not only scholarly journals, but also a number of general magazines of relatively sophisticated content and small circulation. Coverage of foreign material largely ceased during the Second World War and was not resumed afterward, so that the index could better accommodate an ever-increasing number of American periodicals. Ultimately all foreign language publications were dropped and the title of the index was changed to eliminate the word "international." It still includes a number of intellectually sophisticated general magazines, such as Encounter and New Statesman, as well as the leading American journals in the social sciences and humanities and a few of the most important journals of the other English-speaking countries. Thus the Social Sciences and Humanities Index can yield a sample of the journal literature on a very broad range of topics, and a high proportion of its listings will be available in most American college or research libraries, but it is not a suitable tool for comprehensive searching of the literature of any field.

Public Affairs Information Service Bulletin, frequently referred to by its initials as P.A.I.S., is a unique bibliographic tool not readily classifiable in any of the categories which have been delineated, but closer in its general character and approach to the library periodical indexes than to any other type of bibliography. It is an index to publications in all forms relating to "public affairs," by which is meant, roughly, any political, social, or economic topic that relates to matters of public discussion or policy. The Public Affairs Information Service is an association of libraries that instituted the Bulletin in 1916, primarily with the aim of serving the information needs of libraries and research bureaus attached to government agencies, which were being established in substantial numbers at that time. The Bulletin was designed to serve these agencies both as an aid in selection and acquisition of materials and as an identification tool for the publications likely to be in their collections. However, it also proved useful to a much wider public, and is one of the most generally available and heavily used bibliographic tools to be found in American public and academic libraries. It includes material in all forms—books, periodical articles, government documents, and a wide range of pamphlets and reports by a large and varied group of commercial and voluntary agencies—published anywhere in the world in the English language. P.A.I.S. Foreign Language Index was instituted in 1972 for comparable coverage of foreign publications.

As would be expected in view of the subject range and purpose of P.A.I.S., a high proportion of the listings are factual and descriptive publications. The substantial quantities of scholarly literature in political science, economics, and sociology that are also included tend to deal principally with topics bearing on specific public policy issues, rather than with the more abstract and theoretical aspects of those disciplines. The periodicals scrutinized for P.A.I.S. entries include academic journals in such fields as management, public administration, and social welfare. However, the indexing of the periodicals is selective, and only articles falling within the scope of the index are listed.

Education Index indexes about 200 English-language education periodicals, and some other materials such as yearbooks of education associations. It affords good coverage of education publications likely to be most widely held and most frequently consulted in American libraries but it does not attempt to establish a comprehensive record of the literature of the field, and may thus be distinguished from Research in Education and Current Index to Journals in Education, described above. While Education Index and Current Index to Journals in Education overlap in coverage to some extent, there is a fairly clear difference in emphasis. Education Index is geared toward educational practice as much as toward research and scholarship. Many of the periodicals it indexes are addressed to classroom teachers and school administrators, and treat research mainly in terms of its application to current activities and problems in schools. Nearly all the periodicals indexed are American publications and focus mainly on education in this country. Current Index to Journals in Education, on the other hand, is oriented toward the theoretical and scholarly literature and, while definitely American in emphasis, attempts a more world-wide perspective.

Index to Periodical Articles By and About Negroes indexes about twenty periodicals. Included in the group are both scholarly journals in the general area of Negro life and history, such as Phylon and the Journal of Negro Education, and general magazines addressed mainly to Negro readers such as Crisis and Ebony. The index consists of two separate parts. One, compiled by the staff of the library of Central State University in Ohio, is intended to provide an index for periodicals not covered by commercial indexing services such as Reader's Guide. This section includes most of the popular magazines and lists all articles that appear in the periodicals selected for indexing. The second section of the index is compiled at the Schomburg Collection of Negro Literature and History, a unit of the New York Public Library. This index is designed as a bibliographic tool for research in Negro literature and history. It covers mainly scholarly journals in the general area of Negro studies and indexes these selectively, listing only the articles judged to have research value within the subject range of the index. Both sections of the Index employ an alphabetical arrangement, which includes author and subject headings in a single sequence, but due to differences in the character of the materials indexed the subject headings are not uniform for both sections.

The Index to Legal Periodicals indexes about 300 periodicals, mainly university law reviews and journals of bar associations. Most of this material is outside the scope of the social science literature as such, but there is a degree of overlap with the concerns of some social science fields, most notably political science.

The Essay and General Literature Index, while not an index to periodicals, is based on a similar rationale. It is an index to separately written chapters in books, and thus, like the periodical indexes, serves to afford access to materials which are not ordinarily identified by library catalogs. The books included are anthologies, symposia, and similar collections, in all fields of the humanities and social sciences. Some of the disciplinary bibliographies, notably Sociological Abstracts, Psychological Abstracts, and Index of Economic Articles list essays published in books in the same manner as journal articles and in these fields Essay and General Literature Index would have little importance except, perhaps, for identification of some of the older literature. However, when the disciplinary bibliographies list only book titles, and not the individual contributions that they contain, as is generally the case, for example, in history, political science, and anthropology, the Essay and General Literature Index can identify materials not pointed out by other bibliographic sources.

Africa South of the Sahara: Index to Periodical Literature 1900–1970 is not a continuing index issued on a periodic basis, but the publication, in book form, of an index maintained on file cards in the African Section of the Library of Congress. It encompasses the major scholarly journals devoted to Africa, with emphasis on recent years. Several other compilations along similar lines have been published (all by G. K. Hall & Co.), including Index to Periodical Articles, 1950-1964, in the Library of The Royal Institute of International Affairs (London), and Economics and Finance: Index to Periodical Articles, 1947-1971. The latter index derives from the joint World Bank-International Monetary Fund library in Washington, D.C.

Library Catalogs

Like the familiar card catalog, many printed library catalogs are limited to the books and periodical titles in the library's collection, and do not list individual articles in periodicals. Some, however, are very detailed and contain entries for journal articles, chapters in essay collections, and other materials of less than book length. Ordinarily the catalogs are not limited or restricted in any way with regard to the language or publication date of the works listed. Updating tends to be quite slow, however, and supplements listing new acquisitions appear less frequently than even the slowest among the recurrent disciplinary bibliographies. Thus the catalogs of comprehensive library collections can be highly useful as identification tools for the older literature of a field, particularly that which antedates the inception of a recurrent disciplinary bibliography, but are generally unsuited to searching the recent literature.

A highly significant published library catalog for the social sciences is the London Bibliography of the Social Sciences, a combined list of the holdings of several large social science collections in London. It was first published in 1931 and has been supplemented periodically since. This bibliography is about the fullest listing available of social science books[41] published before the inception of the comprehensive disciplinary bibliographies in the 1950s. It is particularly comprehensive in the fields of political science and economics.

A large number of library catalogs have been published in recent years by the Boston firm of G. K. Hall & Co., which specializes in this type of publication. Of particular interest in relation to the social science literature are the catalogs of the Library of the Peabody Museum of Archaeology and Ethnology at Harvard University, the Schomburg Collection of Negro Literature and History of the New York Public Library, and the Library of the American Geographical Society. (See Appendix G for further details on these works.) Other catalogs that may be available in a particular library can usually be identified in that library's catalog under the subheading "catalogs" of the listings for bibliographies of a subject: for example, "Anthropology—Bibliographies—Catalogs."

FOOTNOTES

1. Jean Meynaud and Jean Meyriat, "Prefatory Note," International Bibliography of Political Science, vol. 1. (Paris: UNESCO, 1954), p. 7.

2. A list by disciplines appears as Appendix G, Part 1. Additional details concerning each title may be found in the alphabetical list, Appendix G, Part 2.

3. During the same year a similar bibliography was begun in a German psychological journal, Zeitschrift für Psychologie und Physiologie der Sinnesorgane, published in Hamburg.

4. John Higham, History (Englewood Cliffs, N.J.: Prentice-Hall, 1965), p. 7. By permission of Prentice-Hall, Inc.

5. Ibid., p. 6.

6. For example, in Germany, Bibliographie zur deutschen Geschichte...1889–1927 (Leipzig, annual). This was later continued by Jahresberichte für deutsche Geschichte 1929–1939 (Leipzig, annual) and Jahresberichte für deutschen Geschichte 1949–   (Berlin, biennial). A comparable series for France is: Répertoire méthodique de l'histoire moderne et contemporaine de la France, 1889–1913 (Paris, annual), followed by Répertoire bibliographique de l'histoire de France (Paris, annual, 1923–38), and Bibliographie annuelle de l'histoire de France du cinquième siècle à 1939; Année 1955–   (Paris).

7. The publication is issued as Part 2 of the Annual Report of the Association, as part of the duty imposed upon the society by its act of incorporation "to report annually...concerning...the condition of historical study in America." (Annual Report, 1910.)

8. "Foreword," in each volume. Before 1935, Canada, the West Indies, and Pacific Islands were included.

9. Constitution of the International Committee of Historical Sciences, Article I. In: International Committee of Historical Sciences, Bulletin (October 1926): 119.

10. See the Editorial Bureau Circular in International Committee of Historical Sciences, Bulletin (December 1927): 403.

11. American historians have not infrequently criticized the selections as haphazard and inappropriate. See, for example, the following reviews in the American Historical Review: vol. 60 (1955) p. 398; vol. 63 (1958) p. 452; vol. 68 (1962), p. 168.

12. International Committee of Historical Sciences, Bulletin (October 1926):35.

13. The matter is further discussed below under "Technical Reports," in Appendix H. See also p. 60, above:

14. See Stuart F. Chapin, "Social Science Abstracts—an Institution in the Making: an Example of Social Invention and Social Engineering." American Journal of Sociology 36 (1930): 406–422.

15. Social Science Research Council, Decennial Report 1923–1933. (New York, 1934), p. 8.

16. "Bibliographical Services in the Social Sciences," Library Quarterly 20 (1950): 83.

17. United Nations Educational Scientific and Cultural Organization, Bibliographies in the Social Sciences: A Selected Inventory of Periodical Publications. (Paris, UNESCO, 1951). See the introduction.

18. International Social Science Council, International Sociological Association, International Economic Association, International Political Science Association, International Committee of Comparative Law, International Union of Scientific Psychology, International Federation for Documentation, International Federation of Library Associations.

19. International Bibliography of Economics 1 (Paris: UNSECO, 1953): 7.

20. See Appendix G for details.

21. The number of journals that would need to be included for "comprehensive" coverage is difficult to state. The International Bibliography of Political Science lists over 2,000, but this is not a suitable yardstick because the four parts of the International Bibliography of the Social Sciences use the same list.

22. A similar emphasis on data and on policy related topics will be noted in the "mission-oriented" bibliographies discussed below. From some points of view, Economic Abstracts belongs logically in that group, although it has a broader subject range than is characteristic of the mission-oriented bibliographies.

23. Harold H. Weissman, "Editorial Comments," Abstracts for Social Workers 1 (Spring 1965).

24. David Fanshel, "Editorial Comments," Ibid. Reprinted with permission of the National Association of Social Workers.

25. A list of earlier reports of research supported under federal programs was issued by the U.S. Office of Education in 1967 under the title Research Reports, 1956–1965.

26. For description of ERIC searching services see John M. Morgan, "Information Retrieval Systems for ERIC," RQ 11 (Summer 1972): 374–375.

27. A separate publication, Thesaurus of ERIC Descriptors, 2d ed., Washington, D.C., GPO 1969, lists and classifies the terms employed in the system, indicating the scope of each and the relationships among them.

28. He also founded the American Behavioral Scientist (see Appendix B) and the ABS Guide to Recent Publications in the Social and Behavioral Sciences, described below.

29. By L. N. Rieselback, American Political Science Review 58 (1964): 577–588.

30. See, for example, the comments of Clifton Brock in his essay "Political Science" in Robert B. Downs, ed., Bibliography: Current State and Future Trends (Urbana, Ill.: University of Illinois Press, 1967), p. 300.

31. See Chapter 1 for explanation of the term "behavioral sciences."

32. The bimonthly list is described below under "Current Awareness Lists," in Chapter 8.

33. From the statement of purpose, published in each issue.

34. Statement on cover of each issue.

35. Vol. 1, no. 1, p. 3.

36. By Louis A. Ferman, vol. 4, no. 6, 1969.

37. The division into "academic" and "library" categories is, like most such distinctions, seldom wholly consistent. Atypical characteristics are to be found among members of both groups, and some works are classifiable in either. Among the "academic" bibliographies discussed above, the Royal Anthropological Institute Library's Anthropological Index, and Arms Control and Disarmament, issued by the Library of Congress, are, in point of fact, "library-generated." They were considered among the academic tools because they are directed mainly at specialist groups, rather than library users at large, and because, apart from the specific fact of their origin, they more closely resemble the disciplinary than the library tools.

38. cf. Raynard Swank, "Subject Catalogs, Classifications or Bibliographies? A Review of Critical Discussions, 1876–1942," Library Quarterly 14 (1944): 331.

39. For example, in the classification employed by Sociological Abstracts the general heading "Complex Organizations" embraces the related subdivisions "Industrial Sociology," "Military Sociology," and "Bureaucratic Structures," and all are grouped together. In the alphabetical arrangement of the library-generated Social Sciences and Humanities Index each topic stands separately, so that "Bureaucracy" appears between "Bulgaria" and "Burglary Insurance," and so forth.

40. As noted in the descriptions of the individual works, the classified bibliographies typically include detailed subject indexes in addition to the classification. The aim is to permit access to the materials in terms of either their specific information content or the broader research areas to which they pertain.

41. Periodical holdings (i.e., titles of journals only, not individual articles) of the British Library of Political and Economic Science were included up to 1936, but not afterward. It is planned eventually to issue a complete list of periodicals as a separate section.

Appendix G

Comprehensive Recurrent
Bibliographies Recapitulated

LIST BY DISCIPLINES

The following tables indicate the availability of comprehensive bibliographic records in the social science disciplines. Fuller details concerning each title are given in the alphabetical list below. For identification of the most recent literature, reference should be made also to the current awareness bibliographies described in Chapter 8.

ANTHROPOLOGY

Period of Coverage	Title	Scope Restrictions	Abstracts
—to 1970	Peabody Museum Catalogue		no
1907 –	Social Sciences and Humanities Index (International Index before 1965)	articles only; after 1965 English language only	no
1950 –	Bibliographie der Sozialwissenschaften		no
1955 –	International Bibliography of Social and Cultural Anthropology		no
1961 –	Bulletin Signaletique		yes
1963 –	Anthropological Index	articles only	no
1970 –	Abstracts in Anthropology		yes
1973 –	Social Sciences Citation Index	articles only	no

AREA AND ETHNIC STUDIES

Period of Coverage	Title	Scope Restrictions	Abstracts
−to 1967	Schomburg Collection of Negro Literature and History, Catalogue	books only	no
1900 −	Africa South of the Sahara	articles only	some
1936 −	Handbook of Latin American Studies		some
1936 −	Bibliography of Asian Studies		no
1950 −	African Abstracts	articles only	yes
1950 −	Index to Periodical Articles By and About Negroes	articles only	no
1956 −	American Bibliography of Russian and East European Studies		no
1964 −	America: History and Life	articles only	yes
1970−	Black Information Index	English language only	yes

ECONOMICS

Period of Coverage	Title	Scope Restrictions	Abstracts
−to 1968	London Bibliography of the Social Sciences	books only	no
1886 −	Index of Economic Articles	articles only; English language	no
1905 − (lacks 1943–49)	Bibliographie der Sozialwissenschaften		no
1907 −	Social Sciences and Humanities Index (International Index before 1965)	articles only; after 1965 English language only	no
1916 −	Public Affairs Information Service Bulletin	English only	no
1928–32	Social Science Abstracts	articles only	yes
1947–71	Economics and Finance; Index...	articles and reports only	some
1952 −	International Bibliography of Economics		no
1953 −	Economic Abstracts		yes
1963 −	Journal of Economic Literature		some
1966 −	Poverty and Human Resources		yes
1972 −	P.A.I.S. Foreign Language Index		no
1973 −	Social Sciences Citation Index	articles only	no

EDUCATION

Period of Coverage	Title	Scope Restrictions	Abstracts
1927–40	Bibliography of Research Studies in Education	research reports only	some
1927 –	Child Development Abstracts		yes
1929 –	Education Index	English language only; omits most books	no
1958 –	Mental Retardation Abstracts		yes
1961 –	Bulletin Signaletique		yes
1966 –	Research in Education	research reports only; English language only	yes
1969 –	Current Index to Journals in Education	articles only	yes
1973 –	Social Sciences Citation Index	articles only	no

GEOGRAPHY

Period of Coverage	Title	Scope Restrictions	Abstracts
1891 –	Bibliographie Géographique Internationale		no
1907 –	Social Sciences and Humanities Index (International Index before 1965)	articles only; after 1965 English language only	no
1923–62[1]	American Geographical Society Research Catalogue		no
1966 –	Geographical Abstracts		yes
1973 –	Social Sciences Citation Index	articles only	no

[1] Includes journal articles published since 1923; some earlier books. Updated by Current Geographical Publications, described in Appendix I.

HISTORY

Period of Coverage	Title	Scope Restrictions	Abstracts
1878–1913	Jahresberichte der Geschichtswissenscraft		some brief comments
1902 – (lacks 1904–05, 1941–47)	Writings on American History[1]		no
1907 –	Social Sciences and Humanities Index (International Index before 1965)	articles only; after 1965 English language only	no
1926 – (lacks 1939–46)	International Bibliography of Historical Sciences		no
1928–32	Social Science Abstracts	articles only	yes
1955 –	Historical Abstracts	articles only; modern period (1775–) only	yes
1973 –	Social Sciences Citation Index	articles only	no

[1] See Guides to the Literature, Appendix K, for sources of information about foreign national historical bibliographies.

POLITICAL SCIENCE

Period of Coverage	Title	Scope Restrictions	Abstracts
–to 1968	London Bibliography of the Social Sciences	books only	no
1905 – (lacks 1943–49)	Bibliographie der Sozialwissenschaften		no
1907 –	Social Sciences and Humanities Index (International Index before 1965)	articles only; after 1965 English language only	no
1908 –	Index to Legal Periodicals	articles only; English language	no
1916 –	Public Affairs Information Service Bulletin	English language only	no
1928–32	Social Science Abstracts	articles only	yes
1950 –	International Political Science Abstracts	articles only	yes
1950–64	Index to Periodical Articles (Royal Institute of International Affairs)	articles only	no
1952 –	International Bibliography of Political Science		no
1957 –	Recent Publications in the Social and Behavioral Sciences (ABS Guide. . . 1957–64)		yes
1961 –	Abstracts on Criminology and Penology		yes
1964 –	Arms Control and Disarmament		yes
1966 –	Universal Reference System		yes
1966 –	Poverty and Human Resources		yes
1972 –	P.A.I.S. Foreign Language Index		no
1973 –	Social Sciences Citation Index	articles only	no

PSYCHOLOGY

Period of Coverage	Title	Scope Restrictions	Abstracts
1890–1935	Psychological Index		no
1927 –	Psychological Abstracts		yes
1927 –	Child Development Abstracts		yes
1957 –	Recent Publications in the Social and Behavioral Sciences (ABS Guide. . . 1957–64)		yes
1958 –	Mental Retardation Abstracts		yes
1961 –	Bulletin Signaletique		yes
1973 –	Social Sciences Citation Index	articles only	no

SOCIOLOGY
Including Demography and Social Work

Period of Coverage	Title	Scope Restrictions	Abstracts
–to 1968	London Bibliography of the Social Sciences	books only	no
1907 –	Social Sciences and Humanities Index (International Index before 1965)	articles only; after 1965 English language only	no
1916 –	Public Affairs Information Service Bulletin	English language only	no
1928–32	Social Science Abstracts	articles only	yes
1931 –	Population Index		yes
1950 –	Bibliographie der Sozialwissenschaften		no
1952 –	International Bibliography of Sociology		no
1953 –	Sociological Abstracts		yes
1957 –	Recent Publications in the Social and Behavioral Sciences (ABS Guide. . . 1957–64)		yes
1961 –	Bulletin Signaletique		yes
1961 –	Abstracts on Criminology and Penology		yes
1965 –	Abstracts for Social Workers		yes
1966 –	Poverty and Human Resources		yes
1969 –	Crime and Delinquency Literature	articles only	yes
1972 –	P.A.I.S. Foreign Language Index		no
1973 –	Social Sciences Citation Index	articles only	no

ALPHABETICAL LIST

Bibliographic details for each of the titles mentioned in Chapter 7 are given below. Numbers in parentheses following the entries refer to the pages in the text where the work is discussed.

Abstracts for Social Workers. 1965 – . New York: National Association of Social Workers. quarterly. (155–156)

Abstracts social work books and articles, as well as publications in fields such as psychology and law that have relevance for social work. Coverage limited to English language, mainly American, publications. Classified arrangement with subject and author indexes.

Abstracts in Anthropology. 1970 – . Westport, Conn.: Greenwood Periodicals. quarterly. GN1.A15 (155)

Abstracts journal articles, monographs, and papers presented at meetings in four subfields of anthropology: cultural anthropology, archaeology, linguistics, and physical anthropology. No restrictions on language or place of publication, but depends heavily on abstracts submitted by authors and editors, and coverage so far is limited and uneven. Broad subject classification, with author and subject indexes.

Abstracts on Criminology and Penology. 1961 – . Amsterdam: Criminologica Foundation. bimonthly. HV6001.E9 (163)

Abstracts of the world literature, including publications in all forms and all languages. Abstracts in English, with titles in other languages translated into English. Detailed classed arrangement with author and subject indexes. Volumes 1–8, 1961–68, published under the title Excerpta Criminologica.

Africa South of the Sahara: Index to Periodical Literature 1900–1970. 4 vols. Boston: G. K. Hall & Co., 1971. Z3503.U47 (168–169)

Index to periodical literature on sub-Saharan Africa prepared in the African Section of the Library of Congress. Includes indexing done at the Library, and also some cards received from several European documentation centers that concentrate on Africa. A number of major Africana journals are covered from their beginning dates of publication, but the file's major emphasis is on the period 1967–1970. Arrangement is by region, and by subject within regions. Some entries include abstracts, but many of the abstracts originate with the European services and are in French.

African Abstracts. 1950 – . London: International African Institute. quarterly. DT1.I553 (162)

Abstracts of articles relating to African studies from about 150 journals published all over the world. Monographic publications are not included. All abstracts in English, and foreign titles translated into English. Basic arrangement is by region, with subject designation of each entry indicated by a code number. Annual ethnic and linguistic index, and author index.

Note: During its early years this publication had a strong anthropological emphasis. It was subtitled "Review of Ethnographic, Social, and Linguistic

Studies," and the abstracts were listed in two categories, "ethnographic and social studies" and "linguistic studies." More recently the scope has widened to encompass African studies generally, and in 1967 the subtitle was changed to "Review of Articles Appearing in Current Periodicals." At the same time a subject classification consisting of eleven broad categories pertaining to history, contemporary culture, and the arts was adopted.

America: History and Life. 1964 – . Santa Barbara, Calif.: American Bibliographic Center-Clio Press. quarterly. Z1236.A48 (162)

Abstracts of the journal literature pertaining to United States and Canadian history and culture. Books consisting of separate articles are occasionally listed, but monographic literature is ordinarily excluded. Classification scheme based on regional and chronological categories; annual subject and personal name indexes.

American Bibliography of Russian and Eastern European Studies. 1956 – . Bloomington, Ind.: Indiana University. annual. Z2483.A65 (162)

Inventory of scholarly articles and monographs, mainly in English, issued under the sponsorship of the Modern Languages Association and the Slavic Studies program of Indiana University. No annotations; classified arrangement with author index. At its inception the bibliography focused principally on studies in language, literature, folklore, and pedagogy, but the social sciences and history have been well covered since about 1960. Beginning with 1965, reviews are cited with entries for books.

American Geographical Society. Library. Research Catalog. Boston: G. K. Hall & Co., 1962. Z6009.A48 (169)

Lists books, periodical articles, government documents, maps, and miscellaneous publications. Entries are classified in a scheme consisting of topical and regional categories. More recent additions to the library's collection are listed in its monthly bulletin, Current Geographical Publications.

Anthropological Index to Current Periodicals Received in the Library. 1963 – . London: Royal Anthropological Institute of Great Britain and Ireland. quarterly. (155)

Indexes about 500 anthropological journals published all over the world. No annotations. The basic arrangement is by region, subdivided into broad topical categories: physical anthropology, cultural anthropology, etc. It is planned to supplement this very general classification with detailed subject and author indexes, but these have not been issued as yet.

Arms Control and Disarmament: a Quarterly Bibliography with Abstracts and Annotations. 1964 – . Washington, D.C.: U.S. Library of Congress, for the U.S. Arms Control and Disarmament Agency. JX1974.A1A7 (163)

Fairly detailed abstracts of a broad range of literature in its subject field, somewhat broadly interpreted to encompass a number of topics relating to world politics. To be discontinued in 1973, due to lack of funding.

Bibliographie der Sozialwissenschaften. 1905 – . (n.F. Jahrg. 1– , 1950– .) Gottingen, Vandenhoeck, and Ruprecht. 3 issues per year. Z7163.K85 (146)

Unannotated listing of books and articles in all western languages dealing with economics, political science, sociology, and anthropology. Arranged in broad subject classification with annual author and subject indexes. Published monthly 1905–43, covering economics and political science only. Issued at times under title Bibliographie der Staats-und-Wirtschaftswissenschaften. Publication suspended 1943–50. Beginning with 1950 appeared in three issues per year and scope expanded to include sociology and anthropology, but continues to stress economics.

Bibliographie Géographique Internationale. 1891 – . Paris: Colin. annual. Z6001.B57 (144–145)

Comprehensive listing of books and articles of scholarly interest published anywhere in the world. Issued under the auspices of L'Union Géographique Internationale. Classified arrangement, utilizing both topical and regional categories; author index. Occasional brief annotations (in French) included when content of item is not sufficiently indicated by its title.

Bibliography of Asian Studies. 1941 – . Ann Arbor, Mich.: Association for Asian Studies. annual. Z3001.B5 (162)

Inclusive list of books and articles in occidental languages pertaining to all aspects of the culture and history of Asia. Entries, unannotated, are listed by country, with topical subdivisions. There is an author index, but no subject index.

This bibliography began in 1936 as Bulletin of Far Eastern Bibliography, a separate publication issued five times per year from 1936 to 1940. In 1941 it became an annual supplement to Far Eastern Quarterly, later, Journal of Asian Studies, and continued in this form until 1969, when it became an independent publication.

A cumulation covering the years 1941–1965 was published in 1969 by G. K. Hall & Co. under the title Bibliography of Asian Studies.

Bibliography of Research Studies in Education. 1926/27–1939/40. Washington, D.C.: Government Printing Office. annual. Z5811.U44 (148)

Compiled by the Library, U.S. Office of Education. Listed American research reports in all fields of education. Occasional brief annotations; detailed subject classification with author, subject, and institution indexes.

Continued after the Second World War as Research Studies in Education 1941–51, and annually thereafter, by the education fraternity Phi Delta Kappa. Coverage of this publication limited to doctoral dissertations completed and in progress, and selected published literature in research methods.

Black Information Index. 1970 – . Herndon, Va.: bimonthly. Z1361.N39B554 (162)

A classified, annotated list covering books and articles in all subject areas relating to blacks in the United States and abroad, and to minorities and race relations generally. The Index covers about fifty academic journals in various fields, and many popular magazines and newspapers. Reviews are frequently cited with listings for books.

Bulletin Signaletique: sect. 20: Psychologie, Pedagogie; sect. 21: Sociologie, Sciences du Langage. 1961 – . Paris: Centre Nationale de la Recherche Scientifique. quarterly. Z5813.B84 (155)

World-wide, classified list of books and articles, with additional subject index. Brief, Indicative abstracts, in French, for some items, and foreign titles translated into French.

Child Development Abstracts and Bibliography. 1927 – . Lafayette, Ind.: Purdue University for the Society for Research in Child Development. 3 issues per year. HQ750.A1N3   (161)

Abstracts of English-language and foreign materials pertaining to child development, from the literatures of psychology, psychiatry, medicine, education, and social welfare. Classified arrangement with annual author and subject indexes.

Crime and Delinquency Literature. 1970 – . New York: National Council on Crime and Delinquency. quarterly. HV6001.C67 (163)

Abstracts from about 150 journals, published in the U.S. and abroad, mainly in the fields of law, social work, and criminology. Each issue also contains a review article. Annual subject index.

Current Index to Journals in Education. 1969 – . New York: CCM Information Corporation. monthly. Z5813.C8 (157)

Index, with brief descriptive abstracts, to scholarly articles appearing in about 700 U.S. and foreign education journals. The journals are scanned and indexed by the ERIC clearinghouses, and the indexing scheme parallels that of Research in Education (q.v.).

Economic Abstracts: semimonthly review of abstracts on economics, finance, trade and industry, management and labor. 1953 – . The Hague, Nijhoff. semimonthly. HB1.A1E2 (154–155)

Edited by the Library of the Economic Information Service, Netherlands Ministry of Economic Affairs, in collaboration with the Library, Netherlands School of Economics and the Library, Ministry of Social Affairs. Covers publications in all forms published anywhere in the world, with emphasis on economic policy and applied problems. Most of the publications are in English, French, or German, with abstracts in the language of the original.

Economics and Finance: Index to Periodical Articles, 1947–1971. 4 vols. Boston: G. K. Hall & Co., 1972. (169)

Publication in book form of a card index maintained in the joint World Bank-International Monetary Fund Library. Extensive coverage of journal articles and reports in the field of international economics, with descriptive annotations for some of the entries.

Education Index. 1929 – . New York: H. W. Wilson Co. monthly, except July and August. Z5813.E23 (167)

Subject index to approximately 200 English-language education periodicals. Also includes some material in book form, such as yearbooks of education associations. Unannotated entries are arranged according to an alphabetical list of subjects. Author entires were included until 1961, then discontinued. Monthly issues are cumulated annually.

Essay and General Literature Index. 1900 – . New York: H. W. Wilson Co. annual. A13.E752 (168)

Index to books that are collections of separately written essays. Includes English-language books in all fields of the social sciences and humanities. Unannotated entires listed by author and subject in a single alphabetical sequence. An initial volume covered the years 1900 to 1933; subsequent volumes issued annually, with five-year and ten-year cumulations.

Geographical Abstracts. 1966 – . London: London School of Economics, Department of Geography. bimonthly. (154)

Published in four parts: A) Geomorphology, (published 1960–65 as Geomorphological Abstracts); B) Biogeography, Climatology, and Cartography; C) Economic Geography; D) Social Geography and Cartography. Comprehensive, world-wide coverage of books and articles of interest to professional geographers. Abstracts arranged in a subject classification with annual regional and author indexes.

Handbook of Latin American Studies. 1936 – . Gainesville: University of Florida Press. annual. Z1605.H23 (162)

Inventory of publications in all fields of the social sciences and humanities relating to Latin America, issued under the auspices of the Hispanic Foundation of the Library of Congress. Aims to list all publications, issued anywhere in the world and in all forms, judged to have permanent value for scholarship. Subject chapters are written by specialists in each field, and contain brief introductory accounts of the nature and status of current research, followed by an annotated list of the publications. Since 1964 the Handbook has been divided into two sections—social sciences and humanities (including history)—each appearing in alternate years. Each volume contains an author and subject index. A combined author index covering 1936–1966 has been issued, and a similar subject index is in preparation.

Historical Abstracts: A Bibliography of the World's Periodical Literature. Part A: Modern History Abstracts, 1775–1914; Part B: Twentieth Century Abstracts, 1914 to the Present. 1955 – . Santa Barbara, Calif.: American Bibliographic Center-Clio Press. quarterly. D299.H5 (153)

Abstracts of selected articles published anywhere in the world in historical journals and selected periodicals in cognate fields. Since 1964, articles dealing with the internal history of the United States and Canada have been excluded, since another bibliography produced by the same publisher now covers these (see America: History and Life). Prior to 1971, when publication in two parts (as indicated above) was instituted, coverage was limited to articles dealing with the period 1775–1945. Classified arrangement, with author and subject indexes.

Index of Economic Articles in Journals and Collective Volumes. 1886 – . Homewood, Ill.: Irwin, 1961 – . annual. Z7164.E2I45 (154)

Publication sponsored by the American Economic Association. Currently indexes English-language articles in about 150 major economic journals, and articles in collective books, such as conference proceedings and essay collections. Vols. 1–5, covering 1886–1959, and supplements covering 1960–63 and 1964–65 indexed journal articles only, and were issued between 1961 and 1967 under the title Index of Economic Journals. Two supplementary volumes covering articles in books from 1960 to 1965 were issued under the title Index of Economic Articles in Collective Volumes. Since 1966 the index has covered both journals and collective books under the title given above, and the volumes now appear annually. Entries provide bibliographic information only. The index utilizes a very detailed subject classification, with subject index to the classification but not to individual entries. There are also author indexes.

Index to Legal Periodicals. 1908 – . New York: H. W. Wilson Co. quarterly (168)

Subject index to English-language legal periodicals. Unannotated entries are arranged under an alphabetical sequence of headings.

Index to Periodical Articles By and About Negroes. 1950 – . Boston: G. K. Hall & Co. annual. AI3.04 (168)

Consists of two parts: an index to popular magazines aimed at Negro readers and not covered by Readers' Guide, prepared by the staff of the Hallie Q. Brown Memorial Library of Central State University, Ohio, and an index to scholarly articles compiled by the staff of the Schomburg Collection of Negro Literature and History, New York Public Library. Both parts are unannotated, with author and subject entries listed in a single alphabetical sequence. Issued under the title Index to Selected Periodicals until 1966.

International Bibliography of Economics. 1952 – . Chicago: Aldine. annual. Z7164.E2I58 (152)

World-wide listings of publications of scientific value in all forms. No annotations, but reviews of books listed often cited. Classified arrangement with author and subject indexes.

International Bibliography of Historical Sciences. 1926 – . Paris: Colin, for the International Committee of Historical Sciences. annual. Z6205.I61 (147–148)

Books and articles in all fields of history, published anywhere in the world in occidental languages, selected as pertinent to the interests of the international community of historians. Listings are unannotated; reviews of books listed are cited. Classified arrangement stressing topical, rather than chronological or geographical, categories, with geographic and author indexes.

The bibliography is produced by the cooperative effort of several national historical associations. Listings are selected by national committees, then screened by an over-all editorial committee. Five "official" languages (English, French, German, Spanish, and Italian) are utilized in annual rotation for editorial content, and titles in languages other than one of the five are translated into the language of the volume in which they are listed.

Not published 1940–46.

International Bibliography of Political Science. 1952 – . Chicago: Aldine. annual. Z7163.I64 (152)

World-wide listing of publications of scientific value in all forms. No annotations, but reference is made to listings in International Political Science Abstracts (q.v.) and to reviews of books. Classified arrangement with author and subject indexes.

International Bibliography of Social and Cultural Anthropology. 1955 – . Chicago: Aldine. annual. Z7161.I593 (152)

World-wide listing of publications of scientific value in all forms, covering most branches of anthropology, with physical anthropology the most notable exception. No annotations, but reviews of books listed often cited. Classified arrangement with author and subject indexes.

International Bibliography of Sociology. 1952 – . Chicago: Aldine. annual. Z7161.I594 (152)

World-wide listing of publications of scientific value in all forms, covering all branches of sociology with exception of social psychology and demography. No annotations, but reviews often cited for books listed. Detailed classification scheme, with author and subject indexes.

"International Bibliography of the Social Sciences."

General title of a group of annual bibliographies issued under the sponsorship of UNESCO and its International Committee for Social Sciences Documentation. See International Bibliography of Economics, International Bibliography of Political Science, International Bibliography of Social and Cultural Anthropology, International Bibliography of Sociology.

International Political Science Abstracts. 1951 – . Oxford, Blackwell. quarterly. JA36.I5 (152–153)

Sponsored by UNESCO and its International Committee for Social Sciences Documentation. Abstracts journal articles only, from over 200 major political science journals published all over the world. English-language abstracts of articles published in English; all other abstracts in French. Classified arrangement. Subject index in each issue, cumulated annually, and annual author index.

Jahresberichte der Geschichtswissenshaft; im Auftrage der Historischen Gesellschaft zu Berlin. 1878–1913. Berlin: Mittler, annual. Z6201.J25 (144)

Comprehensive, classified inventory of books and articles in European languages dealing with all branches of historical study. Publication ceased due to World War I; resumed in 1920 as Jahresberichte der deutschen Geschichte, covering German history only.

Journal of Economic Literature. 1969 – . Washington, D.C.: American Economic Association. quarterly. HB1.J6 (154)

Comprehensive listing of current books, and articles in about 150 journals, both English language and foreign. Book listings classified by subject, with brief annotations. Articles listed by subject and also by journal. Also contains longer reviews of significant books, abstracts of selected articles, and review articles.

This journal is the successor to Journal of Economic Abstracts, which was published from 1963 to 1968 and contained abstracts of selected articles from a small group of economic journals, beginning with about thirty journal titles in 1963 and reaching about seventy journals by 1968.

A London Bibliography of the Social Sciences. London: London School of Economics and Political Science, 1931. Supplements 1934–1968. Z7161.L84 (169)

Combined subject catalog of several large social science libraries in London. The initial volumes listed the collections of ten institutions as of 1929, but the number of libraries covered has been reduced in later supplements. The most recent supplements list the holdings to 1968 of two particularly strong collections in the London School of Economics, the British Library of Political and Economic Science and the Edward Fry Library of International Law. The rate of publication is somewhat irregular, but in recent years supplements have appeared at approximately five-year intervals.

The bibliography includes books only. The entries are unannotated, and arranged by subject in a detailed alphabetical scheme with many cross references. There is also a classified list of the headings and subdivisions used, designed to aid in identifying all the locations in the bibliography that might contain relevant material. Author indexes were included in the volumes published up to 1936, but not since. The catalog is updated by a Monthly List of Additions to the Library, issued by the British Library of Political and Economic Science.

Mental Retardation Abstracts. 1964 – . Washington, D.C.: National Institute of Mental Health. quarterly. RC570.M4 (162)

Abstracts articles relevant to study and treatment of mental retardation from about 1,000 journals in the fields of psychiatry, psychology, education, medicine, social work, and sociology. Classified arrangement, with subject and author indexes in each issue cumulated annually. The initial volume, issued in 1964, covered the literature from 1958 to 1963, and was followed by the quarterly publication.

Peabody Museum of Archaeology and Ethnology, Harvard University. Library. Author and Subject Catalogues. Boston: G. K. Hall & Co., 1963. Supplement 1970. Z5119.H36 (169)

Author and subject catalog, including entries for journal articles as well as books and other separate publications.

Population Index. 1935 – . Princeton, N.J.: Population Association of America. quarterly. Z7164.D3P83 (150)

Abstracts of population literature and reports and documents that are sources of population data, published anywhere in the world in occidental languages. Classified arrangement with geographic and author indexes in each issue, cumulated annually.

Since 1969, in order to stabilize the size of the Index in the face of an increasing volume of publication, coverage has been limited to the "core" literature of demography, excluding relevant works in cognate fields such as local history and human genetics. Headnotes to each section of the classification define the scope of the listings in detail and cite the bibliographies providing more extensive coverage of peripheral topics.

A cumulated index covering the years 1935–1968 has been published by G. K. Hall & Co.

Poverty and Human Resources: Abstracts and Survey of Current Literature. 1966 – . Beverly Hills, Calif.: Sage Publications, for University of Michigan-Wayne State University Institute of Labor and Industrial Relations. quarterly. (163)

Abstracts encompassing both the formally published and the "report" literature arranged in broad subject categories with author and subject indexes. Also contains review articles and reports of current governmental problems and policies.

Psychological Abstracts. 1927 – . Washington, American Psychological Association. monthly. BF1.P65 (148–149).

Abstracts of the world-wide psychological literature, in all forms. Classified arrangement, with author and subject indexes in each issue cumulated semiannually. Cumulated author and subject indexes have been published by G. K. Hall & Co. The author index covers Psychological Abstracts and its predecessor, Psychological Index, from 1894 to 1958, with supplements to 1963. The subject index covers Psychological Abstracts from 1927 to 1960, with supplements to 1965. Presumably, supplements will continue to appear.

Psychological Index: an Annual Bibliography of the Literature of Psychology and Cognate Subjects. 1894–1935. Princeton, N.J.: Psychological Review Corp. Z7203.P97 (144)

Books and articles published all over the world, listed in a classified subject arrangement with author index. No abstracts or annotations. Abstracts of many of the listings, as located in a number of journals, are listed in the following: Psychological Index: Abstract References. Edited by H. L. Ansbacher. 2 vols. Columbus, Ohio: American Psychological Association, 1940–41.

Public Affairs Information Service. Bulletin. 1915 – . New York. weekly. Z7163.P9 (166–167).

Index to a wide range of books, articles, and separate reports, including government publications, in all fields pertaining to public affairs published in English anywhere in the world. Entries are unannotated, and listed according to an alphabetical list of subjects. There are also a few author entries, for well-known authors. Weekly issues are cumulated quarterly and annually. Usually cited as PAIS. P.A.I.S. Foreign Language Index, designed for comparable coverage of foreign publications, is a quarterly instituted in 1972. It covers publications in French, German, Italian, Portuguese and Spanish.

Recent Publications in the Social and Behavioral Sciences. 1966 – . Beverly Hills, Calif.: American Behavioral Scientist. annual. Z7161.A42 (161)

A listing, with brief annotations, of significant behaviorally oriented publications in all fields of social science. Based on bimonthly list in each issue of the journal American Behavioral Scientist. Arrangement is by author, with subject index. An earlier volume was issued in 1965 under the title ABS Guide to Recent Publications in the Social and Behavioral Sciences, containing the listings from the inception of American Behavioral Scientist in 1957 to 1964.

Research in Education. 1966 – . Washington, D.C.: U.S. Office of Education. monthly. Z5813.R4 (157)

Abstracts of research reports selected by the ERIC clearinghouses for reproduction and dissemination via the ERIC system. Listings include price and ordering information, in addition to standard bibliographic data, and the descriptors, or indexing terms, used to index the document. Detailed, multi-faceted subject index in each issue, cumulated semiannually and annually.

Royal Institute of International Affairs. Index to Periodical Articles, 1950–1964, in the Library of the Royal Institute. Boston: G. K. Hall & Co., 1964. 2 vols. AI3.R6 (169)

Publication in book form of a card index maintained at the Royal Institute. Selective indexing of about 200 periodicals. Arrangement follows the Library's classification scheme, which includes designations for regions and topics.

Schomburg Collection of Negro Literature and History. Dictionary Catalog. Boston: G. K. Hall & Co., 1962. Supplement 1967. Z881.N592S35 (169)

Holdings of this specialized research unit of the New York Public Library. The collection encompasses materials relating to all aspects of the history and culture of Negroes, everywhere in the world and in all periods of history; also works, regardless of subject, by Negro authors. The catalog lists books and other separate publications, and periodicals by the title of the journal only. There are occasional entries for materials of less than book length, such as papers comprising the proceedings of a conference, but not for most journal articles. Author, title, and subject entries are arranged in a single alphabetical sequence.

Social Science Abstracts; a comprehensive abstracting and indexing journal of the world's periodical literature in the social sciences. 1928–1932. New York: Social Science Abstracts, Inc. monthly. H1.S6 (149–150)

Abstracts of articles selected from about 4,000 journals published all over the world. Main fields covered were economics, political science, sociology, statistics, and history, with lesser coverage of cultural anthropology, psychology, and human geography. Classified arrangement with annual subject index. A cumulated subject index covering the entire span of the publication was also issued.

Social Sciences and Humanities Index. 1907 – . New York: H. W. Wilson & Co. quarterly. AI3.R49 (166)

Indexes about 200 English language periodicals, including scholarly journals in the social sciences and humanities and some general literary and political magazines aimed at an educated readership. Journals in psychology and education are not included. Unannotated entries are listed by subject and author in a single alphabetical sequence. Quarterly issues are cumulated annually.

Published 1907–1965 as International Index to Periodicals. Under the earlier title it included some foreign language periodicals.

Social Sciences Citation Index. 1973 – . Philadelphia: Institute for Scientific Information. 3 issues per year. (160)

Index to articles cited in about 1,000 journals, predominantly but not exclusively in English, in all fields of social science. Also includes a "Permuterm" subject index based on key words in article titles, and an index of institutional affiliations.

Social Work Abstracts. See Abstracts for Social Workers.

Sociological Abstracts. 1953 – . New York: American Sociological Association, Eastern Sociological Society, Midwest Sociological Society. 8 issues per year. HM1.S67 (153)

Comprehensive coverage of the world-wide sociological literature in all forms. Classified arrangement with author and subject indexes, cumulated annually. Supplementary issues contain abstracts of papers read at sociological conferences.

Universal Reference System: Political Science, Government and Public Policy Series. 1966 – . Princeton, N.J.: Princeton Information Technology. 10 vols., plus annual supplement. Z7161.A1U6 (158–160)

Selective abstracts of the political science literature, mainly English language, with highly detailed, multi-faceted indexes. See text for further explanation.

Writings on American History. 1906 – . Washington, D.C.: American Historical Association. Z1236.I331 (145–146)

Comprehensive listing of books and articles classified in regional and topical categories with place and personal name indexes. Usually gives bibliographic data only; occasional brief annotations to clarify meaning of a title.

Canada, West Indies, and Pacific Islands included in coverage until 1935; limited to United States history since 1935. Included references to reviews of books listed until 1940, when discontinued. A consolidated subject and author index covering volumes for 1902–1940 was published in 1956.

Publisher varies. Volumes for 1906–1908 published by the Macmillan Company with a subsidy from the American Historical Association. Since 1909 published by the American Historical Association as Part 2 of its Annual Report. Two earlier volumes preceded the series. A volume covering 1902 was compiled by Professor Ernest C. Richardson, librarian of Princeton University, and published by the University. A volume covering 1903 was compiled and published under the auspices of the Carnegie Institution. No volumes have been issued for 1904–05, and 1941–47.

Appendix H

Some Brief Notes on Technical Reports and Translations

BIBLIOGRAPHIES OF TECHNICAL REPORTS AND OTHER UNPUBLISHED LITERATURE

For the most part, the disciplinary bibliographic records in the social sciences confine their attentions to the writings appearing in the formal, established channels of book and journal publications. Except in education, there is little systematic attempt to provide for the dissemination and retrieval of materials that do not reach the formal channels. Such materials include research reports produced in mimeographed or other "near print" form and given limited distribution among people in contact with the author or institution producing the report, the texts of lectures or papers delivered orally at scientific meetings, and other unpublished manuscripts. These writings are on occasion cited in publications by authors who have had access to them, but they are not ordinarily accessible to the scholarly community at large.[1]

There is some difference of opinion among scholars as to whether such "unpublished papers" or "technical reports" ought to be considered part of "the literature" of a field and hence taken into account in the field's bibliographic arrangements. On the negative side, it is argued that the collective character of science, which is critical for the development and advancement of knowledge, depends on an open literature, fully and equally accessible to all participants in the scientific enterprise. It is further maintained that communication on any other basis circumvents the processes of editorial screening and selection that are built into the formal publication system, thereby diluting the quality of scientific communication while needlessly inflating its quantity. Opposing this is the view that valuable information should not be spurned on account of the form in which it appears, and that the formal publication channels are too slow, cumbersome, and crowded to keep pace with the current rate of scientific output.

The prevalance and importance of communication outside the formal publication channels varies from one field to another. It tends to be more characteristic of applied and mission-oriented research areas, where research is not infrequently carried on in association with operating agencies which have facilities for producing and distributing reports. In traditional academic disciplines, research is mainly university-based and alternatives to established journals and publishers as communications media are seldom available and hence seldom used.[2]

This situation is reflected in the diversity of bibliographic arrangements pertaining to unpublished and quasi-published communications. In education such materials have been institutionalized, under the ERIC program, as basic components of the communication structure of the discipline and have been accorded their own bibliographic record, Research in Education. Some of the mission-oriented bibliographies, or those with a pronounced leaning toward applied areas of social science, include these materials to some extent. Reports issued by various field agencies are listed in Poverty and Human Resources, for example, and P.A.I.S. lists a substantial number of reports and pamphlets issued outside the main publication channels. Some of the bibliographies of the disciplines may occasionally include such materials, but for the most part these works concentrate on books and journals.[3]

A United States government agency, the National Technical Information Service, operates a program for collecting, reproducing, and distributing the technical report literature of all fields. Most of its activities are in the area of the physical sciences and technology, but it also encompasses reports of social and behavioral science research conducted in government agencies, university-based research institutes, and comparable settings. The service publishes a semimonthly abstracting bibliography entitled Government Reports Announcements, with an accompanying set of indexes under the title Government Reports Index. This information has been published since 1946, under several different titles and with several variations in format.

A large producer of technical reports, in the social sciences as well as physical science and technology, is the Rand Corporation, an organization located in California that does a great deal of research under contract to the United States government. Rand studies in the social sciences touch on many topics, with emphasis on problems bearing on aspects of government policy, domestic and foreign. Nonclassified reports issued by the Rand Corporation are distributed through a network of subscribing libraries, and are listed in Selected Rand Abstracts (1963–), a quarterly bibliography.

A new system for dissemination of technical reports and limited-distribution papers in economics, called Economic Working Papers, was announced for inception in 1973 by Trans-Media Publishing Company of New York, in collaboration with Warwick University, England. The papers, expected to number about 1,000 per year, are to be issued on microfiche together with a quarterly Bibliography of Economic Working Papers in hard copy.

Doctoral dissertations are a special form of unpublished literature, and occupy a somewhat ambiguous status in the scientific communication system. They are generally regarded as contributions to knowledge and are not infrequently cited in publications. On the other hand, they are not usually considered among the components of a subject's literature (reviews of the literature, for example, typically do not recognize them) or included in the bibliographic records of a discipline. Some dissertations are ultimately published as monographs or, in much abbreviated form, as journal articles, but a very large number are not. About 250 universities—mostly American institutions—now participate in a system whereby dissertations are microfilmed by University Microfilms, a commercial enterprise, and made available for distribution in this form. A monthly bibliography, Dissertation Abstracts International, contains author-written abstracts of the dissertations. The abstracts are listed by discipline, with a few large subdivisions within disciplines, and there are indexes of subjects and authors in each issue, cumulated annually. Psychological Abstracts lists the psychology dissertations with references to Dissertation Abstracts International, so that the dissertations in that field are recorded and classified with the related literature, but this practice is not a general one among the disciplinary bibliographies.

TRANSLATIONS

References to publications in foreign languages are encountered frequently in scholarly bibliographies. In the majority of instances, a reader who does not know the language in which a work is written is simply without access to the publication, since only a very small proportion of the scholarly literature of any field is ever published in translation. Some works are translated, however, and the following is a brief account of some important sources of translations or of information about the availability of translations.

Translations of books are normally listed in the relevant subject bibliographies in the same manner as the original publications. In addition, UNESCO issues an annual bibliography of books published in translation, under the title Index Translationum. This is a list of the translated books published in each country, arranged, by country, in broad subject categories. There are also author indexes. The annual Index Translationum has been issued since 1949, and is a continuation of an earlier bibliography under the same title, which was issued quarterly from 1932 to 1940 by UNESCO's predecessor, the International Institute of Intellectual Cooperation.

The proportion of journal articles available in translation is even smaller than that of books. Of this small number, nearly all the translations into English are articles published originally in slavic or oriental languages. English translation of the periodical literature of Western Europe is exceedingly rare. The principal sources of translated journal articles are a group of periodicals consisting wholly of translations, and materials translated by the Joint Publications Research Service, a United States government agency.

International Arts and Sciences Press, a commercial publisher, issues a group of journals composed of articles translated from Soviet and Chinese periodicals in various fields.[4] Each of the translation journals covers a designated group of periodicals, but only a small portion of the original content, judged to be of interest to American scholars, is selected and published by the editors.

Soviet Geography: Review and Translation contains translations of selected articles from the leading geographical journals of the Soviet Union and the translated tables of contents of the journals. It is a publication of the American Geographical Society, was begun in 1960, and is issued ten times per year.

The Joint Publications Research Service (JPRS) is a federal agency established in 1957 to translate foreign materials as needed and requested by other government agencies. The portion of its output that is not classified for security reasons is available for general distribution. Much of the work of JPRS deals with physical science and technology. In subjects germane to the social sciences there is considerably more social data, in the form of newspaper reports, laws, political speeches, statistical reports and the like, than contributions to the social science literature as such, but scholarly books and articles are included to a limited extent. JPRS translations are distributed by the National Technical Information Service, and listed and indexed in the Service's Government Reports Index (see above, p. 190) and in the Monthly Catalog of United States Government Publications issued by the U.S. Superintendent of Documents. In addition, CCM Information Corporation, a commercial organization, issues microfilm sets of the JPRS translations with bibliographic indexes. These bibliographies provide more detailed breakdowns of the content and subject matter of the translated materials than is given in the government-issued lists.

FOOTNOTES

1. See above, Chapter 3, for more extended discussion of this matter.

2. In this regard, as in others, the social sciences mirror on a smaller scale the pattern of natural and physical science. The technical report is a widespread and burgeoning natural science phenomenon, but much more so in applied science and technology than in basic research.

3. In 1965, a group of sociologists at the University of Wisconsin at Milwaukee announced the formation of a Clearinghouse for Sociological Literature, which was to reproduce and distribute manuscripts submitted by authors on a fee and royalty basis. Abstracts of these papers were to be published in Sociological Abstracts.

4. The titles (which generally indicate the subject range) and starting dates are as follows: Chinese Economic Studies, 1967– ; Chinese Education, 1968– ; Chinese Law and Government, 1968– ; Chinese Studies in History and Philosophy, 1967– ; Chinese Studies in Sociology and Anthropology, 1968– ; Problems of Economics (translations from Soviet economic journals) 1958– ; Soviet Anthropology and Archeology, 1962– ; Soviet Education, 1958– ; Soviet Law and Government, 1962– ; Soviet Psychology, 1962– ; Soviet Review (translations from several fields in social science and the humanities) 1960– ; Soviet Sociology, 1962– ; Soviet Studies in World History, 1962– .

Comprehensive Recurrent Bibliographies: Summary

To the extent that all the publications comprising the literature of a field are recorded in systematic and permanent fashion, there is said to be "bibliographic control" of that literature. The foregoing has reviewed the institutions and practices that have been developed to effect bibliographic control over the social science literature, and has attempted to suggest some of the ways in which such control has and has not been achieved. The instrument of bibliographic control is preeminently the comprehensive, inclusive record organized to permit an idea or question to be traced through all its ramifications and connections in the literature. Irrespective of all the shortcomings of the existing tools, this is the ultimate goal of the comprehensive recurrent bibliographies, and, in most instances, this type of tool preempts and monopolizes the function of establishing bibliographic control in a discipline. That is, other types of bibliographies are not ordinarily intended to bring additional works into the record. Their goal is to present certain portions of the record in distinctive ways tailored to particular functions.

The bibliographies directed toward specialized functions and purposes may conveniently be divided into two major types: recurrent publications, which list new materials on a continuing basis, and one-time, retrospective bibliographies, which recapitulate selectively the literature of the past. These are the subjects of the two chapters following.

Chapter Eight

Selective Recurrent Bibliographies

CURRENT AWARENESS LISTS

The main function of current awareness lists is to aid scholars in "keeping up" with the literature by announcing the appearance of new publications likely to be of interest. Bibliographies of this type have some features in common with the comprehensive inventories discussed in the preceding section, notably issuance on a regular, periodic schedule and the listing of current materials. Beyond this, there are differences in scope and style that reflect differences in the purposes the bibliographies in the two groups are designed to serve. While there is no single pattern for a "current awareness" bibliography, any more than for a "comprehensive" bibliography, some characteristics commonly encountered in current awareness lists reflect the distinctive communications role of these works.

Since the main aim of current awareness bibliographies is to alert readers to publications apt to be of immediate interest, exhaustive coverage is not a major consideration. Some of the current awareness bibliographies are deliberately selective, attempting to screen the current output and list the works of more than routine significance. Others are more inclusive. However, all are oriented more toward announcement of the current literature than toward creation of a permanent archival record.[1]

Emphasis on current use is reflected also in the organization of the bibliographies. Rapid listing of new publications and frequent appearance of the list are more important than systematic organization and detailed indexing. The current awareness lists tend to use only relatively rudimentary classification and indexing systems, or none. They are designed to be scanned, in their entirety or in large sections, rather than consulted for specifically defined items. However, a search for literature on a particular topic, begun in the more systematically ordered comprehensive inventories, can be carried forward to the most recent materials by means of the current awareness lists, which may be especially useful in fields where the comprehensive tools are infrequent and subject to long delays.

Announcement of the current literature is a traditional function of journals. As the regularly issued and widely distributed instruments of communication in a field, journals are a major medium for dissemination of current news, including news of new publications. Reviewing of books is a major activity along these lines, and some journals supplement the reviews with more extensive lists of books and articles. The current bibliographies published in journals range in elaborateness from simple lists of titles to quite extensive classified and annotated compilations, but the basic idea is to provide an overview of the current output so as to enable readers of the journal to spot writings likely to be of interest. There has been some tendency lately for journals to abandon this feature[2] probably because a rapidly growing volume of literature coupled with increased awareness of the complexity of scholarly information requirements has led to the conclusion that a useful current awareness service is too large an undertaking to be carried on as a sideline by a publication primarily engaged in other activities. Generally speaking, current bibliographies tend to be found in journals devoted to rather narrowly specialized fields, where the bibliography can be limited to a more restricted range of literature, or in the journals of interdisciplinary or applied areas whose range is not adequately reflected by bibliographies in a traditional, disciplinary focus.

The American Historical Review is a conspicuous exception to the above generalization. Each issue of this journal contains, in addition to an unusually large number of book reviews, an extensive list of current books and articles. The bibliography embraces the full range of historical scholarship, and is arranged by region with chronological and topical subdivisions. Similarly comprehensive in its range of subject matter is the current bibliography published in Current Anthropology. This has had several variations in format and coverage.

Another journal devoted to a broad subject area that includes a current bibliography is the interdisciplinary American Behavioral Scientist. However, its annotated list of "New Studies," appearing in each issue, emphasizes publications utilizing a distinctly empirical or "behavioral" approach. In this way, the bibliography is somewhat specialized in scope, although it covers a wide subject range. As mentioned earlier, the listings are cumulated annually and reissued in separate volumes under the title Recent Publications in the Social and Behavioral Sciences.

Other journals publishing bibliographies of the current literature are, for the most part, devoted to narrower fields. Substantial lists of current publications are to be found in each issue of Journal of American History, International Review of Administrative Sciences, International Organization, Africa, Middle East Journal, and Integrated Education. An extensive, classified list of journal articles on mass communication is published in each issue of Journalism Quarterly.

Foreign Affairs includes in each issue an extensive, classified list, with brief annotations, of current books in international relations. The listings include studies of international relations theory and methodology, but works on recent history and the diplomacy and foreign policies of specific countries tend to predominate. Many of these are descriptive historical narratives or general discussions of policy, rather than works having a specifically scientific orientation. Since its inception in 1919 the list has been cumulated at approximately ten-year intervals and reissued under the title Foreign Affairs Bibliography,[3] a series constituting a comprehensive and well-organized list of book publication in this field during the past fifty years.

The abstracting journals discussed in the preceding section are designed largely to function as tools for current awareness as well as to create a permanent record for use over the long term. Arrangement of the abstracts in a classification that follows the pattern of research specialization in the discipline, as is typically done, facilitates the scanning of each issue's listings in the area of the reader's main interests, and many scholars regularly examine their field's abstracting bibliography in this fashion. Abstracting journals that publish substantive articles as well as bibliographic lists, such as Journal of Economic Literature, Population Index, and Poverty and Human Resources, are clearly meant to be read as well as consulted.

Some bibliographies have as their major focus the announcement of current literature. In recent years, the growth in the volume of literature being produced, elimination of current bibliographies from journals, and development of computerized techniques for rapid compilation of bibliographic listings have all acted to generate interest in this type of tool. Current awareness bibliographies generally employ either of two basic formats. Some are classified lists, usually annotated, consisting of items specifically selected for their pertinence to the scope of the bibliography. Others report, without selection or classification, the contents of current journals in a field. The latter approach may seem cumbersome, but the relative simplicity with which such lists can be prepared makes possible very rapid coverage of a broad range of literature.

A function very close to that of the current awareness bibliographies is performed by the lists of new acquisitions compiled and distributed by some libraries. The acquisitions list of a large and specialized collection generally affords a good overview of the current literature of the field.

Current awareness bibliographies in the social sciences are listed and described in Appendix I. The list is not necessarily complete, but it attempts to cover the works of this type which are more or less widely available in American libraries. In addition, the following compilations identify current bibliographies for many subjects: Serial Bibliographies in the Humanities and Social Sciences, compiled by Richard A. Gray,[4] and Index Bibliographicus, published by the International Federation for Documentation.[5] Serial Bibliographies. . . lists both separately issued bibliographies and those published in journals, but journal bibliographies consisting only of book reviews are not included. The compilation includes both ongoing bibliographies and those no longer published. Index Bibliographicus is limited to current publications, but includes book review sections of journals as well as bibliographies more strictly defined. Both lists are world-wide in scope and are arranged by subject, and both provide such information as frequency, date of inception, number of listings per annum, and extent of annotation, though the Gray work is more detailed in this regard.

Current awareness lists tailored to the interests of individual scholars are a recent innovation which is made possible by computers. The processes involved in production of such personalized bibliographies are referred to generally as SDI (Selective Dissemination of Information) systems. There are many such systems and each may possess certain unique characteristics, but basically they involve the recurrent feeding into a computer of bibliographic data and subject descriptors for a large body of literature. Each participant in the system constructs an "interest profile" based on the descriptors used to tag the documents entering the system. The profiles are stored by the computer, which is then able to produce, as often as desired, bibliographies consisting of the items corresponding to each user's expressed needs and interests.

Many research institutions supply SDI services to their staffs, and the Institute for Scientific Information, a private organization located in Philadelphia, offers such a service on a subscription basis for many fields of physical and behavioral science. Libraries may occasionally provide such services to readers (the Congressional Research Service of the Library of Congress has developed an SDI system for the members and staff of Congress) but thus far they are confined to rather special situations. Most library users are limited to the printed bibliographic apparatus, and SDI systems are mentioned here as a matter of general interest but not as an available retrieval tool.

BOOK REVIEWS

Book reviews are a form of "current awareness" communication, since they are always intended to announce the existence of new books as well as, in some degree, to evaluate them. From this point of view, the book review sections of journals are a running record of a significant portion of the current literature, and similar in function to annotated current bibliographies.

Reviews have an additional function, of course, as vehicles of criticism and assessment, but their operation in this regard is quite variable. An essential difference between reviews and annotations, apart from the fact that the latter tend to be briefer and nonevaluative, is that the annotation ordinarily sticks quite closely to the content of the work being described while the review is likely to introduce a broader frame of reference encompassing, at least by implication, such matters as the over-all state of knowledge of the subject, other works in the field, and the personal viewpoint of the reviewer. It is difficult to generalize, however. Reviews in scholarly journals are ordinarily written at the invitation of the editor of the journal, but there are usually no specifications given the reviewer concerning the approach to be used or points to be covered. Some reviews may relate the book to comparable works or assess its contribution to the progressive cumulation of knowledge in its field. Others may discuss the book strictly in its own terms, focusing on its intrinsic merits and shortcomings. The reviewer's discussion and evaluation may center on any aspect of the work—its data, methodology, theoretical orientation, or policy implications—or the reviewer may ignore all these and similar dimensions and use the review as an occasion for presenting some views or ideas of his own on the book's subject. Thus, about all that can be said about book reviews as a source of information about a book is that they are likely to provide some information. The nature of the information, or what the reader can learn about a book by reading a review, really cannot be specified.

Most academic journals include book reviews, often in sufficient number to provide a good overview of the current book literature of the field. Some journals publish mainly reviews of single books. Others employ a style in which several related works are discussed together in a "review essay." The latter form tends to lend itself to consideration of the book as a contribution to a larger body of literature and encourages assessment of its significance in that context. However, the "review essay" should not be confused with review articles or "reviews of the literature" (see Chapter 4) since the "review essay" is basically a book review concentrating on a specific group of books, rather than an over-all examination of the literature relating to a problem or area of research.

The journal Current Anthropology employs an unusual reviewing system. As many as twenty scholars may be asked to review a given book, and the multiple reviews appear together with a statement by the author of his aims with regard to the book and his response to the reviewers' comments. This arrangement represents an attempt to assess new contributions in the context of existing knowledge in a much more deliberate way than is characteristic of reviewing publications generally. However, only a small number of books—no more than one per issue—is covered in this way.

Contemporary Psychology[6] is a periodical consisting entirely of book reviews, and it is the main book-reviewing medium in that field. Directly comparable is Contemporary Sociology,[7] devoted to reviews of sociological books. Educational Studies[8] contains reviews of books in the "foundations of education"; that is, such areas of basic theory as the history and philosophy of education, and educational psychology. American Anthropologist, described in Appendix B, devotes alternate issues to book reviews and Journal of Economic Literature, noted in Appendix G, contains reviews of major books in addition to its more extensive abstracting of the current literature. A new book reviewing journal, Reviews in American History[9] has been announced for publication beginning in 1973. Yearbook of World Affairs, published in London by the Institute of World Affairs, includes essays describing and commenting on the major books published during the year on subjects pertaining to international affairs. Brief reviews of scholarly books in all fields appear in the journal Choice. This publication is issued by the American Library Association as a book selection aid for librarians, but it can be of interest to a wider audience for its concise description and evaluation of a large number of current books.

Lists of the main book review sources in each social science discipline, with indication of the number of reviews each publishes annually, may be found in Carl M. White's Sources of Information in the Social Sciences.[10] Information of a similar nature is given in Index Bibliographicus, and most periodicals directories (see Appendix K) indicate in their listings whether the journal includes book reviews.

A common literature-searching problem involving book reviews is location of a review of a specific book. While finding a review may present some difficulty, particularly in view of the fact that a large number of books are never reviewed anywhere, a still more difficult, but more significant question is whether the review should be sought at all: that is, whether a book review is likely to provide the information about the book the reader needs. Reference has already been made to the variability and unpredictability of the content and emphasis of book reviews. Another important consideration is that the reviewer's perspective is inevitably time bound. The aspects of the book that the reviewer sees as most worthy of discussion and the criteria by which the work's merits and defects are assessed are all grounded in the outlook and state of knowledge in the field at the time of the book's publication. These do not remain constant, and, in consequence, a review of a book published a decade or more earlier may tell the reader very little about the book's current significance. The literature of any field can yield numerous examples of book reviews which offer no hint of the impact the book was later to have.[11] This point applies particularly to significant works that continue to be considered and referred to for many years following their first appearance, but it is true to a greater or lesser extent of all books and reviews. A recent handbook article, history, or other cumulating publication may provide less extensive consideration of the specific book, but mention of the work in a comparative and more or less up-to-date discussion of the topic to which it contributes may be more useful to the reader than an obsolete review in which the book stands divorced from its current context.

Subject to this caveat, some sources that aid in the identification of book reviews may be noted. Reference was made earlier to the citation of book reviews in several of the social science literature inventories: International Bibliography of Historical Sciences and the four bibliographies in UNESCO's "International Bibliography of the Social Sciences" series. Writings on American History cited reviews until 1940 and then discontinued the practice. Index to Periodical Articles By and About Negroes lists book reviews in the periodicals that it indexes.

Mental Health Book Review Index[12] locates reviews of books in the behavioral sciences appearing in some 200 English-language scholarly journals. The periodicals covered are mainly in the fields of psychology and psychiatry, but a number of sociological and anthropological journals are also included. Book Review Digest indexes selected reviews from selected periodicals.[13] The latter are mainly popular magazines and librarians' reviewing media, but a few academic journals are included. Book Review Index[14] indexes reviews in a wide range of periodicals, including a substantial number of scholarly journals in all fields of the social sciences and humanities. Book Review Index to Social Science Periodicials[15] is an annual listing of reviews in about 400 journals.

Discussions of books or the work of particular writers are sometimes published as chapters in book-length anthologies and collections. Materials in this form are, as noted earlier in Chapter 7, listed in Essay and General Literature Index, and this index may be a particularly fruitful source of discussions of books that have become classics or landmarks in their fields.

In the event that a review of the book in question cannot be located through an index, the remaining possibility is to examine directly the journals publishing reviews in the subject area of the book, for the year of its publication and at least the year following, since reviews are sometimes slow to appear.

FOOTNOTES

1. In a few instances, current awareness lists are periodically cumulated and reissued to form permanent records. Examples are Recent Publications in the Social and Behavioral Sciences (see Appendix G), and Foreign Affairs Bibliography, described below.

2. The Journal of Modern History dropped its current bibliography in 1960; the Journal of Negro Education in 1964. Coverage of articles and documents was eliminated from the bibliographic section of American Political Science Review in 1967, leaving only book reviews. The American Economic Review dropped the listing of articles in 1966, and in 1969 transferred all its bibliographic functions to the Journal of Economic Literature.

3. Foreign Affairs Bibliography; a Selected and Annotated List of Books on International Affairs. 1919–32; 1932–42; 1942–52; 1952–62. (N. Y. Council on Foreign Relations, 1933–64.) Z6463.F73.

4. Ann Arbor, Mich.: Pierian Press, 1969. Z1002.G814

5. 4th ed., Geneva, 1964. Z1002.I38

6. Washington, D.C.: American Psychological Association, 1956– monthly. BF1.C53

7. Albany, N. Y.: American Sociological Association. 1972– . bimonthly. HM1.C65

8. Charlottesville, Va.: American Educational Studies Association, 1970– . quarterly. L11.E463

9. Westport, Conn., Redgrave Information Resources Corp.

10. Totowa, N. J., Bedminister Press, 1964. Further described in Appendix K.

11. Two notable examples are Arthur Bentley's The Process of Government (1908) and Margaret Mead's Coming of Age in Samoa (1928). Both these books are now regarded as very significant contributions, but for reasons not apparent to reviewers at the time they were published. See James Garner's note on the Bentley work in American Political Science Review 2 (May 1908): 457, and Robert Redfield's review of Mead in American Journal of Sociology, 34 (January 1929): 729.

12. New York: Council on Research in Bibliography, Inc. 1965– . annual. Z6664.N5M49

13. New York: H. W. Wilson Co., 1905– . quarterly. Z1219.C95 The selection is based on the number of reviews of a given book appearing in the periodicals covered by the Digest, so that the more widely noted books are the ones for which the reviews are listed.

14. Detroit: Gale Research Co., 1965– . bimonthly. Z1035.A1B6

15. Ann Arbor, Mich.: Pierian Press, 1970– .

Appendix I

Selected Current Awareness
Bibliographies

ABC POL SCI (Advance Bibliography of Contents: Political Science and Government) Santa Barbara, Calif.: American Bibliographic Center-Clio Press. Eight issues per year. Z7161.A214

Lists the contents of about 250 American and foreign political science journals. There is very little duplication of the coverage of Current Contents (below). An author index appears in each issue and is cumulated semiannually, and there is an annual subject index. The publisher offers an article copying service.

CLASS (Current Literature Awareness Service Series): Reading. New York: CCM Information Corp. eight issues per year.

First of a projected group of current awareness bibliographies in specialized fields of education to be issued under the ERIC program (see above, pp. 156–157). CLASS:Reading contains abstracts of journal articles and ERIC reports, with author and subject indexes. There are summaries of highlights of current developments and lists of new reading research projects funded by the Office of Education. The abstracts use copy prepared for Research in Education and Current Index to Journals in Education, and CLASS thus duplicates material also published elsewhere, but uses a framework designed to pinpoint as rapidly as possible materials pertinent to a circumscribed research area.

Contents of Recent Economic Journals. London: United Kingdom Department of Trade and Industry. weekly.

Reports contents of about 200 journals encompassing all fields of theoretical and applied economics. Most of the publications covered are English, American, and Western European.

Current Bibliographical Information. United Nations: Dag Hammarskjold Library. semimonthly.

Lists articles on subjects relating to the activities and interests of the United Nations selected from about 500 journals published all over the world, plus books, government documents, etc. Replaces an earlier publication, Current Issues: a Selective Bibliography on Subjects of Concern to the United Nations.

A Current Bibliography on African Affairs. Washington, D.C.: African Bibliographic Center. monthly.

Classified list of current books and articles in two sections, topical and geographical. In addition to the bibliography, each issue contains brief reviews of a few books of particular significance, a list of forthcoming books, an article on some aspect of the literature of African studies, and an author index.

Current Contents: Behavioral, Social and Educational Sciences. Philadelphia: Institute for Scientific Information. weekly.

"Current Contents" is the over-all title of a group of bibliographic journals covering a large number of subject areas and consisting of the reproduced tables of contents of current periodicals. The title above is the member of the group pertinent to the social sciences. It covers about 1,000 journals (all are not in each weekly issue, of course) mostly in English but including some foreign titles. The publisher also offers a reprint service that supplies, on request and for a fee, copies of the articles listed.

Current Geographical Publications. New York: American Geographical Society. monthly.   Z6009.Z47

Additions to the Research Catalogue of the American Geographical Society library. (See Appendix G for description of the Research Catalogue). The listings include books, periodical articles, maps, and any miscellaneous materials added to the catalog. The bibliography is in two sections, general and regional, with additional subject designations for each entry indicated by a system of code numbers.

Economics Selections: an International Bibliography. Series I: New Books in Economics. Pittsburgh: Department of Economics and University Libraries, University of Pittsburgh. quarterly.   Z7164.E2E25

Classified list, with brief descriptive and critical annotations of each title and an indication of its suitability for library purchase. Books in English are emphasized, with foreign works of special interest or significance also included. Formerly published as Economics Library Selections and International Economics Selections Bibliography. (Series II: Lists in Special Fields is a group of retrospective bibliographies and is described in Appendix J.)

International Bureau of Education Bulletin. Geneva. quarterly.   L10.I72

Lists significant new books in education, encompassing works in all European languages and all subdivisions of the education literature. The listings are annotated and classified by subject. The International Bureau of Education is an affiliate of UNESCO.

Personnel Management Abstracts. Ann Arbor, Mich.: Bureau of Industrial Relations and Graduate School of Business Administration, University of Michigan. quarterly.   HF5549.P452

A service designed "for the conscientious manager who frankly doesn't have enough time to read as much as he should" (editorial statement in each issue), and thus oriented chiefly toward practice in the personnel field, but including many items pertinent to scholarly investigation in areas such as industrial sociology and labor economics. The abstracts represent books and selected articles from about 150 periodicals, and are listed in broad subject categories. A more extensive list of articles is presented without abstracts, arranged by author, title, and subject.

Chapter Nine

Retrospective Bibliographies[1]

Retrospective bibliographies are one-time publications bringing together a body of literature in terms of some common element such as subject matter. In contrast to the recurrent bibliographies, which record the output of a stated time period, retrospective works ordinarily have no chronological limitations and encompass whatever time span is appropriate to the subject or purpose of the bibliography. To place these tools in the over-all context of the system of scholarly communication, it is helpful to recall some observations made earlier concerning recurrent bibliographies.

It was pointed out in Chapter 7 that the tool best suited to the creation and maintenance of a basic bibliographic record in a field of study is the comprehensive recurrent bibliography. A work of this type records the literature pertinent to the interests of the field as the publications are issued, and in this way forms a permanent, continually updated inventory. Current awareness lists, described in the preceding chapter, strengthen one aspect of the basic record by providing rapid announcement of new publications. Against this background, the retrospective bibliography may be seen as carrying out still another kind of intention; that of looking over the literature of the past from the perspective of the present.

The idea or purpose underlying a retrospective bibliography may be anything the compiler sees as useful, but two major and fairly distinctive themes tend to characterize these works. Some retrospective bibliographies are intended primarily to open new routes to the literature. They list materials omitted by the ongoing bibliographic tools, or present the literature in relation to an idea or point of view which is not otherwise accessible. Bibliographies of this kind will be referred to here as "research-oriented" because their principal orientation is toward the process of creating new knowledge.

That is, these bibliographies assemble the literature mainly to serve as a springboard for further exploration, and attempt by means of reexamination and reconsideration of the writings of the past to stimulate new insights and accomplishments.

Another group of retrospective bibliographies is based on a different rationale. The principal aim of these works is to summarize what is already known, rather than to point the way to creation of new knowledge. This is done by identifying the literature that best conveys certain prevailing ideas and viewpoints and presenting an evaluated selection, chosen on the basis of quality, importance, suitability for introductory study, or some similar factor. Works of this type are here termed "didactic" bibliographies because their primary intention is to teach. They are designed to aid less knowledgeable readers to become familiar with what others already know, by offering guidance in the selection of appropriate readings from the total range of a subject's literature.

The distinction between "research-oriented" and "didactic" resembles one made earlier in connection with the cumulating components of the substantive literature. It was pointed out in Chapter 6 that such publications as review journals and handbooks are typically "research-oriented" summaries of a subject, in that their systematic accounts of the work of the past are directed toward solidifying the foundations of subsequent explorations. In contrast, publications such as textbooks, collections of readings, and encyclopedias may be said to employ a "didactic" approach, directed toward summary and systematization of an area of knowledge for readers who are not direct participants in the field's research effort. At a rather rough level of comparison, the various forms of cumulating publications within the two broad categories may be said to have approximate bibliographic counterparts. That is, forms of retrospective bibliography identify the literature with about the same degree of detail or selectivity as the various cumulating publications bring to bear on the content of the subject. This parallel underscores once again the idea that literature and bibliography are two faces of a single coin, which is scientific communication.

This conception of the purpose and functioning of a retrospective bibliographies may be clarified by consideration of some concrete examples. In the following account, research-oriented bibliographies, relatively detailed and inclusive presentations, are considered first, followed by the didactic tools that represent, on the whole, a higher and more generalized level of summary. The works discussed have been selected mainly as examples of certain bibliographic styles and characteristics, which means that many useful bibliographies are not mentioned, and it should not be assumed that the bibliographies cited are necessarily more significant than others that are not. In some instances there is rather detailed consideration and extensive quotation of compilers' statements of their intentions, or of the circumstances that stimulated preparation of the bibliography. This is intended to illustrate some of the factors underlying bibliographic work, but not to suggest that the ideas are unique or especially significant in the case of the particular bibliography under consideration. Sources which may be used to locate additional bibliographies are mentioned at the conclusion of the discussion.

RESEARCH-ORIENTED BIBLIOGRAPHIES

One way in which a retrospective bibliography may open a new avenue of access to the literature is by listing materials not covered, or inadequately covered, by an ongoing bibliographic record. This statement requires further comment, since it contradicts, at least in part, the fundamental idea that retrospective bibliographies are not ordinarily a basic bibliographic record but rather a reworking, for special purposes, of a record created mainly by recurrent tools. The explanation lies, of course, in the late and relatively weak development of continuing bibliographic inventories in many of the social science disciplines.[2] In the absence of ongoing records, a number of retrospective bibliographies have been compiled for the purpose of recording, as inclusively as possible, the literature pertinent to various fields of study. Although works of this kind can probably be expected to decrease in number and importance as comprehensive recurrent bibliographies in the social sciences are developed and improved, at present they sometimes constitute significant searching tools. These are the retrospective tools closest in basic idea and function to the recurrent bibliographies, and as such they offer a useful and interesting contrast to the other uses of the retrospective format, to be considered further on.

An important example of retrospective compilation of a basic bibliographic record is Ethnographic Bibliography of North America, by George P. Murdock, (1960),[3] an inclusive inventory of the anthropological literature relating to North American culture. Professor Murdock began to keep records of ethnographic publications in the 1930s when regular, institutionalized arrangements for doing this did not exist and there was no comprehensive, ongoing bibliography of the literature of anthropology. His work was the basis for successive editions of the Ethnographic Bibliography of North America (1941, 1953, 1960) and for several other regional ethnographic bibliographies published by the Human Relations Area Files.[4] Since 1955, the International Bibliography of Social and Cultural Anthropology has been issued as a continuing record of ethnographic publications, but the retrospective bibliographies described here cover the literature of each region more thoroughly than the international bibliography and, of course, encompass older publications as well as more recent works. Thus they identify otherwise inaccessible writings and compensate to some extent for the deficiencies of the recurrent bibliographic record in anthropology, but their basic task is the same as that of the recurrent literature inventories.

Several bibliographies relating to the Negro may likewise be cited as examples of retrospective inventories of fields in which records of the literature have not been maintained on a continuing basis. A Bibliography of the Negro in Africa and America, compiled by Monroe N. Work (1928) draws together the publications pertaining to its topic that the compiler judged to be of interest for scholarly purposes. Race and Region, compiled by Edgar T. and Alma Macy Thompson (1949) is directed toward a similar end. It has a narrower scope than Work's bibliography, focusing on interracial relations in the United States, but the subject is defined broadly enough to encompass many aspects of Negro life in America, and the bibliography thus continues Work's listings, at least in part. For more recent years, Elizabeth W. Miller's and Mary L. Fisher's The Negro in America: A Bibliography (2d ed., 1970) lists a very comprehensive array of materials dealing with all aspects of its topic. This bibliography emphasizes the period following the 1954 Supreme Court decision on school segregation, but earlier publications of major significance are also included.

Some retrospective bibliographies that have appeared in successive editions or have been recurrently updated by supplements may perhaps be regarded as occupying a borderline status between the recurrent and retrospective categories. An example is the series entitled Metropolitan Communities: A Bibliography with Special Emphasis upon Government and Politics. This consists of an initial volume covering the literature from 1925 to 1955, updated by supplements for 1955-57, 1958-64, and 1965-67. The bibliography encompasses books and articles from the standard literature of such fields as public administration, local politics, and municipal finance, as well as what is described as "soft cover, fugitive material";[5] that is, separately published research reports and compilations of data. Metropolitan Communities affords more extensive coverage of the literature of urban government than Public Affairs Information Service Bulletin, its closest counterpart among the recurrent tools, and its organization is geared to a specific range of interests in a way not usually achieved by the more general tools. (For example, a section headed "Socio-economic Background" lists materials on an array of otherwise rather disparate topics such as race relations, migration, location of industry.) In this regard Metropolitan Communities somewhat resembles the "mission-oriented" recurrent bibliographies. (See pp. 162–163.)

The foregoing are examples of technically "retrospective" bibliographies since they are not issued recurrently on a predetermined schedule, but the functions they are designed to perform do not particularly involve a retrospective orientation and could probably be carried out more effectively on a recurrent basis if the needed resources were available. In the case of many retrospective bibliographies, however, the quality of retrospectiveness, of looking back over the literature of the past from the vantage point of a particular time or a particular stage in the development of knowledge, is central to the aims of the bibliography. The purpose of these works is not simply to record the existence of publications, so as to compensate for the absence of a recurrent inventory, but to perform another kind of identifying function—one which specifically makes use of the distinctive time perspective afforded by the retrospective approach.

Ordinarily the aim is to present the literature in some sort of interpretive framework: to bring together a body of writings in relation to a specific problem or set of ideas, or to assess the literature of the past from the point of view of current criteria and concerns. Since looking backward is intrinsic to such efforts, the resulting bibliographies are necessarily and purposefully retrospective, in contrast to works such as those just described which were compiled retrospectively only because a basic continuing inventory was not created earlier. The more purposefully retrospective bibliographies may be said to have a dual function. They are not only tools for identification of the literature, but also instruments for its summary, assessment, and interpretation. The emphasis placed on each aspect of the dual role varies from one bibliography to another, and the qualities of interpretation and assessment are often implied, rather than overtly stated. However, in viewing retrospective bibliographies overall, a number of ways in which these works serve purposes of explanation, as well as identification and location, may be seen.

Retrospective bibliographies are sometimes compiled as inventories of the literature relevant to subjects that have not been generally regarded as disciplines or distinct research areas but that, in the judgment of the bibliography's compiler, have sufficient interest to benefit from an over-all survey of the literature. This is often the case with regard to subjects that have been pursued independently in several disciplines. In such instances, the bibliography may serve as a vehicle for illuminating the common concerns and points of contact among the various fields, and the possibilities for cross-fertilization and continued research across disciplinary lines. An example is International Bibliography of Research in Marriage and the Family 1900–1964, by Joan Aldous and Reuben Hill (1966). This is an inclusive inventory of research conducted in fields such as sociology, clinical psychology, anthropology, and psychiatry, focused on a wide variety of subjects in which some aspect of marriage or the family figured. The compilers note that the topic is one that is investigated in different contexts and from different points of view by researchers in the different disciplines and points out that "the Bibliography should make it less difficult for the interested person to surmount interdisciplinary barriers and gain a broader perspective on existing knowledge of the family."[6] It was observed earlier that an area of study attracting the efforts of scholars from several disciplines may in time develop a distinctive identity and establish a continuing record of its literature, as in the case, for example, of Child Development Abstracts.[7] A retrospective inventory such as International Bibliography of Research in Marriage and the Family is a way of laying the groundwork for further development of the field by bringing its diverse streams into contact with each other.

In somewhat similar fashion, a retrospective bibliography may be designed to define and organize an emerging area of research, in which the literature is not adequately delineated by recurrent bibliographies because the dimensions of the subject are not yet clearly recognized. An example is A Bibliographic Guide to Population Geography by Wilber A. Zelinsky, (1962). The compiler notes that "because it is one of the youngest of the geographic specialities, the contents, functions, and limits of population geography have not yet become crystallized in theory or practice."[8]   The bibliography's purpose is to identify and organize the pertinent literature in a way that reflects the particular approach of this field, distinguishing it from related or adjacent areas such as demography or urban geography, and in this way helping create a foundation for investigation and analysis centered on the distinctive outlook and concepts of population geography.

The use of retrospective bibliographies as a means to examine and assess the potentialities of an emerging research area is well illustrated by a group of bibliographies in the field of propaganda and mass communication research. Propaganda and Promotional Activities by Harold D. Lasswell, Ralph D. Casey, and Bruce Lannes Smith was the first, published in 1935 as an attempt to bring together the publications pertinent to what was, at the time, a newly emerging area of study. A major aim of the bibliography's compilers, and of its sponsor, the Social Science Research Council, was to stimulate empirical and analytic study of propaganda, in place of the descriptive and polemical approaches, which largely characterized writing on the subject. To this end, the bibliography attempted to identify writing in which "the categories used had promise of being made operational" and in which "authors showed familiarity with empirical work."[9] The listings were organized according to a rigorously logical scheme designed "to outline the entire field of propaganda study" and "to illustrate the potentialities. . .for the development of greater conceptual soundness and methodological skill."[10] Thus, for example, the sections devoted to the theoretical base of the subject encompass not only analyses of propaganda as such, but also "theories of closely related methods of collective management," ranging from physical coercion and bribery to diplomatic negotiation, and "theories of the general patterns of collective response," covering topics such as myths, mass behavior, and public opinion. A section devoted to "the symbols and practices of which propaganda makes use or to which it adapts itself" includes studies of educational systems as "symbols of institutions" engaged in inculcating loyalty to the established order, and studies of mass movements as "systems of symbolic protest." In this way, the bibliography not only identified relevant materials for the propaganda researcher; it attempted to show how the subject might be studied by pointing out the categories and relationships which seemed amenable to scientific investigation.

Propaganda and Promotional Activities was followed at roughly ten-year intervals by two subsequent compilations, each listing the literature since the previous bibliography and examining, by means of review essays, the developing character of the field. These works were Propaganda, Communication and Public Opinion by Bruce Lannes Smith, Harold D. Lasswell and Ralph D. Casey, (1946) and International Communication and Political Opinion by Bruce Lannes Smith and Chitra M. Smith (1956). The latter narrowed the scope somewhat, but its basic frame of reference is much the same as that of the earlier works, and it identifies itself as a successor to them.

As efforts to take stock of the accumulating literature of a research area and direct attention to significant trends and issues, these bibliographies have much in common with descriptive reviews of the literature.[11] The bibliographic format tends to place more emphasis on extensive listing and detailed classification of the literature than is characteristic of reviews, and generally offers less in the way of discussion and comment, but the two approaches to summary of a subject's literature are not dissimilar in their basic intentions.

In International Communication and Public Opinion, the third bibliography in the propaganda series, the original emphasis on promoting the development of the field along scientific lines is less evident, and the bibliography is presented largely as an enumeration of the literature rather than a device for stocktaking and assessment. Possibly this reflected a view that, as the field was no longer in an early, formative stage, its prevailing patterns of analysis were unlikely to be meaningfully influenced by the bibliography. The compiler wrote:

> . . .(R)elevant analytic categories often have not been adopted in spite of their operational usefulness because unfortunately writers in the field have tended to ignore them. For example, "Elites", "Peasantry", "Urban Middle Class" would be desirable differentiations under the general heading of "Audience Characteristics"; we have contented ourselves with primarily geographic differentiations because in the main the available body of writing follows these lines. The temptation to introduce a more analytic structure was thus resisted, on the assumption that the function of this bibliography is to serve as a tool rather than to teach a lesson.[12]

An almost directly opposing view, stressing the capacity of a bibliography "to teach a lesson" while serving as a tool, is put forward by Karl Deutsch and Richard Merritt in Nationalism and National Development: An Interdisciplinary Bibliography, (1970). The subject of this work is not a new area of study—the bibliography updates one published in 1956, which was itself a successor to a 1935 publication[13]—but it is one regarded as intrinsically beyond the range of any single discipline. The introduction contains an unusually explicit statement of the relation between the particular approach to the subject that the compilers seek to advance and the selection and organization of materials for the bibliography, and on this ground is of sufficient interest here to quote at length.

> The organizing principle of this bibliography. . .is the point of view of the unity of science. This viewpoint stems, not from the preconceived notions of the authors, but rather from the experience of conducting research on problems of nationalism and nationality. In this research it very soon became apparent that no single scientific discipline and no single branch of humanistic scholarship was sufficient to deal with such problems. The analytical social sciences seemed shallow without the large processes and long series of data that are recorded by history. Yet history seemed vague or chaotic without the help of the more analytic disciplines. All the social sciences, on occasion, required specific data, or even general answers, from various behavioral sciences—in particular the theory of communication and control—and from such special disciplines as social linguistics, human geography, and economics. Moreover, we believe that quantitative data and various models and methods of mathematical analysis can be and should be applied to the study of nationalism.
>
> Accordingly, the bibliography is broadly inclusive across many disciplines. In listing items in, say, sociology, psychology, or statistical method, we have included not only those showing how a method or concept *has been* applied to the analysis of nationalism. We have also listed items that seemed to us to contain potentially important concepts or methods that *could be* so applied. The bibliography offers, therefore, not only a survey but a provocation. In this regard it serves a double purpose. On the one hand, it is a tool for gathering descriptive materials on nationalism in the form of comparative studies, as well as of historical studies and of the analysis of particular cases, for most of the countries and regions of the world. It also offers, on the other hand, a tentative survey of tools and methods for such research that seems to us possible and worth doing in the future, together with items containing collections or analysis of relevant quantitative data.[14]

Many retrospective bibliographies focus on relatively specific topics, such as federalism or political elites, in contrast to the more broadly gauged "fields" or "research areas" encompassed by the works discussed above. It was earlier observed that distinctions between "narrow" and "broad" subjects are relative, and dependent more on the way research on a topic has developed than on qualities intrinsic to the subject itself.[15] Accordingly, retrospective bibliographies devoted to "specific topics" and "general fields" have similar characteristics and there are a number of direct parallels between the two groups. The essential aim of works of either type is to identify and organize the literature in terms of a perspective not otherwise available through bibliographic tools. However, subjects of the more narrowly gauged bibliographies tend to be topics of current interest that are not necessarily seen as major areas of research specialization over the long term. The range of such topics is wide and diverse, and not readily defined, but a few general types or categories are rather frequently encountered.

A number of retrospective bibliographies deal with topics pertinent to current public issues, such as intergovernmental relations, religion in public schools, poverty, or the "culturally disadvantaged."[16] These bibliographies often draw on the literature of several branches of scholarship, as well as nonscholarly publications. Generally, they are designed to serve a diversified range of prospective users, both within and outside the academic community, and one of their functions may be to suggest ways in which basic research, with its focus on relatively abstract ideas, may bear on specific social questions. For example, Benjamin Schlesinger's Poverty in Canada and the United States (1966), lists publications that deal more or less directly with poverty and related matters, under such headings as "Culture of Poverty" and "Critiques of the 'War on Poverty,' " but also includes pertinent writings in wider areas such as "Family Life and Child Rearing" and "Social Action and Social Change." In this way the bibliography is able to portray the subject in its broader research context and perhaps serve as a kind of bridge between the cumulative results of scholarly investigation and a matter of current public interest.

Retrospective bibliographies are sometimes compiled as a form of summary of activities and research results in one area that are seen as potentially useful to readers in other fields. A notable example is Social Science Literature: a Bibliography for International Law by Wesley L. Gould and Michael Barkun (1972). This work attempts to pinpoint writings across the broad spectrum of social science that may be considered relevant to the study of international law. The classification is designed to organize the listings in relation to legal concepts (e.g., psychological studies of obedience behavior appear in the general category "Conflict, Obligations, Reciprocity, Agreement") and many of the annotations suggest the potential contribution of the listed work to legal scholarship. The bibliography is an extension of the same authors' International Law and the

Social Sciences,[17] an expository account of the field of international law and its research directions which looks toward integration of traditional approaches emphasizing legal norms and procedures with the concepts of modern social science.

Creativity and the Individual: Summaries of Selected Literature in Psychology and Psychiatry by Morris Stein and Shirley Heinze (1960) is another example of a bibliography designed to direct the attention of researchers in one field to accomplishments in related areas. The work was compiled as part of a foundation-sponsored program of publishing "fundamental and applied research that contributes new knowledge and new ideas important for the practice of business," and "reflects an interest in the potential contribution of the behavioral sciences to the field of business administration."[18] To this end, the bibliography presents a "representative sample" of literature on its subject, in chapters devoted to various aspects of creativity (e.g., the creative process) or to subjects that scholars have investigated in relation to creativity (e.g., heredity). Each chapter begins with a brief descriptive summary of the nature of the research that has been done, followed by the listings, which are extensively annotated.

A comparable aim—to supply a "factual basis for informed management judgments"[19] underlies The Developing Nations: A Guide to Information Sources by Eloise G. ReQua and Jane Statham (1965). This work draws together a broad array of factual and interpretive publications emanating from such fields as political science, economics, and area studies, in an attempt to illuminate the relationship between social science research and issues of business and public policy.

Retrospective bibliographies are sometimes vehicles for presenting new research ideas or theoretical concepts that have begun to develop a distinctive literature or are seen as promising focal points for future efforts. Bibliographies on decision making, political elites, alienation, and youth culture[20] illustrate this type of undertaking.

The literature pertinent to a relatively new idea may be difficult to trace in standard bibliographic tools because the concept has not yet been developed to the point where it is a generally understood component of a discipline's vocabulary and hence of its bibliographic classifications. If the dimensions of the topic are not clear, pertinent materials are likely to be scattered among several subject classifications or not adequately distinguished from works on similar topics having a different focus and emphasis. Sometimes the interpretation or approach conveyed by the bibliography is the original contribution of the compiler, who identifies and comments on a body of relevant literature as a way of setting forth his ideas on the subject.

Bibliographies whose focus is a concept or issue in scientific study often go beyond the characteristic bibliographic mode, in which the compiler's ideas about the subject are implied by the selection and organization of materials, but not overtly stated, to include direct consideration of the content of the subject and the relation of the cited literature to particular questions and issues. However, the extent to which this is the case varies. In general, bibliographies focused on topics that have engaged the attention of many scholars are apt to aim for a more or less consensual picture of the nature and directions of research and to stress identification and organization of the literature more than criticism or explanation. Bibliographies inclined to more specific examination and direct comment on the literature tend to be works setting forth the compiler's individual ideas and point of view. (The point is similar to a distinction noted earlier between individual and institutional reviews of the literature).[21] The two approaches are not mutually exclusive, but may perhaps best be seen as the poles of a continuum along which many bibliographies may be ranged at various points. A few examples may illustrate and clarify the idea.

Decision-Making by Paul Wasserman and Fred Silander (1958) is a systematic inventory of the literature relating to a subject which, at the time of the bibliography's compilation, was emerging as a focus of research interest in several fields. The compilers' introduction observes that the literature of decision making is difficult to trace systematically because "attempts to synthesize have been isolated and uncommon" and "the literature's sum total is to be found in a widely scattered group of writings which cut across all the areas of social and scientific inquiry." It is noted also that "one instrument for bringing order to a subject is to attempt to rationally arrange and classify its literature."[22] The bibliography identifies, as its basis of organization, a number of research areas, such as communication, group behavior, and personality characteristics, in which literature pertinent to the idea of decision making has appeared, and lists materials in each category that relate to the central theme. A supplement published six years after the original work employs a somewhat different topical arrangement, to "reflect the differences growing out of the more recent directions of research and subsequent publication in the field."[23]

Thus, while the bibliography is intrinsically a work of synthesis, grounded in the compilers' understanding of the subject and its research implications and embodying their judgments of the meaning and relevance of the publications selected for inclusion, its focus is the concept of decision making as generally manifested in prevailing research approaches, and it does not comment directly on any issues raised by the works listed or put forward a distinct idea or interpretation of its own.

Similar to the above, but reflecting a somewhat more specific viewpoint is <u>Soviet Foreign Relations and World Communism</u>, edited by Thomas S. Hammond (1965) and composed of the contributions of a large group of specialists on various phases of the subject. This bibliography's basic premise is set forth by the editor as follows:

> . . .(I)n many cases the official diplomatic relations of the USSR have been less important than the unofficial ones conducted through the Comintern, the Cominform, "front" organizations and the various Communist parties. Hence books on "World Communism" were added. Also, since the domestic policies inaugurated by the Communist regimes of Eastern Europe and Asia have been in part the result of Soviet influence, and thus are connected with Soviet foreign policy, we have added basic works on the Communist regimes that have appeared since 1917.[24]

The bibliography thus represents a rather definite view of the nature of Soviet foreign policy and the materials germane to its study. However, it does no more than propose the relationships mentioned above, as the basis of its scope and organization, and does not attempt to substantiate or develop the idea through direct consideration of the content of the literature cited. The works listed in the chapters devoted to such areas as mass movements, front organizations, and national communist parties are generally significant writings on these topics and do not necessarily address themselves to problems of Soviet foreign policy. Likewise, the annotations are general descriptions of the contents of the publications and do not pinpoint specific connections to the bibliography's central theme.

An example of a bibliography in which the selection and description of the listings are more closely tied to explicitly stated ideas is <u>The Process of Modernization: An Annotated Bibliography on the Socio-Cultural Aspects of Development</u> by John Brode (1969). This work deals with the concept of "modernization" as developed by a group of researchers associated with the Harvard Project on the Sociocultural Aspects of Development. As viewed by these scholars, modernization represents a specific range of phenomena, distinguishable from other similar concepts such as social change, economic development, or industrialization. The purpose of the bibliography is to develop and explain the idea of modernization by exploring the ways in which the existing literature on development sheds light on it. This is done through the use of closely defined selection criteria, and consideration of the relation of each cited work to the theme of the bibliography. With regard to the first, the aim was not simply to identify writings on a given subject, but rather to select works exemplifying an approach or treatment relevant to the concerns of the bibliography. The listings are described as:

. . .studies of village communities that highlighted the elements of stability, innovation and change; those that threw light on why rural people left the village community in search of new opportunities in factories and urban centers; studies that exposed the problems industry and urban centers have in absorbing and adjusting to the new industrial worker; and particularly those studies that gauge the impact on the new industrial worker of his first experiences in the modern milieu.[25]

Similarly, the annotations are not general descriptions of the content of the listed works, but statements of their bearing on the central hypothesis of the bibliography:

. . .(I)tems have been annotated with an eye only to what they can contribute to an understanding of the process (of modernization): descriptions of social change under the impact of some modern factor are noted; other sociological conclusions are ignored. Annotation does not indicate the over-all worth of the item but only signals its pertinence to the theme of modernization.[26]

There is also a review essay summarizing the general character of the research presented in the bibliography and the inferences and conclusions suggested by the accumulated literature.

Another example of a bibliography designed to illuminate a specific idea is The Emergence of Youth Societies, by David Gottlieb and others (1966). This is a compilation of the literature of adolescent behavior presented in relation to a specific hypothesis that is spelled out in detail as the basis for the bibliographic listings. The underlying idea is that "youth culture," or a distinctive adolescent social pattern, is a function of technological growth and is manifested similarly in many societies, overriding specific cultural differences. The bibliography assembles a number of empirical studies of adolescent behavior in many cultures as a source of further insight into the validity and implications of the hypothesis. A detailed theoretical model sets forth and explains the variables to be pinpointed in the bibliographic listings, followed by the studies arranged in a geographical classification with each regional section introduced by a discussion of the general character and import of the cited literature. Many of the entries are further described in individual annotations. This bibliography brings together a broad, cross-cultural array of studies of adolescence, but it is primarily a vehicle for consideration of certain specific ideas and only secondarily, and more or less incidentally, a general identification tool.

Although The Emergence of Youth Societies is classified in libraries as a bibliography, it can as readily be regarded as a contribution to the theoretical literature, and as such it illustrates the basic convergence between the substantive and bibliographic approaches to the cumulation and ordering of knowledge. Generally a work in which the citations are classified and individually annotated is regarded as a bibliography rather than a review of the literature, and generally the bibliographic format presents a somewhat fuller view of each publication, but the differences may well be rather small and more a matter of emphasis than of basic intention.

Some retrospective bibliographies present the literature in terms of a dimension other than subject matter. For example, Sociological Measurement: An Inventory of Scales and Indices, by Charles M. Bonjean, Richard J. Hill, and S. Dale McLemore (1967) is a compilation listing studies in which specific measurement devices or techniques (e.g., "Nettler's Scale of Alienated Attitude," "Two Factor Index of Social Position") are used in sociological investigation. The bibliography thus attempts to make the literature identifiable and retrievable in terms of the methodological technique employed, something which, as was seen earlier, is not accomplished by the standard recurrent bibliographic tools. Another bibliography organized in terms of a methodological dimension is Survey Research in Comparative Social Change by Frederick W. Frey (1969). It lists reports of survey research conducted cross-nationally or in developing societies. Psychoanalysis, Psychology and Literature by Norman Kiell (1963) lists works dealing with literary writing from a psychological point of view or using literary themes to illustrate psychological ideas, and is thus another example of a bibliography identifying a dimension of literature nor ordinarily brought out in bibliographic records.

Bibliographies such as the three just described serve in part to compensate for the general lack of multi-dimensional approaches in the standard, recurrent bibliographic tools, but there is also a sense in which these works are instruments of assessment and summary as well. Usually the dimension of the literature identified by the bibliography is one regarded by the compiler as needed and useful in his field at the particular time, and worthy of more attention than it has received. For example, the introduction to Sociological Measurement points out that much sociological research lacks comparability and continuity because of a lack of consistency in the use of measurement concepts and techniques.

> When the investigator tries to build continuity in his research, more often than not he is faced with one or both of two major problems. So many different measures are available for some phenomena that the selection of a scale or index may itself be a research problem of no small magnitude. In other cases, an extensive search through the literature may yield no adequate description of a scale or index to measure the phenomenon of concern to the investigator.[27]

The bibliography attempts to meet this problem not only by identifying and classifying the studies that employ various measurement techniques, but also by summarizing and comparing the uses of measurement in the various conceptual areas of sociology. It includes a detailed statistical analysis of the frequency of use of specific measures and the problems and concepts to which they have been applied. Forty-seven scales and indexes found to be in most widespread use are described in critical essays.[28] In this way, the bibliography provides a means of identification otherwise lacking in its field, and also reviews and summarizes an aspect of the field's accomplishment.

Topics for which research depends heavily on relatively obscure materials, not generally encompassed by the standard bibliographic tools, are sometimes the focus of retrospective bibliographies. Several bibliographies in the general area of the history of social movements may be cited as examples.[29] These include not only scholarly publications, but also the publications of the various social and political groups and the writings of their leaders. For the most part, the latter categories can be strictly regarded as data rather than literature, but researchers tend to regard both types of material as intrinsic elements of the literature base of the subject.

In summary, notwithstanding many variations in scope and style, the retrospective bibliographies designated "research-oriented" share a common goal. All are directed toward enlarging the possibilities of access to the literature, by bringing otherwise unrecorded material under bibliographic control or by presenting a body of literature in relation to an idea or approach not otherwise well identified in bibliographic tools. This is done in many ways, from identifying the literature associated with broad trends in the development of an entire field, to detailed and critical examination of the writings bearing on a sharply defined and limited research question. The common quality is the effort to stimulate and facilitate the advancement of knowledge beyond the point represented by the contents of the bibliography. This is the essence of the designation "research-oriented," and the factor differentiating "research-oriented" bibliographies from the "didactic" bibliographies now to be considered.

DIDACTIC BIBLIOGRAPHIES

The primary aim of these works is not to create new routes of access to the literature or add to the body of accessible writings, but rather to aid the reader in selecting from a plethora of available materials. This is generally done by identifying the more highly regarded or useful works, and thus removing from consideration those judged to be of lesser quality, obsolete, or redundant. Identification of the literature in such a framework can be extremely valuable to a reader whose immediate aim is to learn what others already know, in the more or less conventional or traditional divisions of a subject, rather than to investigate new or specialized issues, or to extend the boundaries of existing knowledge. For subjects that have been extensively studied and written about, the most difficult aspect of literature searching is ordinarily not the location of some pertinent writings, but selection of the most suitable works from a vast, unmanageable array whose similarities in subject matter may mask large and important differences in level, approach, current relevance, and general standing in the field. The didactic bibliography is a tool designed to guide readers who are not sufficiently knowledgeable about the subject and its literature to make the necessary judgments for themselves.

The process of selecting certain works out of a subject's literature on the basis of quality or representativeness is clearly analogous to that of selecting a subject's fundamental ideas from the totality of investigation and discussion in the field, and didactic bibliographies thus have much in common with textbooks and other generalized summaries, including the quality of implicitly representing collective scholarly judgment and the prevailing consensus of a field. As was noted earlier, textbooks and similar works do not, for the most part, simply report what has already been defined as "existing knowledge," but themselves formulate and systematize a body of ideas, which come to be regarded as the consensus of the field to the extent that the formulation is accepted and used by other scholars. Similarly the compilers of selective, summary bibliographies do not simply set down titles already recognized as "basic" or "representative" or whatever, but offer these judgments to the scholarly community, whose members endorse the selections to the extent that they make use of the bibliography in their research[30] and teaching. Consonant with this quality of conveying generally accepted evaluation of the literature, many didactic bibliographies are in fact collective or institutional efforts, compiled under the auspices of learned societies or university faculties, by scholars appointed to the task by those groups.

Bibliographies in the didactic category vary principally in their degree of selectivity and, accordingly, in the proportion of the subject's literature they encompass. Without attempting to set down any definite or rigid categories, several characteristic approaches may be delineated.

Many didactic bibliographies are highly selective compilations intended to identify basic works considered most suitable for a first introduction to the subject or a general, over-all account of its content. These bibliographies generally list books only, since they are geared to the broad and basic divisions of the subject and the more cumulated phases of the scholarly discussion, which ordinarily do not involve the level of detail characteristic of the journal literature. They are most often limited to works in English, on the assumption that pertinent foreign contributions will have been assimilated into the basic literature. A prominent example of a bibliography of this general type is the

Harvard List of Books in Psychology,[31] a selective list of significant books representing all the major branches and phases of psychological study, compiled and periodically revised by the psychology faculty at Harvard.

A number of selective bibliographies encompass a somewhat wider range of literature, including journal articles and, in some instances, foreign publications. Works of this type are often conceived as a kind of general summary of available knowledge. That is, they are intended to supply not simply a basic introduction to the subject in the form of its most significant and comprehensive writings, but a broad spectrum of works representative of the subject's literature as a whole and of all the topics and issues that figure significantly in current study. In scope and level these bibliographies are perhaps comparable to handbooks. Their approach to the subject is usually detailed enough to extend to the journal literature as well as books, and may also encompass foreign publications. Examples of bibliographies of this general character are the Harvard Guide to American History, prepared by members of the history faculty at Harvard, and The Economics of Underdeveloped Areas, a reading list issued by the Institute of Commonwealth Studies, Oxford University. These present rather detailed classifications of their respective subjects and list books and articles selected as significant or representative contributions on each topic.

A type of bibliography similar in many ways to the didactic compilations is the list representing a basic library collection in a particular field, intended as a purchasing guide for libraries. A number of such bibliographies are geared to college library collections and encompass, generally, the literature relevant to the main currents of research in the field, and works of historical importance, omitting the more esoteric and specialized materials. The field's major journals are usually listed, but there is naturally no enumeration of individual articles. A characteristic work of this type is A Basic Geographical Library, published by the Association of American Geographers.

A list, with descriptive notes, of didactic bibliographies in the social sciences will be found in Appendix J. The listing is not exhaustive, but it attempts to convey an over-all view of bibliographies of this type and to identify some significant and widely used titles.

RETROSPECTIVE BIBLIOGRAPHIES: SUMMARY OF AIMS AND CHARACTERISTICS

The preceding discussion of retrospective bibliographies has attempted to delineate a number of types and categories of these works and some features of structure and organization generally characteristic of each. It is not suggested that the categorization is in all instances clear-cut and consistent. Characteristics ascribed to several categories may overlap, and many bibliographies may be difficult to class as belonging definitively to one "type" or another. However, the purpose of discussing bibliographies in this way was to suggest the range and variety of purposes toward which retrospective bibliographies may be directed, but not to construct a classification scheme as such. The essential point is that a bibliography "on" a given subject does not function independently and in isolation from other publications and records of the literature, but is part of a wider system of communication, performing certain limited functions within the system. Accordingly, these works should not be viewed as noncommittal lists of publications "on" a subject, put together on the general assumption that it would be convenient to have a number of references on the topic assembled in one place. Examples of such bibliographies may perhaps be found, but much more commonly a retrospective bibliography is designed to carry a specific message about a subject and its literature.

The selection and presentation of materials in a given work represent one set of choices among many possibilities, and derive from the circumstances underlying the compilation of the bibliography and the particular ends it is designed to serve.[32] It follows that the usefulness of a particular bibliography to a given reader or in performance of a given task depends only in part on the range of subject matter covered. Also to be considered is the phase of the scholarly discussion to which the bibliography addresses itself and, in consequence, the particular segment of a subject's literature that the bibliography identifies. All of the bibliographies described above are lists of publications "on" a subject, but none of them would serve all needs for the literature of the subject interchangeably or equally well.

A related point of some importance is the relatively rapid obsolescence of retrospective bibliographies. These works become dated not only because they cannot identify any publications more recent than the bibliography itself, but also because the perspective that a retrospective bibliography brings to bear on the literature is necessarily that of a particular point in time and therefore does not remain relevant forever. In general, the more interpretive and specific the bibliography's approach to the literature, the more it is affected by the passage of time. Bibliographies that are essentially inventories— for example, Work's Bibliography of the Negro—largely retain their usefulness as identification tools for the literature of their subject during the period covered. On the other hand, a bibliography geared to a particular explanatory concept—for example, Brode's Process of Modernization—becomes obsolete not only because it lacks the newest materials, but also because the conception of the subject that is the basis for the bibliography undergoes change as additional research and new ideas are brought to bear on it, with the result that the selection and organization of the literature conveyed by the bibliography become progressively less relevant to scholars' needs and interests. Much the same applies also to the selective, didactic bibliographies. Not only the constant appearance of new publications, but also constant change in the outlook and standards of judgment prevailing in a field cause these works to decline in usefulness as their age increases.

SOURCES FOR IDENTIFICATION OF BIBLIOGRAPHIES

The retrospective bibliographies mentioned in the preceding account and in the appendix following are a cross-section of tools of this type rather than a complete listing of the useful titles, and, of course, the discussion here can take no account of the works appearing in the future. Several sources are generally useful for identifying bibliographies. Library catalogs list the bibliographies in the library's collection under the subject with the subheading "bibliography" (e.g., Economic development–bibliog.). Guides to the literature, discussed in Chapter 10, mention the significant bibliographies in their subject areas. A World Bibliography of Bibliographies by Theodore Besterman[33] is a five-volume compilation listing, without annotation, over 100,000 recurrent and retrospective bibliographies on all subjects. New bibliographies are listed as published in most of the recurrent bibliographic inventories described in Chapter 7. Bibliographic Index[34] appears three times yearly and lists bibliographies consisting of forty entries or more, including both separate publications and bibliographies appended to books and articles.

FOOTNOTES

1. An earlier version of this chapter appeared in RQ 11 (1971) 15–22.

2. See pp. 140–142 above.

3. Bibliographic details for the works mentioned in this chapter may be found in Appendix J.

4. Human Relations Area Files (HRAF) is an organization based at Yale University that has analyzed a large body of descriptive writings concerning the world's cultures, and constructed an extensive, continuing file of ethnographic data. The file is duplicated and distributed to a number of research institutions. The series HRAF Behavior Science Bibliographies includes, in addition to the work cited above, Roman Jakobson and others, Paleosiberian Peoples and Languages, 1957 (GN673.J3); Raymond Kennedy, Bibliography of Indonesian Peoples and Cultures, 2d rev. ed., 1962 (Z5115.K4); H. C. Koh, Korea; an Analytical

Guide to Bibliographies, 1971 (Z3316.A1K64); Timothy J. O'Leary, Ethnographic Bibliography of South America, 1963 (Z5114.O4); Raphael Patai, Jordan, Lebanon and Syria: an Annotated Bibliography, 1957 (Z3013.P3); Karl J. Pelzer, West Malaysia and Singapore: a Selected Bibliography, 1971 (Z3246.P4); Robert J. Theodoratus, Europe: a Selected Ethnographic Bibliography, 1969 (Z5171.T5).

5. Metropolitan Communities 3, 1967, p. vi.

6. Joan Aldous, International Bibliography of Research in Marriage and the Family, p. 3.

7. See pp. 142, 161.

8. Wilbur A. Zelinsky, A Bibliographic Guide to Population Geography, p. vi.

9. Harold Lasswell, Propaganda and Promotional Activities, introduction to 1969 reissue, p. xvii.

10. Harold Lasswell, Propaganda and Promotional Activities, 1935, pp. x–xi.

11. See Chapter 4. The recurrent descriptive reviews generally work on a more frequent schedule than ten years, but reviews from the perspective of a decade or longer have on occasion appeared in a format similar to that of handbooks. See, for example, Joseph B. Gittler ed., Review of Sociology: Analysis of a Decade (New York: John Wiley, 1957). HM51.G57

12. Bruce Lannes Smith and Chitra M. Smith, International Communication and Public Opinion: a Guide to the Literature (copyright © 1956 by the Rand Corporation), published by Princeton University Press, p. 3. Reprinted by permission of Princeton University Press.

13. See in Appendix J: Koppel S. Pinson, A Bibliographic Introduction to Nationalism (1935) and Karl W. Deutsch, An Inter-disciplinary Bibliography on Nationalism 1935–1953 (1956). The 1970 bibliography cited encompasses publications of 1935–1966.

14. Introduction (unpaged). Reprinted from Nationalism and National Development by Karl Deutsch and Richard Merritt by permission of The M.I.T. Press, Cambridge, Massachusetts. Copyright © 1970 by the Massachusetts Institute of Technology.

15. See pp. 61–62.

16. See in Appendix J: Albert A. Liboiron, Federalism and Intergovernmental Relations in Australia, Canada, the United States and Other Countries; Lawrence C. Little, Religion and Public Education; Benjamin Schlesinger, Poverty in Canada and the United States; Robert E. Booth et. al., Culturally Disadvantaged.

17. Princeton: Princeton University Press, 1970. JX1249.G67

18. "Foreword" by W. Allen Wallis.

19. "Preface," by Paul Wasserman, in Eloise ReQua, The Developing Nations. The statement refers to a series of "Management Information Guides," of which the work cited here is one. The other titles in the series deal mainly

with more technical aspects of business, such as real estate or production control, and are only tangentially germane to the social science literature, as considered here.

20. See in Appendix J: Paul Wasserman and Fred S. Silander, Decision-Making; Carl Beck and J. Thomas McKechnie, Political Elites; Mary Lystad, Social Aspects of Alienation; David Gottlieb, Jon Reeves and Warren D. Ten Houton, The Emergence of Youth Scoieties.

21. See Chapter 4.

22. Paul Wasserman, Decision-Making, p. iv.

23. Paul Wasserman, op. cit., supplement, p. iii.

24. Thomas S. Hammond, Soviet Foreign Relations and World Communism (copyright © 1965 by Princeton University Press) p. vii. Reprinted by permission of Princeton University Press.

25. "Foreword," by Alex Inkeles, in John Brode, Process of Modernization, p. vii.

26. John Brode, op cit., p. 2.

27. Charles M. Bonjean, Sociological Measurement (copyright © 1967 by Chandler Publishing Company) p. 1. Reprinted by permission of Chandler Publishing Company, an Intext publisher.

28. In psychology, arrangements for conveying a similar type of information are institutionalized in the Mental Measurement Yearbook. See Appendix C.

29. See in Appendix J: Mouvements ouvriers et socialistes; T. D. Seymour Bassett, Socialism and American Life; Joel Seidman, Communism in the United States; Witold S. Sworakowski, The Communist International and its Front Organizations.

30. A scholar would not ordinarily use a didactic bibliography for literature searching in his area of primary specialization since he is usually sufficiently familiar with that literature not to need the bibliography's guidance. However, he might use such a bibliography to enter an adjacent field with which he was less familiar, and in such instances would be likely to regard with confidence a work whose selections in his own specialty met with his approval.

31. For bibliographic details and additional descriptions of this work and the other bibliographies cited as examples below, see Appendix J.

32. A number of related points are discussed at length in Patrick Wilson, Two Kinds of Power: an Essay on Bibliographic Control (Berkeley: University of California Press, 1968), a work which came to the writer's attention too late to be considered more directly here.

33. 4th ed., Lausanne: Societas Bibliographica, 1965.

34. New York: H. W. Wilson Co., 1938– . Z1002.B594

Appendix J

Retrospective Bibliographies

RESEARCH-ORIENTED BIBLIOGRAPHIES MENTIONED IN CHAPTER 9.

Aldous, Joan and Reuben Hill, International Bibliography of Research in Marriage and the Family 1900–1964. Minneapolis: University of Minnesota Press, 1967. Z7164.M2A48 (211)

Bassett, T. D. Seymour, "Bibliography: Descriptive and Critical," vol. 2 of Donald D. Egbert, ed., Socialism and American Life. Princeton: Princeton University Press, 1952. HX83.E45 vol. 2 (221)

Beck, Carl and J. Thomas McKechnie, Political Elites: a Select Computerized Bibliography. Cambridge Mass.: MIT Press, 1968. Z7164.E4B4 (216)

Bonjean, Charles M., Richard J. Hill, and S. Dale McLemore, Sociological Measurement: an Inventory of Scales and Indices. San Francisco: Chandler, 1967. Z7164.S68B6 (220)

Booth, Robert E. et. al., Culturally Disadvantaged: a Bibliography and Keyword-Out-of-Context (KWOC) Index. Detroit: Wayne State University Press, 1967. Z5814.C52C8 (215)

Brode, John, The Process of Modernization: an Annotated Bibliography. Cambridge, Mass.: Harvard University Press, 1969. Z7164.U5B7 (218)

Deutsch, Karl W., An Interdisciplinary Bibliography on Nationalism 1935-1953. Cambridge, Mass.: MIT Press, 1956. Z7164.N2D4 (214)

Deutsch, Karl and Richard Merritt, Nationalism and National Development: an Interdisciplinary Bibliography. Cambridge, Mass.: MIT Press, 1970. Z7164.N2D43 (214)

Frey, Frederick, W., Survey Research in Comparative Social Change. Cambridge, Mass.: MIT Press, 1969. Z7164.U5F73 (220)

Gottlieb, David; Jon Reeves; and Warren D. Ten Houton, The Emergence of Youth Societies: a Cross-Cultural Approach. New York: Free Press, 1966. Z7164.Y8G62 (219)

Gould. Wesley L. and Michael Barkun, Social Science Literature: a Bibliography for International Law. Princeton: Princeton University Press for the American Society of International Law, 1972. Z6461.G68 (215)

Hammond, Thomas S., ed., Soviet Foreign Relations and World Communism. Princeton: Princeton University Press, 1965. Z2517.R4H3 (218)

Kiell, Norman, Psychoanalysis, Psychology and Literature. Madison: University of Wisconsin Press, 1963. Z6511.K5 (220)

Lasswell, Harold D.; Ralph D. Casey; and Bruce Lannes Smith, Propaganda and Promotional Activities. Minneapolis: University of Minnesota Press, 1935; Chicago: University of Chicago Press, 1969. Z7204.S67L3 (212)

Liboiron, Albert A., Federalism and Intergovernmental Relations in Australia, Canada, the United States and Other Countries: a Bibliography. Kingston, Ontario: Queen's University, 1967. Z7165.A8L5 (215)

Little, Lawrence C., Religion and Public Education. 3rd ed., Pittsburgh: University of Pittsburgh Book Center, 1968. Z5814.C57L5 1968 (215)

Lystad, Mary H., Social Aspects of Alienation: an Annotated Bibliography. Chevy Chase, Md.: National Institute of Mental Health, 1969. Z7204.A5L9 (216)

Metropolitan Communities: a Bibliography with Special Emphasis upon Government and Politics. Prepared by Government Affairs Foundation. Chicago: Public Administration Service, 1956; supplement 1955–57, 1959; vol. 3, 1959–64, prepared by the Institute of Governmental Studies, University of California, 1967; vol. 4, 1965–67, 1969. Z7164.L8G66 (210)

Miller, Elizabeth W. and Mary L. Fisher, The Negro in America: a Bibliography. 2nd ed., Cambridge, Mass.: Harvard University Press, 1970. Z1361.N39M5 1970 (210)

Mouvements ouvriers et socialistes: Chronologie et Bibliographie. 6 vols. Paris: Editions ouvrieres, 1950– . Z7161.M64 (221)

Murdock, George P., Ethnographic Bibliography of North America. 3rd ed., New Haven: Human Relations Area Files, 1960. Z1209.M8 1960 (209)

Pinson, Koppel S., A Bibliographic Introduction to Nationalism. New York: Columbia University Press, 1935. Z7164.N2P6 (214)

ReQua, Eloise G. and Jane Statham, The Developing Nations: a Guide to Information Sources. Detroit: Gale Research Co., 1965. Z7164.U5R4 (216)

Schlesinger, Benjamin, Poverty in Canada and the United States: Overview and Annotated Bibliography. Toronto: University of Toronto Press, 1966. Z7164.C4S37 (215)

Seidman, Joel, Communism in the United States: a Bibliography. Ithaca: Cornell University Press, 1969. Z7164.S67S38 (221)

Smith, Bruce Lannes and Chitra M. Smith, International Communication and Public Opinion. Princeton: Princeton University Press, 1956. Z7204.S67B87 (213)

Smith, Bruce Lannes; Harold D. Lasswell; and Ralph D. Casey, Propaganda, Communication and Public Opinion. Princeton: Princeton University Press, 1946. Z7204.S67S6 (213)

Stein, Morris and Shirley Heinze, Creativity and the Individual: Summaries of Selected Literature in Psychology and Psychiatry. New York: Free Press, 1960. Z7204.C8S72 (216)

Sworakowski, Witold S., The Communist International and its Front Organizations. Stanford, Calif.: Hoover Institute, 1965. Z7164.S67S86 (221)

Thompson, Edgar T. and Alma Macy Thompson, Race and Religion. Chapel Hill: University of North Carolina Press, 1949. Z1361.N39T5 (210)

Wasserman, Paul and Fred S. Silander, Decision-Making: an Annotated Bibliography. Ithaca: Graduate School of Business and Public Administration, Cornell University, 1958; supplement, 1964. Z7204.A6W3 (217)

Work, Monroe N., A Bibliography of the Negro in Africa and America. New York: H. W. Wilson Co., 1928. Z1361.N39W8 (210)

Zelinsky, Wilber A., A Bibliographic Guide to Population Geography. University of Chicago, Department of Geography, Research Paper no. 80, 1962. H31.C514 no. 80 (212)

SELECTED DIDACTIC BIBLIOGRAPHIES IN THE SOCIAL SCIENCES[1]

Social Sciences (all disciplines)

Hoselitz, Bert, ed., A Reader's Guide to the Social Sciences. rev. ed., New York: Free Press, 1970. H61.H69 1970
    A series of bibliographic essays describing the development, research, interests, and literary output of the social science disciplines, with citation of leading or representative works. Covers sociology, anthropology, psychology, political science, economics, and geography. An earlier edition, published in 1959, included history among the disciplines covered, and also contained a general essay on the history of social science during the past 200 years.

White, Carl M., ed. Sources of Information in the Social Sciences. Totowa, N.J.: Bedminister Press, 1964. Z7161.W49
    Bibliographic essays in the fields of history, economics, sociology, anthropology, psychology, education, and political science, outlining the

[1] In addition to the titles listed here, many of the guides to the literature described in Chapter 10 also contain basic bibliographies of their subjects.

nature of study in the field with citation of significant works. More extensive listings than Hoselitz, above, with relatively less emphasis on the landmarks of each field's development and greater concentration on the leading writings pertinent to current work. Also contains extensive lists of bibliographies and reference works, described in further detail in Appendix K. A revised edition is to be published in 1973.

Anthropology

Beckham, Rexford S., "A Basic List of Books and Periodicals for College Libraries," in Mandelbaum, David G., ed., Resources for the Teaching of Anthropology. Berkeley: University of California Press, 1963. pp.77–316. Z5111.M3

A classified list of approximately 1,700 items selected as most useful and important for undergraduate instruction and student research.

Area and Ethnic Studies

American Universities Field Staff. A Select Bibliography: Asia, Africa, Eastern Europe, Latin America. New York, 1960. Supplements 1961, 1963, 1965, 1967, 1969. Z5579.A5

Designed to assist college study and general reading about "nonwestern" civilizations. Lists books and journals recommended for library purchase, with an indication of the "core" works in each subject category. Works listed are mainly, but not exclusively, in English.

Birnbaum, Eleazar. Books on Asia from the Near East to the Far East; a Guide for the General Reader. Toronto: University of Toronto Press, 1971. Z3001.B54

Annotated list of books considered best for the student and nonspecialist. Includes books dealing with all aspects of the history and culture of Asia as a whole, the Islamic world, India and South Asia, and the Far East. Mostly English language; some works in French are included.

Horecky, Paul, ed., East Central Europe: A Guide to Basic Publications. Chicago: University of Chicago Press, 1969. Z2483.H56

Selective, annotated inventory of the most important writings relating to East Germany, Czechoslavakia, Hungary, and Poland. Subject sections compiled by about seventy contributors. Focuses on political, socio-economic and intellectual life; excludes science and technology. Includes books, important periodicals, and some individual articles. Lists works in indigenous languages and some foreign publications, principally English-language.

Horecky, Paul, ed., Russia and the Soviet Union: A Bibliographical Guide to Western Language Publications. Chicago: University of Chicago Press, 1965. Z2491.H64

Conspectus of western language writings, chiefly in book form, considered to be particularly relevant to the study of the political, socio-economic, and intellectual life in the Russian Empire and the Soviet Union. Subject chapters contributed by about thirty specialists. About 2,000 titles listed, with brief annotations. Brief section devoted to bibliographies and reference works.

Horecky, Paul, ed.. Southeastern Europe: a Guide to Basic Publications. Chicago: University of Chicago Press, 1969. Z2831.H67

Similar in scope and format to the compiler's East Central Europe (above), with coverage of Albania, Bulgaria, Greece, Romania, and Yugoslavia.

Porter, Dorothy B. The Negro in the United States: A Selected Bibliography. Washington: Library of Congress, 1970. Z1361.N39P59

About 1,700 significant books touching many areas of the humanities as well as the social sciences. Designed as a basic bibliographic resource for courses in Negro history and culture in schools and colleges. There are brief annotations of some titles.

U.S. Library of Congress. General Reference and Bibliography Division. A Guide to the Study of the United States of America: Representative Books Reflecting the Development of American Life and Thought. Prepared under the direction of Roy P. Basler by Donald H. Mugridge and Blanch P. McCrum. Washington: GPO, 1960. Z1215.U53

Over 6,000 books on all phases of American life, with extensive annotations. An appendix lists 190 "Selected Readings in American Studies"; titles selected as "those. . .which have a synthetic approach, bridge the various academic and scholarly disciplines, and are therefore of special significance to teachers or students pursuing courses in American studies."

Welsch, Erwin K. The Negro in the United States: A Research Guide. Bloomington: Indiana University Press, 1965. Z1361.N39W4

A selection of the most significant works on all aspects of the subject is presented in the form of evaluative, comparative essays offering brief descriptions of the titles mentioned.

Economics

Bibliography for Students of Economics. London: Oxford University Press, 1968. Z7164.E2B519

A basic reading list compiled by economists at Oxford and encompassing all branches of the field in a detailed subject classification. Includes books, also separate essays or chapters in books, and some journal articles. Earlier editions were published in 1948, 1950, and 1957 under the title Bibliography in Economics for the Oxford Honour School of Philosophy, Politics and Economics.

Economics Selections, Series II: Basic Lists in Special Fields. Department of Economics, University of Pittsburgh. Z7164.E2E27

A series of basic book lists in specialized areas of economics. Relatively recent publications in English are stressed, but older and foreign titles are sometimes included. Entries include brief annotations, and an indication of the size and type of library for which the book is recommended. From 1954 to 1963 the series was published by Johns Hopkins University under the title Economics Library Selections. The following lists have been issued:

International Economics (1954); Statistics and Econometrics (1955); Economics Reference Works and Professional Journals (1956); Business

Fluctuations 1957; Economic Theory and History of Thought (1960); Economics of Labor (1961); Economics of Development and Growth (1963); Selected Bibliography of Economics Reference Works and Professional Journals, and Citizenship Reference Library (1965); Selected Bibliography of Books in Public Finance (1966); Special Bibliography in International Economics (1968).

Hazlewood, Arthur. The Economics of Under-Developed Areas: An Annotated Reading List of Books, Articles and Official Publications. 2d ed., London: Oxford University Press, 1959. Z7161.H3 1959

    Prepared for the Institute of Commonwealth Studies at Oxford University. Designed to identify the best English-language economics literature on the subject. Includes about 1,000 items in a classified arrangement. Updated by the same compiler's Economics of Development: An Annotated List of Books and Articles Published 1958–1962 (London: Oxford University Press, 1964.) Z7164.U5H37

Education

Bristow, Thelma and Brian Holmes. Comparative Education Through the Literature: A Bibliographic Guide. Hamden, Conn.: Shoe String Press, 1968. Z5814.C76B7

    A basic list of English-language books, classified and extensively annotated.

Goldberg, I. Ignacy. Selected Bibliography of Special Education. New York: Teachers College, Columbia University, 1967. Z5814.C52G62

    Books and articles in broad subject categories.

Richmond, W. Kenneth. The Literature of Education: a Critical Bibliography, 1945–1970. London: Methuen, 1972. Z5811.R53

    A synoptic view of the education literature of the past twenty-five years, in the form of "a selection of some of the more notable books and major reports which have appeared in the English language. . ." (p.1). Each chapter is introduced by a review of research trends in the subject, followed by the annotated bibliography.

Geography

Church, Martha. A Basic Geographical Library: A Selected and Annotated Book List for American Colleges. Washington, D.C.: Association of American Geographers, 1966. Z6001.C48

    Over 1,300 titles in a classified arrangement with very brief annotations. Contains mainly English-language publications, but important foreign works unavailable in translation are also included.

History

American Historical Association. Guide to Historical Literature. Board of Editors: George F. Howe and others. New York: Macmillan, 1961. Z6201.A55

    A listing of the most significant publications in all branches and periods of historical study, compiled by a committee of the American Historical

Association. Lists mainly books, but also some journal articles; mainly English-language publications, but some foreign materials. A section is devoted to bibliographies and reference materials.

Bibliography of British History: Tudor Period, 1485–1603. 2d ed. Edited by Conyers Read. Oxford: Clarendon Press, 1959. Z2018.R28

Bibliography of British History: Stuart Period, 1603–1704. Edited by Godfrey Davies. Oxford: Clarendon Press, 1928. Z2018.D25

Bibliography of British History: The Eighteenth Century, 1714–1789. Edited by Stanley Pargellis and D. J. Medley. Oxford: Clarendon Press, 1951. Z2019.P3

    Extensive listings of books, journal articles, and printed source materials judged useful for both beginning and advanced historical study. There are brief annotations of some items. Some sections have introductory notes commenting on the character of the works listed and the leading publications. The titles above are the product to date of a project jointly undertaken prior to World War I by the American Historical Association and the Royal Historical Society, which was designed to continue Charles Gross' The Sources and Literature of English History, from the Earliest Times to About 1485 (2d ed., London, Longmans Green, 1915.) Z2016.G87 1915

Bullock, Alan and A. J. P. Taylor. A Selected List of Books on European History, 1915–1914. Oxford: Clarendon Press, 1957. Z2000.B8 1957

    Major works in English and Western European languages, arranged in geographical categories with chronological and topical subdivisions. Few annotations, but the best books on a subject or outstanding characteristics of a book are occasionally pointed out.

Crowther, Peter A. A Bibliography of Works in English on Early Russian History to 1800. New York: Barnes and Noble, 1969. Z2506.C75 1969b

    Patterned on David Shapiro's Bibliography of Russian History (see below), extending coverage back to an earlier time period.

"Goldentree Bibliographies in American History," Series editor, Arthur S. Link. New York: Appleton-Century-Crofts. 1969– .

    A series projected to number about twenty-five bibliographies, each devoted to a specialized area of American history. Aimed at undergraduate research needs, the lists include books and journal articles and attempt to identify all works considered still useful in relation to the mainstream of current knowledge. Entries are arranged in detailed chronological and topical classifications, and are unannotated. The following titles have appeared:

Bremner, Robert H. American Social History Since 1860. 1971. Z1361.C6B7

Burr, Nelson R. Religions in American Life. 1970. Z7757.U5B8

Donald, David. The Nation in Crisis 1861–1877. 1969. Z1241.D57

Fehrenbacher, Don E. Manifest Destiny and the Coming of the Civil War, 1841–1860. 1970. Z1236.F34

Greene, Jack P. and E. P. Papenfuse. The American Colonies in the Eighteenth Century, 1689–1763. 1969. Z1237.G74

Grob, Gerald N. American Social History Before 1860. 1970. Z1361.C6G7
Link, Arthur S. and William M. Leary, Jr. The Progressive Era and the Great War, 1896–1920. 1969. Z1244.L56
Taylor, George Rogers. American Economic History Before 1860. 1970. Z7165.U5T37

Handlin, Oscar et. al. Harvard Guide to American History. Cambridge, Mass.: Harvard University Press, 1954. Z1236.H27

Presents a detailed outline of important topics in the study of American history, with references to the most significant books, articles, and data sources pertinent to each. Has been an extremely important bibliographic tool, but its age has begun to detract seriously from its usefulness. A substantial portion of the work is devoted to methods and sources of historical research. This aspect is described further under "guides to the literature," in Appendix K.

Nevins, Allan; James I. Robertson, Jr.; and Bell I. Wiley, Civil War Books: A Critical Bibliography. 2 vols. Baton Rouge: Louisiana State University Press, 1967. Z1242.N35

A list of some 6,000 titles (selected from an estimated 50,000 books in existence dealing with the Civil War) designed to identify works of greatest probable interest to researchers. The bibliography focuses on the war as such, rather than its causes, antecedents, or aftermath. There are brief annotations.

Roach, John, ed. A Bibliography of Modern History. Cambridge: Cambridge University Press, 1968. Z6204.R62

Bibliographic supplement to the encyclopedic survey, New Cambridge Modern History (see Appendix E). Following the organization of the parent work, the bibliography indicates the most significant literature on each topic for purposes of introductory reading or the beginning stages of research.

Shapiro, David. A Select Bibliography of Works in English on Russian History, 1801–1917. Oxford: Basil Blackwell, 1962. Z2509.S5

Includes books and articles considered useful for scholarly purposes. Arranged chronologically and by subject, with brief introductory notes to each section indicating the most significant studies or best introductions. Reviews of books are cited in some instances.

Political Science and International Relations

A Bibliography for Students of Politics. London: Oxford University Press, 1971. Z7161.B5526

A guide to reading prepared by political scientists in Oxford University for students in the Oxford Honour Schools of Philosophy, Politics, and Economics. Includes mainly English-language books; also some journal articles. Emphasis is on political history and institutions, especially in Great Britain, and international relations.

Carnell, Francis. The Politics of the New States; A Select, Annotated Bibliography with Special Reference to the Commonwealth. London: Oxford University Press for the Institute of Commonwealth Studies, 1961. Z7164.C7C3

A comprehensive listing of the literature pertinent to current study of the subject. Mainly English-language books, but some journal articles and foreign publications are included. There are brief annotations, and a few books on each topic are identified as basic, introductory works.

Conference on North Atlantic Community, Bruges, 1957. The Atlantic Community: An Introductory Bibliography. 2 vols. Leyden: A. W. Sythoff, 1962. Z2000.6 C6 1957i

Books and articles selected as "a basic reading list for any study of the Atlantic Community" (foreword). Lists works in English, French, German, and Italian, with annotations in English.

Foreign Affairs 50-Year Bibliography: New Evaluations of Significant Books on International Relations 1920–1970, edited by Byron Dexter. New York: Bowker, for the Council on Foreign Relations, 1972. Z6463.F62

A selection of some 2,000 books on international relations published between 1920 and 1970 which are considered to be landmarks of the field or to have current significance. Brief reviews by many contributors indicate the book's impact and current standing.

Harmon, Robert B. Political Science: A Bibliographical Guide to the Literature. Metuchen, N. J.: Scarecrow Press, 1965. Supplements 1968, 1972. Z7161.H27

A comprehensive list of books, mainly in English but including some foreign titles, arranged according to a systematic outline of areas of study in political science.

Kolarz, Walter. Books on Communism. 2d ed., New York: Oxford University Press, 1964. Z7164.S67K666

An annotated, classified list of 2,500 significant books in English published since 1945.

Speeckaert, G. P. Bibliographie selective sur l'Organisation internationale; Select Bibliography on International Organization, 1885–1964. Brussells: Union of International Associations, 1965. Z6464.I6S68 1965

Over 1,000 significant books in all languages. Includes 350 works on international organization in general, and 730 titles dealing with 214 individual organizations.

Psychology

The Harvard List of Books in Psychology. 4th ed. compiled and annotated by the psychologists in Harvard University. Cambridge: Harvard University Press, 1971. (1st ed. 1949, 2d ed., 1955, 3d ed., 1964) Z7201.H28 1971

Lists the most significant English-language titles in the major divisions of psychology, with brief annotations.

Sociology

Blum, Eleanor. Basic Books in the Mass Media: an Annotated, Selected Booklist Covering General Communications, Book Publishing, Broadcasting, Film, Magazines, Newspapers, Advertising, Indexes, and Scholarly and Professional Periodicals. Urbana: University of Illinois Press, 1972.   Z5630.B55

Includes basic texts and also handbooks, bibliographies, and other reference materials in each of the categories enumerated in the subtitle.

Chapter Ten

Guides to the Literature and Directories of Periodicals

GUIDES TO THE LITERATURE

This term refers to works that present in systematic fashion the over-all information system of a field. Ordinarily this encompasses the basic pattern of organization of the literature, and the major publications and retrieval tools. It sometimes includes other matters as well, such as sources of data relevant to the field (statistics, laws, etc.), organizations acting as sources of information, descriptions of major library collections and archives. Many guides identify the classic or landmark books in their fields, or include basic bibliographies of the type described in the preceding section, but the essential difference between a guide and a didactic bibliography is that the emphasis of the former is on the mechanisms and over-all structure of the field's information system, rather than on the identification of specific works. That is, the didactic bibliography suggests what to read on a given subject, but the essential message of the guide concerns how to find out what to read.

Beyond this general characterization, guides vary a good deal in their content and specific aims. Some devote considerable attention to the processes and techniques of literature searching, offering rather detailed instructions on procedures to be followed in library research, from the selection and definition of a topic to final preparation of the manuscript. Such guides are apt to include fairly extensive consideration of the various types of publications and bibliographic tools, and of the usefulness of each of the information seeker.

In contrast, many guides focus quite narrowly on identification and description of specific information sources, and say little or nothing about the relation of the sources to each other or to an over-all communication pattern. Ordinarily the listings are categorized in terms of various types of material— encyclopedias, bibliographies, etc.—but it is assumed that the reader is familiar with the characteristics and information potential of each category and thus aware of the type of publication which will best serve his needs. Accordingly, the guide emphasizes the details of composition and content of individual works.

Most guides may be placed somewhere between these two extremes. In all instances, however, these works can be most effectively used when the reader approaches them with some prior understanding of the type of information he is seeking and, accordingly, the desired characteristics of the information tool to be identified by the guide. A reader who understands that he needs, say, a handbook or introductory bibliography can use the guide to identify a work of that type in the appropriate subject range, but without such a conception of what is being sought, the guide's enumeration of categories and titles is often more bewildering than helpful.

These cautionary comments apply in some degree to all guides, even those that include explanation of literature-searching procedures and the characteristics of the various types of sources. Ultimately, it rests with each user of the literature to define the connections between his particular information requirements and the system of communication created by the publications and bibliographic tools of a field, and in this way to select the appropriate sources on the basis of the descriptions offered by the guide. The preceding discussion has endeavored to show the distinctive roles played by the various forms of publications in the process of creating a body of knowledge and recording what is known. In this way, one may conceive of literature searching as an attempt to "tune in" on the scholarly discussion at some designated point, by means of the publications and bibliographic tools pertaining to that phase and level of the over-all communication process. The guide to the literature is a device which can aid in identifying a given type of publication for a given range of subject matter.

Listed in Appendix K are some widely used guides to the literature in a number of social science fields. The annotations attempt to indicate the basic approach and orientation of each title.

DIRECTORIES OF PERIODICALS

Directories of periodicals identify and describe the journals pertinent to a field of study. Their function resembles that of guides to the literature in that, like the guides, the directories do not point out specific writings on a topic, but rather suggest the publications likely to contain certain types of material.

Periodicals directories have a number of uses in connection with selection and acquisition of journals in libraries, but these tools do not usually figure importantly in literature searching. In a thoroughly exhaustive investigation, or a search focused on an obscure point or topic about which little has been written, the reader may be obliged to go beyond the coverage of the literature afforded by indexes and abstracts, and examine all the available journals directly, issue by issue and article by article. In such cases the periodicals directories can aid in identifying the appropriate titles, and particularly the more obscure publications not covered by the bibliographic tools. The directories may also be used to point out the specialized journals that a reader with a continuing interest in a subject may wish to read regularly, or to suggest sources of book reviews or special types of materials such as chronologies or texts of documents.

Most periodicals directories organize their listings in terms of a subject classification. Basic bibliographic data such as sponsorship, address, frequency, and starting date are usually given for each title, and features such as book reviews, advertising, or professional news are noted. In some instances there is additional description of the scope and content of the journals.

A list of directories of social science periodicals appears in Appendix K. It may be noted that most of the directories are addressed to specialized fields or research interests. The most comprehensive, world-wide compilation is UNESCO's World List of Social Science Periodicals. This is updated by an annual listing of new periodicals, with brief descriptive notes, which has appeared since 1968 in International Social Science Journal.

Appendix K

Guides to the Literature and Directories of Periodicals

GUIDES TO THE LITERATURE

Social Sciences (all disciplines)

Clarke, Jack Alden. Research Materials in the Social Sciences. Madison: University of Wisconsin Press, 1959. Z7161.C56

  Annotated listing of indexes, bibliographies, etc., including general works as well as those specialized in the social sciences.

Lewis, Peter R. The Literature of the Social Sciences: An Introductory Survey and Guide. London: The Library Association, 1960. Z7161.L45

  The principal guides to the literature, bibliographies, journals, basic textbooks, and data sources for economics, political science, law, international affairs, and sociology are identified and briefly described. Each subject chapter includes a chronology of landmarks in the history of the field and identifies major schools of thought and their representative writings. Also discusses the availability and organization of each field's literature in libraries, and methods and tools of book selection and acquisition. British materials are emphasized.

White, Carl M. Sources of Information in the Social Sciences. Totowa, N.J.: Bedminister Press, 1964. Z7161.W49

  Describes bibliographies and other reference materials in the social sciences generally, and in history, economics, sociology, anthropology, psychology, education, and political science. Includes guides to the literature, current and retrospective bibliographies, sources of book reviews, directories and biographical compendia, encyclopedias, dictionaries, handbooks, chronologies, and current news publications, journals, and monographs, in classified lists with fairly extensive annotations. There are rather full details on individual titles, but only brief discussion, in the introductory chapter, of the characteristics and use of the various types of tools. Particularly valuable as a source of information about bibliographic and reference tools in the fields in which there is no specialized guide to the subject. (Also contains bibliographic essays on the basic literature of each field. This material is described in Appendix J.) A revised edition is to appear in 1973.

Anthropology

Mukherjee, A.K. Annotated Guide to Reference Materials in the Human Sciences. New York: Asia Publishing House, 1962. Z5111.M8

Introductory essay on types of references and bibliographic works in anthropology and their range and characteristics, followed by classified listing with brief annotations of each title. Fairly extensive lists of journals and standard texts in anthropological subfields and specialized areas. Similar, though briefer, treatment given also to sociology and social psychology.

Area and Ethnic Studies

Berton, Peter and Eugene Wu. Contemporary China: A Research Guide. Hoover Institution Bibliographical Series XXXI. Stanford, Calif.: Hoover Institution, 1967. Z3106.B39

Extensive listings, with detailed annotations, of bibliographies, encyclopedias, sources of laws and other documentary materials, periodicals, newspapers, translation and monitoring services, and other information resources.

Johnson, Donald Clay. A Guide to Reference Materials on Southeast Asia, Based on the Collections in the Yale and Cornell University Libraries. New Haven: Yale University Press, 1970. Z3221.J63

An extensive, unannotated list encompassing bibliographies, dictionaries, encyclopedias, atlases and comparable materials in European languages. Arranged in broad subject categories, subdivided by country.

Miller, Elizabeth W. and Mary L. Fisher. The Negro in America: a Bibliography. 2d rev. and enl. ed. Cambridge, Mass.: Harvard University Press, 1970. Z1361.N39M5 1970

This bibliography is principally an inventory of the literature of its subject (see above, p. 210). However, the final chapter, entitled "A Guide to Further Research," identifies and describes indexes, abstracts, bibliographies, serials, checklists, and other major research tools.

See also under Political Science: McGowan, P. J. African Politics. . .

Economics

Andreano, Ralph L.; Evan Ira Farber; and Sabron Reynolds. The Student Economist's Handbook: A Guide to Sources. Cambridge, Mass.: Schenkman Publishing Co. Inc., 1967. Z7164.E2A63

A manual of basic instruction on how to use library materials for research in economics. Discusses the usefulness of various types of works (e.g., bibliographies, periodicals) and presents descriptions of major publications. Considerable emphasis on data sources: statistics, government documents, etc. Also contains list, with descriptive notes, of major economics journals and business magazines.

Fletcher, Arthur, ed. The Use of Economics Literature. Hamden, Conn.: Archon Books, 1971.

Contributions by a number of authors cover publication and literature-searching patterns in economics, the major bibliographies and journals, specialized resources such as U.S. and British government publications, and the publications of international organizations, and the major writings and bibliographies in such subdivisions of economics as labor economics, economic development, and economic history. The orientation is basically British, but there is very good coverage of American materials.

Maltby, Arthur. Economics and Commerce: The Sources of Information and Their Organization. Hamden, Conn.: Archon Books, 1968. Z7164.E2M38

Descriptions in essay form of the major categories of economics reference tools: encyclopedias, directories, bibliographies, journals, government documents, statistical sources. Orientation is mainly British, but good coverage of American works also. Of particular interest for comparisons of alternative sources, and explanation of what they can and cannot do in connection with various information-searching purposes.

Education

Burke, Arvid J. and Mary A. Burke. Documentation in Education. New York: Teachers College Press, 1967. (Revision of How to Locate Educational Information and Data by Carter Alexander and Arvid J. Burke, 4th rev. ed. 1st ed. published 1935.) Z711.B93 1967

A basic outline of publication patterns, organization of materials in libraries, procedures in analyzing questions and searching for information are presented in Part 1, "Fundamentals of Information and Storage and Retrieval." Part 2, "Locating Educational Information or Data," describes sources useful for locating factual information on education and other topics, and how to use them. Part 3, "Bibliographic Searching in Education," presents an extensive discussion of procedures, with annotated lists of major bibliographic sources. This guide encompasses English-language materials in virtually all fields, but its major emphasis is on education.

Manheim, Theodore; Gloria L. Dardarian; and Diane A. Satterthwaite. Sources in Educational Research: A Selected and Annotated Bibliography. Vol. 1. Detroit: Wayne State University Press, 1969. Z5811.M25

Annotated lists of bibliographies, encyclopedias, periodicals, research monograph series, and miscellaneous reference works selected as most useful to undergraduate and graduate students in education. Volume one, cited above, covers education research in general and nine specialized subject areas. Future volumes are planned to cover additional topics, such as history of education, educational sociology, educational administration.

Geography

Lock, C.B. Muriel. Geography: A Reference Handbook. London: Clive Bingley, 1968. Z6001.L58

Alphabetical list, with descriptions, "covering some of the main focal points of geographical study" (Foreword). Includes important publications, organizations and institutions, people. Arrangement lends itself most readily to supplying information about single items, but there is a subject index useful for locating entries by category, such as "Bibliographies," or "Geography, History of."

Wright, John Kirtland and Elizabeth T. Platt. Aids to Geographical Research: Bibliographies, Periodicals, Atlases, Gazetteers and Other Reference Books. 2d. rev. ed., New York: Columbia University Press for the American Geographical Society, 1947. (American Geographical Society Research Series no. 22) Z6001.A1W9 1947

A fairly lengthy introduction considers characteristics of geographical study and the relation of research aids, as described in the book, to the range of scholarly and professional activities in geography. This is followed by an extensive and detailed bibliography, arranged by major topics and regions, with descriptive annotations. The listings are updated by Chauncy D. Harris, Bibliographies and Reference Works for Research in Geography (Department of Geography, University of Chicago, 1967), an annotated list of recent titles.

History

American Historical Association. Guide to Historical Literature. Board of Editors: George F. Howe et. al. New York: Macmillan, 1961. Z6201.A55

Annotated listings of major bibliographies, indexes, sources of book reviews, statistics, etc. Little consideration of search methods or use of materials, but a number of significant tools for historical research are identified. (For description of the basic bibliography comprising the bulk of this work, see Appendix J.)

Gray, Wood, et. al. Historian's Handbook: a Key to the Study and Writing of History. 2d ed. Boston: Houghton Mifflin Co., 1964. D23.G78 1964

A concise manual for history students, covering the nature of historical study, tools, methods and mechanics of research. Chapter 2, "Pursuit of Evidence," contains extensive lists of bibliographies, major texts, and other reference materials.

Handlin, Oscar and others. Harvard Guide to American History. Cambridge, Mass.: Harvard University Press, 1954. Z1236.H27

Part I, "Status, Methods and Presentation" contains a series of essays on the nature and evolution of the historical discipline, and methods of research. Part II, "Materials and Tools," discusses a wide range of historical source materials and finding tools. Encompasses "materials of history" (e.g., maps, manuscripts, films), "aids to historical research" (bibliographies, indexes, etc.), "historical sources" (public documents, journals, textbooks, encyclopedias, biographies, historical fiction, etc.). In addition to the above, there is an extensive basic bibliography, as described in Appendix J.

Hockett, Homer C. The Critical Method in Historical Research and Writing. New York: Macmillan Co., 1955. E175.7 H6446

Mainly a discussion of methods of historical investigation, presenting extended consideration of such matters as choice of a topic for a historical research paper, critical textual analysis, mechanics of note taking and form for footnotes and bibliographic entries. Also considers the characteristics and use of major types of historical information sources, such as bibliographies, journals, government documents. An extensive, systematic bibliography listing guides, bibliographies, indexes and a variety of important data sources supports the text.

Kitson Clark, G. Guide for Research Students Working on Historical Subjects. 2d ed., Cambridge: At the University Press, 1969. D16.K58 1968

Introduction to methods and procedures in historical research: choosing a topic, reviewing and presenting evidence, keeping notes, etc. Oriented toward doctoral students in British universities, but has more general applicability. Appendix has brief descriptions of major bibliographic tools, guides to manuscripts, and "working tools" such as dictionaries, and biographical compendia. Main focus is British and French history.

Morley, Charles. Guide to Research in Russian History. Syracuse: University Press, 1951. Z2506.M85

An annotated list of bibliographies, encyclopedias, biographical compendia, chronologies, chronicles, and similar materials.

Poulton, Helen. The Historian's Handbook: a Descriptive Guide to Reference Works. Norman: University of Oklahoma Press, 1972. Z6201.P65

Description in narrative form of a variety of reference materials useful to history students: library catalogs, bibliographies, encyclopedias, almanacs, legal sources, government publications, etc. Includes some discussion of the general characteristics and uses of works of a given type, and some comparison of similar or related works.

Political Science

Brock, Clifton. The Literature of Political Science: A Guide for Students, Librarians and Teachers. New York: Bowker, 1969. Z7161.B83

Describes the major bibliographic tools and sources of factual information pertinent to the study of political science. Considerable emphasis on methods and procedures of literature searching and the usefulness of various types of materials in the information-gathering process. The organization and style of presentation of information in the major tools is presented in considerable detail and illustrated by reproduced pages.

Holler, Frederick. The Information Sources of Political Science. Santa Barbara, Calif.: American Bibliographic Center-Clio Press, 1971. Z7161.H64

Extensive listing, with annotations, of guides, bibliographies, directories, dictionaries, and documentary and statistical sources for political science and about ten subfields.

McGowan, Patrick J. African Politics: A Guide to Research Resources, Methods and Literature. Occasional Paper 55, Maxwell Graduate School of Citizenship and Public Affairs, Syracuse University, 1970.   DT1.S915   no. 55

Extensive compilation of bibliographic tools, data sources and basic writings. Individual listings are unannotated, but each category of material is introduced and explained by introductory comments.

Mason, John Brown. Research Resources: Annotated Guide to the Social Sciences. Vol. 1: International Relations and Recent History; Indexes, Abstracts and Periodicals. Santa Barbara, Calif.: American Bibliographic Center—Clio Press, 1968.   Z7161.M36

Annotated list of about 1,200 bibliographic and reference publications, including one-time and continuing bibliographies, significant journals, biographical and organization directories, chronologies and dictionaries. Major emphasis is on identification and description of individual titles, with only brief comments on the characteristics and uses of the various types of tools. Volume 2 (1971) deals with official publications of the United States and international organizations, and statistical sources.

Merritt, Richard L. and Gloria J. Pyszka. The Student Political Scientist's Handbook. Cambridge, Mass.: Schenkman Publishing Co. Inc., 1969.   JA86.M4

Brief discussion of the character of modern political science and some basic considerations in formulating and attacking a problem for research. Most of the work consists of descriptions of resource materials: bibliographies, government publications, sources of factual political information, periodical literature.

U.S. Library of Congress. General Reference and Bibliography Division. A Guide to Bibliographic Tools for Research in Foreign Affairs. 2d ed. Compiled by Helen F. Conover. Washington, D.C.: 1958.   Z6461.U49

Designed as a basic list for "initial steps in reference work" or "preliminary research." Cites bibliographic sections of major journals, both U.S. and foreign, research journals and magazines of news and comment, annual surveys and chronologies, sources of statistics and biographical information, organization directories. Covers general and regional materials. Listings are extensively annotated, but there is little over-all discussion of the characteristics of materials or searching problems.

Wynar, Lubomyr R. Guide to Reference Materials in Political Science: A Selective Bibliography. 2 vols. Denver: Colorado Bibliographic Institute, 1966. Z7161.W9

A comprehensive list, with brief annotations, of bibliographies and informational materials in the social sciences generally, and in political science and its subfields. Includes guides to the literature, bibliographies, indexes and library catalogs, encyclopedias and dictionaries, directories, statistical compendia, atlases. For political science and six subfields (political theory, ideology, international relations, public administration, political behavior and comparative political systems) includes extensive lists of textbooks and monographs.

Zawodny, J.K. Guide to the Study of International Relations. San Francisco: Chandler, 1966. Z6461.Z3

Concise descriptions of bibliographic tools and other resources (encyclopedias, document and manuscript collections, chronologies and news summaries) pertinent to the study of international relations. Emphasis is on characteristics of individual titles, rather than consideration of the uses of the various categories of materials.

Psychology

Daniel, Robert S. and C.M. Louttit. Professional Problems in Psychology. New York: Prentice-Hall, 1953. BF76.D35

Part II, "Psychological Literature," discusses general characteristics of psychological publications, with citation and description of important bibliographies, abstracting publications, dictionaries, encyclopedias, etc. Also considered are problems and techniques of report writing and manuscript preparation.

Elliott, C. K. A Guide to the Documentation of Psychology. London: Clive Bingley, 1971. BF76.8.E4

An outline of literature-searching strategies and procedures useful in psychological research and study, with discussion of the characteristics and uses of the major types of documentary resources: journals, reviews, abstracts, handbooks, textbooks, etc. Unannotated lists of titles are contained in appendixes.

Sarbin, Theodore R. and William C. Coe. The Student Psychologist's Handbook: a Guide to Sources. Cambridge, Mass.: Schenkman Publishing Co., Inc., 1969. BF77.S28

A brief guide to research procedures and major information sources. Describes the content of the main divisions of psychology, the basic characteristics of a research paper, the major journals, handbooks, and similar sources. A glossary of statistical terms explains, in less detail than a textbook but more extensively than a dictionary, about fifty basic quantitative concepts.

See also under Anthropology: Mukherjee, A. K., Annotated Guide. . .

DIRECTORIES OF SOCIAL SCIENCE PERIODICALS

America's Education Press. 31st ed. Syracuse, New York: Educational Press Association of America, 1971. Z5813.E24

A classified list, frequently revised, of educational periodicals issued in the United States and Canada. Covers periodicals of national, state and local organizations and agencies, as well as journals in many specialized areas of education. The list has been issued annually or bienially since 1926.

Boehm, Eric H. and Lalit Adolphus. Historical Periodicals: An Annotated World List of Historical and Related Serial Publications. Santa Barbara, Calif.: American Bibliographic Center-Clio Press, 1961. Z6205.B6

Includes journals in the historical discipline, and periodicals in other fields such as education or literature that contain articles on historical topics. Includes annuals, transactions of societies, and other relatively infrequent serial publications, and many periodicals devoted to local history. Coverage is world-wide, including titles in oriental languages. Entries are arranged geographically, and provide bibliographic data and brief descriptions of contents.

Camp, William L. Guide to Periodicals in Education. Metuchen, N.J.: Scarecrow Press, 1968.   Z5813.C28

Periodicals published in the United States, classified by subject. Entries provide bibliographic data plus a statement of general editorial policy and information pertaining to preparation and submission of manuscripts.

United Nations Educational, Scientific and Cultural Organization. Liste mondiale des périodiques spécialisés dans les sciences sociales: World List of Social Science Periodicals. 3d ed., Paris: UNESCO, 1966.   Z7163.U52   1966

Includes scholarly journals in all social science fields, but omits psychology except for social psychology, and history is limited to economic and social history. Arranged by country, with subject and title indexes. Entries provide basic bibliographic data, description of the contents of a typical issue of the journal (number of pages, number and length of articles, special features) and sometimes additional descriptive notes. The language (or languages) used by each journal, and inclusion of summaries of articles in other languages, are noted.

U.S. Bureau of the Census. Bibliography of Social Science Periodicals and Monograph Series. (Foreign Social Science Bibliographies, Series P-92, nos. 1–22) Washington, D.C.: G.P.O., 1961–1965.   Z7161.U43

A group of annotated lists of periodicals and monograph series devoted to the social sciences published in selected foreign countries. Each list is classified by subject and contains basic bibliographic data and brief descriptions of the contents of each of the publications listed. The countries and years covered are: Rumania, 1947–60; Bulgaria, 1944–60; Mainland China, 1949–61; Republic of China, 1949–61; Greece, 1950–61; Albania, 1944–61; Hong Kong, 1950–61; North Korea, 1945–61; Republic of Korea, 1945–61; Iceland, 1950–62; Denmark, 1945–61; Finland, 1950–62; Hungary, 1947–62; Turkey, 1950–62; Norway, 1945–62; Poland, 1945–62; U.S.S.R., 1950–63; Yugoslavia, 1945–63; Czechoslovakia, 1948–63; Japan, 1950–63; Soviet Zone of Germany, 1948–63; Sweden, 1950–63.

U.S. Library of Congress. African Section: Serials for African Studies. Compiled by Helen F. Conover. Washington, D.C.: G.P.O., 1961.   Z3503.U48

Lists publications in western languages published in Africa and abroad, including periodicals, monograph series, some annual reports of institutions and the like, but not government documents. Entries provide basic bibliographic data, plus additional notes on the publishing history of the item, holdings of the Library of Congress and, in some cases, a brief description of the character of the publication. Arrangement is alphabetical by title, with a subject index and an index of institutions.

U.S. Library of Congress. African Section. Sub-Saraharan Africa: A Guide to Serials. Washington, D.C.: G.P.O., 1970.   Z3503.U49

Periodicals and other serials published in or concerning sub-Saharan Africa, published in western or African languages using the Roman alphabet. In addition to periodicals, includes monographic series, yearbooks and annual reports of institutions, but excludes most government publications. Listing is alphabetical, with subject and country index of organizations. Entries include basic bibliographic data and holdings of the Library of Congress and other large research libraries, and indicate where the periodical is indexed.

U.S. Library of Congress, Slavic and Central European Division. East and East Central Europe: Periodicals in English and Other West European Languages, compiled by Paul L. Horecky with the assistance of Jania Wojicka. Washington, D.C.: G.P.O., 1958.   Z6955.U5

Journals published in, or concerning, the area encompassing Albania, the Baltic Countries, Bulgaria, Czechoslovakia, Hungary, Poland, Rumania, U.S.S.R. and Yugoslavia. Arranged geographically, giving basic bibliographic information and a brief description of the contents of each publication.

Zimmerman, Irene. A Guide to Current Latin American Periodicals: Humanities and Social Sciences. Gainesville, Fla.: Kallman Publishing Co., 1961. Z6954.S8Z5

A comprehensive listing of periodicals considered valuable for research purposes or likely to be cited in scholarly work. Arranged by country, with each national list introduced by a general discussion of the characteristics of periodical publication in the country, with references to sources of more detailed information. The listings for individual titles provide the basic bibliographic facts and relatively extensive descriptions of the subject coverage and point of view of the periodical. A subject section identifies the journals pertinent to eighteen fields in the social sciences and humanities, and also contains brief accounts of the over-all nature of journal publication in each of the fields and reference to the major bibliographic tools for identification of individual articles. A chronological section describes the main currents in Latin American periodical publications from the mid-nineteenth century to the present, and lists the journals by their starting dates.

Chapter Eleven

The Organization of Scholarly Bibliography: Summary

In every field of scholarship there is a group of publications whose function is to track the discussions in the field by recording its published output. These bibliographic records take various forms, each identified with a more or less distinctive communication function. Again it may be observed that "each type of source has its job to do."

The comprehensive, recurrent bibliography is the inclusive and permanent inventory, encompassing all contributions to the literature of a field of study. By affording a means of access to the total range of the scholarly effort, it forms the foundation of the bibliographic system. Beyond this, the other forms of bibliography record selected segments of the literature for a variety of special purposes. The current awareness list provides rapid announcement of the new works likely to be of greatest interest. It is designed to assist scholars to monitor the literature most suitable for their immediate concerns. Retrospective bibliographies look back over the literature, reevaluating and reorganizing some portion of the work of the past in terms of current perspectives. Research-oriented compilations in this format seek to illuminate a new question or idea by identification of the pertinent literature, and thus to "tune in" on the scholarly discussion as it bears on a particular approach or point of view relative to a topic. Didactic bibliographies, through their identification of the core literature of a subject, point the way to widely accepted knowledge at the more generalized levels of discourse. Finally, the guide to the literature surveys the over-all communications picture in a field and identifies the available tools in the various categories.

This overview depicts the types of bibliographic publication commonly encountered in the social sciences, but it does not portray the bibliographic structure of any single discipline. The several fields of social science differ considerably with regard to their bibliographic tools and practices. What follows does not attempt to recapitulate all the works discussed in the preceding chapters, but it can perhaps summarize the account by sketching in gross outline the bibliographic apparatus of each field.

Psychology has, in Psychological Abstracts, a highly developed and effective comprehensive bibliography. On the other hand, this discipline makes little use of retrospective bibliographies for selective and interpretive presentation of the literature. The Harvard List of Books in Psychology is a well-known and widely used compilation of basic books, and there are several guides to the literature geared principally to the needs of beginning students. However, at more intermediate levels, between comprehensive recording of the research literature and highly selective introductory book lists, the work of summary and cumulation tends to be conveyed by substance-oriented publications such as handbooks and reviews of the literature, rather than by bibliographies.

In sociology, good inclusive coverage of the literature has been attained in recent years by Sociological Abstracts, and there is also the International Bibliography of Sociology, providing somewhat more attention to foreign publications, but lacking abstracts. The research-oriented retrospective bibliography is encountered quite often as a device for summarizing and assessing accumulated work in various segments of the discipline, but there seems to be less attention to compilation of basic bibliographies. About the best listings available of the field's core literature are the chapters devoted to sociology in Hoselitz's Reader's Guide to the Social Sciences, and White's Sources of Information in the Social Sciences. Similarly, there is no separately published guide to the sociological literature, and the best source for identifying bibliographic resources in the field is the appendix to the sociological chapter in White's book.

Anthropology still lacks a satisfactory running inventory of its literature. The International Bibliography of Social and Cultural Anthropology most closely approximates this, but it appears only annually, and lacks annotations. The Anthropological Index provides more rapid coverage of the journal literature, but with rather sketchy indexing and, again, without abstracts or annotations. The new Abstracts in Anthropology may bring about substantial improvement in time, though its coverage so far is limited. Fairly complete retrospective bibliographies may be found for a number of subjects, doubtless in response to the lack of regular bibliographic recording on a comprehensive and continuing basis. There are some basic bibliographies and guides, though this work has not received a great deal of emphasis.

Education is unique among the social sciences in the attention given to bibliographic control and dissemination of the technical report literature, by means of the ERIC system and Research in Education. The Current Index to Journals in Education provides a fairly good record of the journal literature, though coverage of foreign materials is quite selective, and books are, of course, omitted. Bulletin Signaletique has a more international perspective, or, at least, offers a good route to the foreign literature. Retrospective bibliographies at all levels are numerous. Among guides to the literature, Burke's Documentation in Education has, through its successive editions, become established as a "standard" work.

In geography, a basic record of the literature extends back to the last century, in the form of Bibliographie Géographique Internationale, and inception of Geographical Abstracts in 1966 represents a significant advance in promptness and in fullness of description. Retrospective bibliographies are often used to focus on specific topics and research issues. Somewhat less attention has been given to compilation of basic bibliographies and guides, though examples of these may be found.

A major move toward attainment of adequate comprehensive records in economics is represented by the inception of the Journal of Economic Literature in 1969. This publication added abstracting and a relatively frequent publication schedule to the more rudimentary facilities offered by the International Bibliography of Economics and the Index of Economic Articles. Since the Journal of Economic Literature is also a vehicle for review articles, on both the specific problem and broader trend report levels, its development may stimulate economists to place more emphasis on cumulation and assessment in the review format, and less on retrospective bibliographies. There are several basic bibliographies and guides, with the Oxford reading list a notable example in the former category.

Political science remains rather badly in need of a comprehensive abstracting service encompassing the full range of its literature. International Political Science Abstracts is limited to journals. The Universal Reference System compilations offer some noteworthy indexing innovations, but are limited in coverage. The International Bibliography of Political Science is comprehensive, but appears only annually and lacks abstracts or other description. This field makes relatively heavy use of specific subject bibliographies as a means of organizing the literature. There are several guides to the literature and didactic-type bibliographies, but a well-selected compilation of major books, comparable to the Harvard List of Books in Psychology or the American Historical Association's Guide to Historical Literature is lacking. The chapter on political science by Heinz Eulau in Hoselitz's Reader's Guide to the Social Sciences provides a good basic selection.

The comprehensive bibliographic record in history shows many inadequacies. The International Bibliography of Historical Sciences encompasses all branches of the discipline, but it lacks abstracts, appears only annually, and is probably more selective in its coverage of the literature than most historians would desire. Historical Abstracts is restricted to journal articles pertaining to a limited chronological period. In the field of American History, <u>Writings on American History</u> has all the shortcomings of other unannotated annual bibliographies, plus extremely long delays in publication and an uncertain future. On the other hand, extensive use is made in history of one-time retrospective bibliographies, both to collect and organize the literature for specific research topics and to identify the core writings in broad fields. Guides to the literature are also quite numerous, probably in part because the use of published materials as data plays such an important role in historical research. The American Historical Association's <u>Guide to Historical Literature</u> is a central tool in the field, combining the functions of basic bibliography and guide to the literature, and tracking the mainstream of historical scholarship and research resources.

In this cursory survey of bibliographic arrangements in the social science disciplines, two generally contrasting approaches or patterns of emphasis are discernible. One places its major stress on comprehensive and continuing records of the literature. The other is characterized by rather weak comprehensive records, and extensive use of the one-time retrospective bibliography as a significant identifying tool.

Psychology affords a good example of the first approach. In that field the continuing record of the literature is quite well developed and effective, but the device of the selective retrospective bibliography is relatively little used. Preference is given instead to summary and cumulation in substantive formats. This discipline also has more regularized and long standing arrangements for reviewing of the literature than prevail generally among the social sciences.

A marked contrast to this is offered by history. In this field there is no really adequate running inventory of the literature, and substantive cumulating devices such as periodic review publications and handbooks are almost unknown. On the other hand, retrospective bibliographies, which select and systematize segments of the literature in terms of particular perspectives or purposes, are numerous.

Psychology and history present perhaps the sharpest contrast along these lines among the social sciences, with the other disciplines occupying more or less intermediate positions. Several factors can be cited to account for these differences. For one thing, irrespective of underlying causes, the existence in a field of a well established ongoing comprehensive bibliography is likely in itself to encourage assessment and cumulation in substantive, rather than bibliographic terms. Since a basic record of the literature is collectively and continuously maintained, the attention of individual scholars centers on interpretation and commentary, rather than identification of materials as such. Another important consideration (or perhaps just another way of saying the same thing) is the extent to which there is agreement within a field regarding its appropriate concerns and its standards and methods of scholarship. When the outlook is relatively unified, cumulation of knowledge in relatively explicit terms, as manifested in summaries and critical evaluations of the work in various research areas, is seen as both feasible and important. On the other hand, the more diffuse and non-committal bibliographic orientation lends itself more readily to situations in which standards and basic assumptions are relatively heterogeneous, and many different perspectives are apt to be brought to bear on the literature.

Consideration of the differences in bibliographic organization among the disciplines should not obscure their fundamental similarity. The variations relate to the extent to which different bibliographic devices are used, and each field has its own areas of emphasis and omission. But the basic configuration of the bibliographic structure, meaning the functions of the several types of bibliographic tools and the interrelations among them, is essentially the same in all fields. In each instance there is some approximation of an inclusive, continuing record of the literature in its entirety. These vary in their adequacy, but not in their basic intention. Supplementing the comprehensive record is an assortment of more selective records designed to carry out a range of special and limited purposes. Again, these vary in detail, but are alike in function.

This basic bibliographic structure mirrors the structure of scholarly literature. As was seen earlier, the scholarly discussion, as conveyed by the literature, tends to move from inclusive detail to more selective generalization.[1] This is reflected in the progression from research reports to encyclopedias, and, in roughly analogous fashion, in the bibliographic progression from comprehensive literature inventories to more selective records designed for special purposes. Jointly, though in different ways, the systems of literature and bibliography convey and keep track of the scholarly discussion. The correspondence and interplay between the two modes of communication can provide the basis for a systematic understanding of literature searching, the matter to be explored in the concluding section.

[1] See Chapter 6.

PART IV

Recapitulation and

Some Conclusions

LITERATURE AND BIBLIOGRAPHY AS PARALLEL COMMUNICATION SYSTEMS

I have repeatedly observed that the literature and the bibliographical apparatus of scholarship manifest many organizational and functional similarities because both are shaped fundamentally by the character of scientific communication. A dominant theme of the discussion has been that both literature and bibliography are means for conveying "what is known" in science; the former in direct, substantive terms, and the latter in the compressed, abbreviated form of bibliographic citation.

Scientific literature consists of explanations and their supporting data. These are successively transformed and reformulated at the several levels of scholarly discussion, so that the concrete and limited observations and inferences drawn directly from research are eventually cumulated to form the basis for generalized, abstract explanatory statements. In the case of the bibliographic tools, the component elements are the citations identifying the literature. The citations, of course, do not in themselves change from one bibliographic compilation to another. However, new ways of thinking about a subject are suggested by new selections and descriptions of its literature, and in this way the bibliographic tools which track the scientific discussion also help to organize and define its content.

Literature searching was described earlier as a procedure by which the searcher tunes in on the scholarly discussion at the level of generality corresponding to his familiarity with the subject, and then follows the discussion through closer analysis of more specific matters to reach the level of detail and currency indicated by the problem.[1] Because of the basic parallels in structure and function between the literature and the bibliographic apparatus, the writings relating to a given subject can be located by means of either facet of the communication system.

For example, using the literature directly, a searcher might begin his investigation with an encyclopedia article, follow up its references to the major books on one or more smaller aspects of the subject, and be led from these, by means of their footnotes and bibliographies, to more detailed summary publications such as handbooks, and ultimately to the primary research reports. A parallel path employing the bibliographic tools could start with a guide to the literature to identify either a bibliography listing basic books or the books themselves, then return to the guide in search of routes to larger and more detailed segments of the literature, in the form of research-oriented bibliographies on selected phases of the subject, annual reviews, review journals, and, ultimately, the inclusive bibliographic inventories affording maximum coverage of the primary contributions in the area. In an actual instance the two paths would probably be intermingled, with elements of either or both employed at various stages. The essential point is that at each level of scientific communication, the substantive and the bibliographic modes of presentation can perform quite similar functions, and publications in either group can be called upon to locate and track the discussion.

This returns to the observation, made earlier, that "literature" and "bibliography" are not distinct categories, but closely related and overlapping terms describing two somewhat different ways of doing similar things.[2] Every scholarly publication identifies related works and is thereby in some degree bibliographic, and every bibliography, through its selection and organization of materials, communicates some understanding of its subject, at least by implication. Conventionally, "literature" refers to works primarily intended to convey substantive information, in which bibliographic references play an ancillary role, while "bibliography" refers to works in which identification of the literature is the central purpose, and exposition of the subject ancillary. Another way of putting it is that literature generally means high information content relative to the number of citations, and a stress on interpretation and evaluation of the cited works over identification as such, while in bibliographic tools these proportions and relationships tend to be reversed. But these differences are only relative, and, as was seen earlier, some works are difficult to assign definitively to either category.

From the point of view of the reader and literature-searcher, a distinction between "bibliography" and "literature" as terminological labels is unimportant. However, a given publication's position along what has been described as "a continuum between high coverage of the literature with low direct provision of information at the one end and low coverage of the literature with high provision of direct information at the other"[3] has some noteworthy consequences and implications.

Learning about something is never a matter of stringing together unconnected bits of information, but rather involves relating new information to an existing stock. A significant asset of the "high provision of information" publications (i.e., "literature") as identification tools is that they provide a context that helps the reader to judge the import and potential usefulness of the bibliographic references. The perspectives from which the cited publications are seen as relevant to the subject under consideration are indicated by the discussion, and the references lead to materials relating directly and specifically to those perspectives. Such citations may encompass not only works "on" the subject as such, but also writings viewed as pertinent on grounds of methodological similarities, shared theoretical assumptions, or in other ways. In this way, references from the substantive literature not only reveal the existence of publications relating to the topic, but also help provide a foundation for making use of them.

In contrast, publications in the "high literature coverage" vein tend to establish the connections between a subject and its literature rather more loosely. The writings grouped under a given subject heading in a bibliography may relate to various aspects of the subject in a variety of ways, but there may be little in the listings themselves to suggest this. Authors' names, the terminology used in titles, date or place of publication, or the journal or series in which a work appears may furnish clues, but these are meaningful only to knowledgeable readers. The same is true, though to a lesser extent, when abstracts and annotations are used. Since these summarize the content of each work separately and in its own terms, it is left to the reader to relate the cited works to the needs of his investigation.

A major drawback of searching the literature via footnote tracing in substantive publications is that the process normally moves only backward through time, and cannot be used to investigate the subsequent development of an idea. The new technique of citation indexing, described in Chapter 7, is designed to deal with this problem. Yet, at all events, the advantages of tracking the literature via its own references are greatest when the problem under consideration is an extensively studied one, or when the searcher seeks to carry an idea forward along lines essentially similar to those pursued by previous investigators. In such instances, the reader is able, through following up citations, to tune in on a clearly defined and delimited discussion among writers who repeatedly address each other and direct their attention to the same range of issues. The picture is somewhat different when the intention is to break new ground and approach a subject in terms that depart from generally recognized perspectives and the traditional lines of work in a discipline. In such cases, the ability of the substantive publications to identify the literature relevant to an ongoing discussion offers little advantage. Since the contexts in which the topic has previously been considered are not seen as directly germane to the new approach, the view of the literature afforded by earlier discussions is apt to be too highly structured, restricted to selected aspects of the topic, and liable to have omitted potentially useful materials whose relevance to the problem was not previously recognized. The more wide-ranging and relatively noncommital qualities characteristic of the bibliographic tools can then be seen as assets. However, the inherent difficulties of the bibliographic mode of communication remain, meaning that it devolves on the reader to supply the contextual framework necessary to reach the appropriate citations and judge their relevance.

The principle of tuning in on the scholarly discussion at a point corresponding to the reader's level of familiarity with the subject applies to the choice of tools and procedures for locating the literature as well as to the choice of the works to be read. Just as comprehension of the more detailed substantive accounts of a subject rests on a foundation conveyed at the more generalized levels of the literature, successful use of the compressed and cryptic information provided by bibliographic listings depends on the reader's ability to supply an interpretive context. In general, the demands on the reader's prior knowledge increase as he moves from the "substantive" communication vehicles, emphasizing content, to the "bibliographic tools," emphasizing identification.

LITERATURE SEARCHING AS TUNING IN

The essential message of the foregoing is that literature searching is an intrinsic part of scholarship, and should not be regarded as an extraneous, mechanical chore. Students sometimes assume that the most efficient way to prepare a research paper is to assemble the entire bibliography at the start, thus clearing the way for the "real" task of reading and writing. The defect in this procedure is that the literature is thus selected at a point when the student's understanding of his topic is yet unformed.

At the start of an investigation of a relatively unfamiliar subject, the searcher is apt to have only a vague conception of what "information about" the matter might mean. He is unlikely to have particular questions in mind, because he does not yet understand the subject well enough to imagine the kinds of questions that can be raised about it or the ways it might be explored. In consequence, he has no basis for differentiating among the references he encounters; everything that seems to touch on a term or phrase connected to the subject appears about the same as everything else. In the manner of someone putting together a balanced menu, he may choose a few books and some periodical articles and perhaps a selection or two from an encyclopedia or newspaper, but this usually reflects a desire for variety for its own sake, rather than the requirements of the problem. Since there is no central idea or question to give direction to the search, the resulting paper can do no more than summarize whatever was fortuitously encountered in the literature. It cannot attempt to probe a question in any depth or report on the state of knowledge with regard to an issue, because it taps only an indeterminate portion of a larger scholarly effort, whose over-all character and results remain unknown.

Similar hazards are presented by another familiar and often automatic procedure, which is to start the search at the library card catalog. The difficulty here is that the catalog is an unselective inventory of the total holdings of the library. Most subject headings will yield many more books than the searcher can reasonably expect to read, and these include, without discrimination or distinction, the excellent and the mediocre, the authoritative and the obscure, the currently valid and the obsolete. Since the catalog cards provide only bibliographic information, it may not be possible to distinguish basic texts and other comprehensive treatments from reports of single, narrowly gauged research studies. There is nothing to indicate a connection between any of the works listed and the larger processes of cumulative scholarship relative to the subject. As with other inclusive, nondescriptive bibliographic tools, the user must rely heavily on oblique clues such as the terminology of titles, authors' names, sponsoring institutions and the like. However, these are apt to have little meaning for the searcher unfamiliar with the subject,[4] and, again, the closer the student is to the start of his investigation, the less knowledgeable he is apt to be. Thus, again, an approach which separates the processes of searching from the process of learning about a subject is apt to eventuate in the collection of a tenuously related assortment of materials and a paper which summarizes them somehow but cannot report systematically "what is known" about a deliberately chosen problem.

A more purposeful approach would center on the idea that both the focus of the paper and the literature relevant to it will be progressively clarified as the investigation proceeds and the searcher gains understanding of the subject. Accordingly, the first step would be to locate a discussion at the level of generality corresponding to the searcher's degree of acquaintance with the topic, and read that before seeking further references. In this way the search proceeds by stages, and each forward step is informed by the searcher's growing expertise.

To illustrate very roughly and generally what this might involve, a student preparing a term paper might decide to begin with a basic, comprehensive books, as a generalized overview of the subject. This is ordinarily a good procedure when the searcher has no firm ideas about a specific problem for the paper, or how to "narrow down" a broad and complex topic to manageable size. A guide to the literature might therefore be consulted first, for direct identification of a suitable book, or for a basic bibliography from which such a work could be chosen. Presumably the book would set forth the dimensions of the subject as scholars have dealt with it, and provide some indication of the prevailing consensus and current state of knowledge. It might stimulate some ideas about narrower issues that could be investigated more intensively for the paper, and supply references to the literature dealing more specifically with such points. These, and the further references that they in turn supplied, could be followed up until the material began to seem tangential to the central issue.

At that point the reader might return to the guide, this time seeking a more detailed presentation of the literature pertinent to the problem, in the form, possibly, of research-oriented bibliographies, handbooks, or annual reviews. If, at the start of the project, the student had already been sufficiently familiar with the subject to have a fairly definite problem in mind, he might have begun the search at this level, omitting the introductory book. In any event, his prior acquaintance with the scholarly background of his subject will help the student to comprehend the discussion and bibliographic connections presented at more detailed levels of analysis. As the topic is no longer entirely unfamiliar, he is able to recognize the value of materials whose relevance might not be evident to the uninformed searcher, and to pinpoint his specific interests amid the variety of perspectives and approaches represented.

If a suitable handbook or review publication is not available, the student may be obliged to do without the advantages of a selected, structured overview of the subject, and survey the literature more inclusively by means of the comprehensive, recurrent bibliographic inventory. Ultimately he would probably have had to do this anyway, to find the most recent publications or to explore a specific point more exhaustively than is done by the reviews and cumulations. Again, the more he understands about the subject on the basis of his previous reading, the better he will be able to cope knowledgeably with the multitude of references and absence of substantive guidance characteristic of the inclusive bibliographic tools, and to spot the most useful materials and avoid unproductive leads.

This description of literature searching is necessarily quite general. The steps to be followed in any actual research would depend a great deal on the character of the question and the amount of scholarly attention it has received, the extent and depth of the inquiry, and other matters, even though the basic procedure and its underlying rationale would be much the same. An additional, and very significant, consideration, would be the adequacy of the bibliographic resources relating to the subject in question.

As the preceding account has repeatedly indicated, the communication structure of the social sciences has many deficiencies. A given form of publication or retrieval tool may be very little developed, or lacking altogether, in one or another discipline, and in all the fields it is possible to identify useful communication functions for which no adequate instrument exists. A reader may recognize that the approach characteristic of a particular type of publication—handbook, or basic bibliography or whatever—would be likely to supply just the information he needs, but find that such a work does not exist for his subject, or is too old to be of use. There may often be no choice but to improvise and make do with materials less than optimally suited to the purpose at hand.

It is especially important that the idea of the literature as a coherent, functionally differentiated system of communication not be lost sight of under these conditions. A reader who understands the essential qualities of scientific communication and the various roles carried out within the system is in the best position to exploit whatever resources are available with maximum effectiveness. In the absence of a systematic conceptualization, the assortment of publications and bibliographies are an indistinguisable mass of "information sources." The reader is unlikely to find even as much as inadequate resources have to offer, because he is unaware of what might be found, or what to look for. Difficult though it is to locate an authoritative, introductory text through a library card catalog, or a review article by means of a general periodical index, it can often be done, given some luck and diligence—but only by someone able to make these distinctions and recognize what he needs when he finds it.

Another value of a systematic view of communication is that it offers a measuring rod with which to assess existing facilities and arrangements, and can thus help librarians and social scientists to sharpen their perceptions of what the communication structure lacks and how improvements might be made. This returns, in conclusion, to one of the basic tenets of science, with which this account began: "The present state of knowledge is of importance chiefly as a basis for future operations."[5]

FOOTNOTES

1. See Chapter 6.
2. See pp. 134–135.
3. Patricia B. Knapp, "The Meaning of the Monteith College Library Program for Library Education," Journal of Education for Librarianship 6 (Fall 1965): 123. Mrs. Kanpp continues, "the usefulness of any source on this continuum depends upon the amount of information the user brings to his search," the basic point elaborated here.
4. Cf. Patricia B. Knapp, The Monteith College Library Experiment (New York: Scarecrow Press, 1966) pp. 40–41, 67.
5. James B. Conant, Science and Common Sense (New Haven: Yale University Press, 1951) p. 25.

Name and Title Index

This index lists titles of journals, series, and composite reference works such as handbooks and encyclopedias. Other books mentioned in the text are listed under authors' names. Page numbers in boldface refer to the principal descriptions of the works listed.

Subject Index

Abstracts, communication role, 153, 164-165
    content, 147-148, 164-165
    coverage of literature, 143, 152
    current awareness use, 197
Afro-American studies, bibliographies, 162, 174, 233
    guides to literature, 244
Anthropology, bibliographic records, 151, 155, 209, 254
    bibliographies (lists), 173, 232
    books about, 47-48
    cumulating publications, 128
    dictionaries, 119
    guides to literature, 244
    histories, 107
    journals, 66, 69
Applied fields, 20, 40
    bibliographies, 142, 162-163
    technical reports, use in, 190
Archives, governmental, 24
Area studies, bibliographies, 142, 161-162, 232-233
    guides to literature, 244

Behavioral sciences, 20, 38
    bibliographies, 161, 196
Bibliographic control, 192-193
Bibliographic essays (*see* Research reviews)
Bibliographic system, adequacy, 140-142, 150-151
    communication roles, 135, 192-193, 253, 257, 259-260
    disciplinary patterns, 254-257
    parallels to literature, 134, 219-220, 257, 259-261
Bibliographies, annotations in, 143, 147-148, 164-165
    classification of entries, 137, 143, 153, 165

Bibliographies *(continued)*
    communication roles, 132-134, 139-140, 192-193, 195, 207-208, 221
    computer searches, 149, 157
    as cumulating publications, 208
    dimensions of, 135-137
    and disciplinary identity, 140-141, 147-148, 150, 155-156, 256-257
    inclusiveness in, 139-140, 142-143, 209
    indexing of entries, 143, 158-160
    as interdisciplinary connectors, 142, 211, 215-216
    interpretive functions, 211, 213-214, 217, 219, 221-222
    library-produced, 143, 163-166, 197, 223
    methodological designations in, 137, 157, 158, 220
    and new research areas, delineation of, 212-213, 216-217
    obsolescence, 224-225
    scope of, 136, 142, 164
    selectivity in, 152, 195, 222-223
    sources identifying, 225
    types of, 133-134, 253
Book reviews, communication role, 58, 198-199
    content, 199, 200
    obsolescence, 200-201
    sources identifying, 201
Books, research reports in, 60-61
Business administration, 19, 20

Citation indexing, 160, 261
Communication, scientific, functions, 12-13
    shortcomings, 126-127, 265
    as system, 53-55, 265
Concepts, 6
Consensus, scientific, 11-12